FirstBus

Britain's largest bus operator

incorporating

Badgerline & Grampian

Keith A. Jenkinson

An Autobus Review Publication

First published December 1997

ISBN 0 907834 38 8

Printed by Bakes & Lord Ltd.
Beacon Road, Bradford BD6 3NB

AUTOBUS REVIEW PUBLICATIONS LTD.
42 Coniston Avenue, Queensbury,
Bradford, West Yorkshire BD13 2JD

Pictured travelling along the guided busway in Scott Hall Road, Leeds on a demonstration run is Leeds City Link silver & blue Superbus-liveried Alexander Strider-bodied Scania N113CRB 8635 (K1YRL). (Yorkshire Rider)

FOREWORD

Formed in June 1995 FirstBus plc was a major new public company with over 14,500 employees and 5,600 vehicles operating throughout the UK. In just over two years the group has grown to become the largest UK bus operator, employing some 23,500 staff and operating almost 9,000 vehicles throughout Britain. FirstBus is also a major rail operator. We were awarded the seven year Great Eastern Train franchise in January 1997 and have a 24.5% interest in Great Western and North Western Train franchises. The recent purchase of a 51% stake in Bristol Airport emphasises its position as a major public transport group.

Our aim is to be the industry leader. This can only be achieved through the involvement of our staff and the delivery of high quality, reliable and cost-effective public transport to our customers. The group's long term success will be achieved through organic growth which is why we are investing in new high specification vehicles, monitoring customer satisfaction and developing other customer initiatives such as real time information, guided busways and bus priority measures.

We operate in exciting times for the transport industry and are pleased that the first history of the new group is being published. This book will undoubtedly become a real collectors item. Congratulations to Keith and his team for a well documented publication which we hope you will enjoy.

Trevor Smallwood
Executive Chairman

Moir Lockhead
Group Chief Executive

November 1997

INTRODUCTION & ACKNOWLEDGEMENTS

Although FirstBus plc did not come into being until June 1995, its ancestry dates back to 1986 when National Bus Company subsidiary Badgerline was sold to the private sector and Council-owned Grampian Regional Transport was re-formed as a free standing company. During the next nine years, both companies developed into important groups within the road passenger transport industry, gaining expansion through acquisitions and establishing a presence in many different parts of Britain.

Due to the individuality of the two groups who ultimately joined together to form FirstBus, this book has been divided into three separate sections, one tracing the development of Badgerline, one following the expansion of Grampian Regional Transport and the other taking account of FirstBus which has now achieved the position of Britain's largest bus operating company in addition to having rail, airport and retail involvements. It was only in this manner that the history of the latter could be unfolded and I hope that readers will find this understandable.

Surprisingly, comparatively little has been written previously on the subject of FirstBus and its predecessors and I hope, therefore, that this book might fill that void. Without the help of others, however, it would have been extremely difficult to unravel all the events leading up to, and indeed beyond, June 1995 or to assemble such a comprehensive selection of photographs and I acknowledge the contribution made by several individuals as well as a number of enthusiast groups. Amongst these are Terry Blackman, Murdoch Currie, Bernard Davies, Malcolm Flynn, John Hobbs, Paul Kay, Thomas W.W.Knowles, Campbell Morrison, John Podgorski, Steve Procter, the late John Whitmore, Fred York, FirstBus Enthusiasts Group, PSV Circle and the West Yorkshire Metro Transport News. A special 'thank you' must also be extended to Trevor Smallwood and Moir Lockhead for giving up their precious time to reading - and correcting - my draft text and for offering additional information and greatly valued comments to ensure that this history is both comprehensive and accurate. If I have overlooked any others who have contributed in any way, then I apologise and hope that they will forgive me.

Despite much burning of the midnight oil, checking and re-checking reams of paper containing various references to Badgerline, Grampian and FirstBus and trying to select what amounts to only a few photographs from well over two thousand, I have nevertheless gained much pleasure from these tasks and hope now that those who read the 'finished work' will find it both enjoyable and informative.

Keith A.Jenkinson.
Queensbury, Bradford
November 1997

FIRSTBUS PLC PORTFOLIO

Badger Retail Limited (B)

The Berks Bucks Bus Company Limited
- *Beeline*
- *London Buslines*

A.E. & F.R.Brewer Limited (B)
- *United Welsh Coaches*

Bristol International Airport (51%)

Bristol Omnibus Company Limited (B)
- *Badgerline*
- *City Line*

CentreWest London Buses Limited
- *Ealing Buses*
- *Gold Arrow*
- *Uxbridge Buses*

Comlaw No.313 Limited #
- *GCT*

Eastern Counties Omnibus Company Limited (G) #
- *Blue Bus*
- *Rosemary Coaches*
- *Waylands Minibus Services*

Eastern Scottish Omnibuses Limited (G) #

Essex Buses Limited
- *Eastern National*
- *Thamesway*

FB Properties Limited

Grampian Regional Transport Limited (G) #

Great Eastern Railway Limited

Greater Manchester Buses North Limited

Great Western Holdings Limited (24.5%)
- *Great Western Trains*
- *North Western Trains*

Kelvin Central Buses Limited #

Kirkpatrick of Deeside Limited (G) #

Leicester CityBus Limited (94%) (G) #

Lowland Omnibuses Limited (G) #
- *FifeFirst*
- *SMT*

Mainline Partnership Limited (20%)

G.E.Mair Hire Services Limited (G) #

Midland Bluebird Limited (G) #
- *SMT*

Midland Red West Limited (B)

Northampton Transport Limited (G) #

Portsmouth Transit Limited

PMT Limited (B)
- *Crosville*
- *Pennine*
- *Red Rider*

The Provincial Bus Company Limited

Quickstep Travel Limited (B)

Rider (York) Limited (B)

Skillplace Training Limited (B)

Southampton CityBus Limited
- *Hants & Sussex*

The South Wales Transport Company Limited (B)

Sovereign Quay Limited (B)

Strathclyde Buses Limited #
- *Greater Glasgow*

Tramtrack Croydon Limited (20%)

Wessex National Limited (B)
- *Sky Blue*

Western National Limited (B)

Yorkshire Rider Limited (B)
- *Bradford Traveller*
- *Calderline*
- *Kingfisher Huddersfield*
- *Leeds City Link*

(B) signifies a former Badgerline company.
(G) signifies a former GRT company.
signifies companies registered in Scotland (All others are registered in England and Wales)
Names in italics are those of operating units within the parent company.

COVER PHOTOGRAPHS

Front upper : Resting at St.Andrew bus station, Edinburgh is Lowland's Wright Axcess Ultralow-bodied Scania L113CRL 505 (P505XSH) painted in FifeFirst livery and lettered for operation on its new Edinburgh - Ballingry service. (S.R.Procter)

Front lower left : Sporting Wells fleet names, Badgerline ECW-bodied Bristol RELH6L 2076 (GHY138K) leaves Wells bus station in August 1991 on the 126 service to Weston-super-Mare. (P.Horrex)

Front lower right : One of a large number of Alexander-bodied Leyland Atlanteans operated by Grampian Regional Transport, 296 (LRS296W) at Guild Street, Aberdeen carries an exact fare notice in its destination screen. (J.L.Hobbs)

Rear upper left : Painted in Leeds City Link's attractive new livery, Alexander-bodied Scania N113DRB 8005 (G805JYG) approaches Bradford Transport Interchange at the end of its inter-city journey from Leeds. (K.A.Jenkinson)

Rear centre left : Seen at Swansea bus station still painted in South Wales Transport livery and showing an SWT logo below its windscreens, ECW-bodied Bristol VRT 972 (BEP972V) had gained a Brewers vinyl on its side panel after its transfer to the latter company in 1992. (D.P.B.Davies)

Rear lower left : Leaving Buchanan bus station, Glasgow on a journey to Drumchapel is Greater Glasgow Alexander-bodied Volvo B6LE MV33 (P513VOS) which in addition to carrying SuperBus fleet names also carries promotional lettering on its cove panels. (K.A.Jenkinson)

Rear upper right : Great Eastern Trains 321-364 wearing its owner's new livery approaches Colchester station on the London to Ipswich service in October 1997. (J.Podgorski)

Rear upper centre right : Greater Manchester Northern Counties-bodied MCW Metrobus 5209 (C209FVU) in its owner's new all-over orange livery leaves Bolton bus station on the 400 service to Stockport. (K.A.Jenkinson)

Rear lower centre right : Travelling along High Street, Colchester in August 1995 is Eastern National Plaxton Pointer-bodied Dennis Dart 811 (L811OPU) which sports a badger logo behind its rear wheel arch. (D.W.Rhodes)

Rear lower right : Having been registered by Western National by whom it was briefly operated, all-red liveried low-floor Plaxton Pointer-bodied Dennis Dart 3307 (P889TCV) was devoid of fleet names when seen at Yeadon in September 1997 whilst operating for Quickstep Travel. (K.A.Jenkinson)

Badgerline

FROM STATE OWNERSHIP TO INDEPENDENCE

Although a comparatively new company set up in 1995, the foundations of FirstBus were laid some ten years earlier as a consequence of the 1985 Transport Act under which the National Bus Company was to be sold to the private sector and municipal transport undertakings had to be reformed into separate companies.

In preparation for the National Bus Company sell-off, several of its larger subsidiaries were split into smaller companies to make them more attractive to prospective purchasers and amongst these was the mighty Bristol Omnibus Company Limited which was divided into three separate operating companies - The Cheltenham & Gloucester Omnibus Company Limited, Bristol Omnibus Company Limited and Badgerline Limited - on 28 November 1985. The new companies became operational on 1 January 1986 with Cheltenham & Gloucester taking over the services operating in and around those towns, Bristol Omnibus Co. (City Line) retaining the Bristol city services and Badgerline taking over the former 'Country Services' covering an area bounded in the west by the Bristol Channel, in the north by Berkeley and Tetbury, in the east by Devizes and Warminster and in the south by Frome, Street and Bridgwater. Under these changes, Badgerline set up new headquarters at Weston-super-Mare from where all its administration was to be carried out. A new livery of yellow, emerald green and white and the Badgerline fleetname had already been adopted by Bristol Omnibus Co. on 29 April 1985 for its vehicles employed on 'Country Services', and this was retained by the newly-created company although at the time of transfer a large number of buses still wore NBC's corporate leaf green and white colours to which new Badgerline logos had been applied.

Amongst the 400 buses and coaches inherited from Bristol Omnibus Co. were 47 Ford Transit van-converted minibuses which had made their debut in 1985, Bristol REs and LHs, Leyland Nationals, Bristol VRTs, a small number of Leyland Olympians and MCW Metrobuses and a quantity of Leyland Leopard and Tiger coaches. Continuing the policy adopted by Bristol Omnibus Co., Badgerline used local Bath, Bristol, Weston and Wells fleet names for its vehicles operating in those areas as well as the Minilink name on its small capacity buses, Swiftlink on its non-National Express liveried coaches and express vehicles and Coastrider on its open-top double deckers based at Weston-super-Mare. The Swiftlink name was, however, to prove short lived as it was found that having certain vehicles marked for specific routing was a restriction which caused too much inflexibility for the company's vehicle schedulers.

Still painted in NBC leaf green livery with Weston fleet names and additionally adorned with Badgerline logos on its between deck white band, Roe-bodied Leyland Olympian 9512 (JHU911X) leaves Bristol at the start of its journey to Weston super Mare. (Travelscene)

Being one of the first National Bus Company subsidiaries to be offered for sale to the private sector, Badgerline's senior management team headed by Managing Director Trevor Smallwood and supported by around 80 staff members at all levels formed a new company under the title of Quayshelfco 135 Limited on 18 June 1986 and immediately set about putting together an offer for their company, submitting this to the NBC for consideration alongside bids from other sources. After what seemed like a never-ending wait, the announcement was eventually made that the management team's bid had been successful and on 23 September 1986 Badgerline became

Wearing Badgerline's green & yellow livery and displaying Bristol fleet names, ECW-bodied Bristol RELL6L 1331 (OAE953M) was one of a number of buses of this type inherited by the newly privatised company from its NBC predecessor. (J.Whitmore)

One of a large number of Ford Transits operated by Badgerline, Dormobile-bodied 4452 (B452WTC) is seen in Weston super Mare operating a contracted service to the local Leo's Supermarket. (T.W.W.Knowles)

Passing through Bath whilst working the city tour is Roman City Plaxton-bodied Leyland Leopard NAE887L which was adorned with ***appropriate lettering. (T.W.W.Knowles)***

the third company to be transferred from the National Bus Company into private ownership following the renaming of Quayshelfco 135 to Badgerline Holdings Limited on 1 September.

Although Badgerline had a number of ideas as to its future development, initially few changes were implemented and the policies and strategies currently in force continued although with deregulation being but a few weeks away, a watchful eye was being kept on the possible new competitors believed to be waiting in the wings for their own opportunities to expand. Prior to Badgerline leaving the NBC it had already registered the services it wished to operate after D-day on 26 October and had additionally submitted tenders to the various local authorities for services financially supported by them which had not been registered commercially. Almost before it had chance to assess its new position in the private sector, the company was faced with the threat of new competition, giving it an uneasy start to its new-found freedom. In the event, however, competition from other independent operators was not as bad as had first been expected, although in some of its established areas Badgerline now found that it was having to pull out all the stops in order to retain its market share. More services were converted to minibus operation in order to offer a higher frequency of service and penetrate housing estates which were inaccessible to conventional size buses and new networks were established in an attempt to attract more passengers to public transport. To cater for new tendered services gained around Midsomer Norton and Trowbridge, Badgerline opened new out stations in each of these towns and for its Bristol city operations it adopted the name 'City Badger'. Unlike many other operators around Britain, however, the company did not find it necessary to purchase any secondhand vehicles to counter competition from deregulation which initially proved to be negligible.

Soon after it had settled in to the new deregulated scene, Badgerline upon learning on 20 November of the collapse of Bath-based coach operator Roman City Ltd. immediately stepped in and purchased the company together with its associate Roman City Holidays from the receiver. This 17-coach company in addition to operating a tours and holiday programme also ran a daily express service from Bath to the capital under the name of 'London Connection' and thus Badgerline was able to diversify into the tours market with a ready-made programme with a high quality reputation. Although Roman City's fleet was not included in the purchase, its two recently-delivered Duple-bodied DAFs and a Jonckheere-bodied DAF double decker were used on the London service for a short period of time on a lease basis until new replacements were found. To this end, 2 Leyland Tigers were hired from Wessex National on 4 December to allow the pair of DAF single deckers to be returned to their rightful owner while 2 new Leyland Royal Tiger Doyens were purchased and after being fitted with toilets and serveries replaced the Wessex vehicles at the end of that month.

At this time Badgerline had a number of new Volvo B10Ms on order for which Alexander bodywork had been specified for 14 dual-purpose single deckers and 12 dual-purpose double deckers and Plaxton bodywork for 10 coaches. Due to the inability of Plaxton to deliver on time, however, the coach bodywork order was cancelled and replaced with Van Hool of Belgium who was able to meet the required date. Thus, the company's first new full-size vehicles took up their duties in the late spring of 1987 as planned. These were operated under the first major application of Volvo's 'mileage contract' concept by which a set rate per mile was paid for the supply of the vehicles and their routine maintenance for a period of five years. The deal did not, however, include body repairs or faults which were the responsibility of Badgerline.

TFB216M, one of Roman City's Plaxton-bodied Leyland Leopards is *pictured at Moreton in Marsh whilst working an excursion. (T.W.W.Knowles)*

1987

The new year started with the relicensing of Bristol LH6L 435 which was immediately loaned to the Bristol & Weston Health Authority for staff transport duties while on 1 February several service changes were implemented in Bath and Weston-super-Mare. In connection with these, an evening service was reintroduced on Bath service 8 (Bus Station - Larkhall) in competition with Streamline Taxis who had gained an Avon County Council contract for its operation following its non-registration by Badgerline whereas in Weston-super-Mare full-size buses were returned to town service 7 as part of a general revision of local operations.

Seeking further expansion, Badgerline submitted a bid for another National Bus Company subsidiary, this time Wilts & Dorset in March 1987, but this too proved unsuccessful and the company was ultimately sold to its management team on 24 June. In preparation for what turned out to be its abortive bid, Badgerline had registered a new company under the title Quayshelfco 172 Limited on 10 April which it renamed Badgerline South Limited on 17 July. Meanwhile, at the end of May Badgerline discontinued its twice daily 'London

The first new single decker buses ordered by Badgerline following its passage to the private sector was a batch of Alexander-bodied Volvo B10Ms, one of which - 111 (D111GHY) - is seen parked in High Street, Weston-super-Mare in June 1987 with a Weston fleet name above its ***front wheel arch. (A.Gilmour)***

Plympton Coachlines Plaxton Supreme IV-bodied Ford R1114 MPH5W typifies that operator's fleet at the time of its merger with Western National. (T.W.W.Knowles)

Having been given Western National fleet number 811 but still wearing Plympton Coachlines livery and fleet names, ex.Plymouth Citybus MCCW-bodied Leyland Atlantean MCO258H prepares to take up its next duty on service 11 from Plymouth to Derriford Hospital on 20 June 1988. (J.Whitmore)

Connection' service, passing this to National Express who then contracted Badgerline to provide the vehicles for its operation. Announcing that bookings for the 1987 Roman City Holidays programme were well ahead of the levels of the previous year, it was also stated that the optional excursions offered with its holidays would now be included in the overall price which would not be increased as a result. At this same time, Badgerline recommenced operation of the hour-long Roman City open-top bus tour of Bath which ran on a 20 minute frequency using Leyland Atlanteans supplemented by Bristol VRTs which were repainted into Roman City's livery of yellow with bands of red and blue upswept at the rear and fitted with both Roman City and Badgerline fleet names. Additionally, on 23 May Badgerline vacated its distinctive Beach Bus Station, depot and offices at Weston-super-Mare and moved into a new purpose-built depot on the Oldmixon Industrial Estate, enabling its original site and buildings to be sold for redevelopment. Simultaneously, and as part of its diversification plans, Badgerline opened its first newsagents shop in part of its group of office and shop units at High Street, Weston-super-Mare and, trading under the title of Badger News this also acted as an outlet for the company's ticket sales. Soon after these events, Badgerline reorganised its company structure and created several operating subsidiaries including Badgerline Ltd., Roman City, Roman City Travel (in which it held a 65% share) and Badger News.

Equally important was the bid submitted by JayIsle Ltd. who traded as Plympton Coach Lines, for the purchase from the National Bus Company of its subsidiary Western National. Plympton Coach Lines was a Plymouth-based independent operator whose fleet comprised a mere 17 vehicles, 9 of which were double deckers used in competition with midibuses operated by municipal-owned Plymouth Citybus on local services. 3 of the double deckers were MCW Metropolitans while the remainder were ex.Plymouth Citybus Leyland Atlanteans while the coaches comprised 5 Ford R1114s, a Volvo B58 and a Bedford YMT. One of Plympton's directors, John Preece, was also managing director of Plymouth Computers, one of the largest computer supply companies in the south-west and was thus well versed in business matters. In support of his bid, he invited the

Adorned with Hoppa lettering on its side panels and in the top of its windscreen, Western National Reeve Burgess-bodied Mercedes Benz L608D 69 (C687ECV) is seen at Plymouth bus station. After later passing to Badgerline, it ultimately joined the fleet of Eastern National in September 1993. (J.Whitmore)

Still painted in NBC-style green livery and displaying Cornwall Busways fleet names, ECW-bodied Bristol VRT 1150 (AFJ752T) rests in Plymouth bus station during the late summer of 1987. (J.Whitmore)

Western National management team to join him despite it having made its own offer of purchase, and also gained backing from Badgerline to achieve his goal. The outcome, announced at the end of July, was that Western National had been sold to Quayshelfco 176 Limited, a company set up on 6 May by Plympton Coach Lines and Badgerline, in which the latter had a 39% stake, John Preece and Ashley Taylor 41% and merchant bankers Hill Samuel 20%, and that the date of transfer would be 6 August. Thus Badgerline had gained success at last and had added another company - or at least part - to its growing portfolio. Following this acquisition, Quayshelfco 176 Ltd. changed its name to Western National Holdings Limited on 27 August.

BATTLE FOR EXPANSION

Whilst the battle for control of Western National had been taking place, Badgerline on 28 June launched an attack on Wilts & Dorset in Salisbury when it formed a subsidiary under the title of Badgerline South and began two minibus routes from the city centre to Bemerton Heath housing conurbation in direct competition with the incumbent operator. Wilts & Dorset responded on 4 July by doubling its service frequency on the two routes concerned using conventional size vehicles whilst almost immediately Badgerline began minibus operations on three more services from Salisbury city centre to Paul's Dene, Bishopdown and West Harnham. To launch its new services, Badgerline used television star Ronnie Corbett together with a minibus cavalcade around the city which Wilts & Dorset followed with its own vehicles, whilst the latter introduced a variety of promotions in a bid to retain passenger loyalty. Such was the initial success of Badgerline's new venture that on 7 September it introduced yet another new route serving Laverstock and thirteen days later began frequent services to Newbridge and Odstock Hospital. All the routes were maintained by new 19-seat Robin Hood-bodied Iveco 49.10s sporting Minilink fleetnames. Not losing sight of its existing operations whilst all these events were taking place, Badgerline sought to improve its services around Keynsham and enhanced its double deck and minibus frequencies to Bristol and Bath under the 'Keynsham Konnection' name.

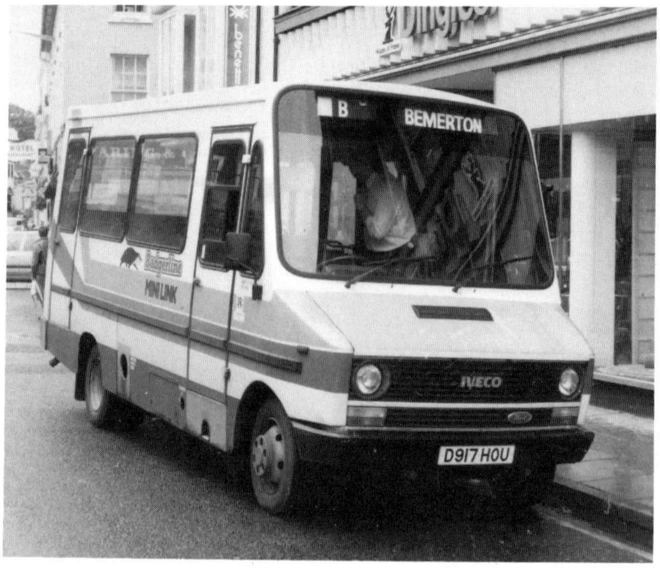

Badgerline's Robin Hood-bodied Iveco 49.10 4917 (D917HOU) in Salisbury in July 1987 is working its owner's recently-introduced service B to Bemerton which ran in competition to Wilts & Dorset. (T.W.W.Knowles)

Meanwhile, prior to its sortie into Salisbury, Badgerline had joined forces with Southern Vectis on 1 May when together they set up a new company named Quayshelfco 175 Limited in which Badgerline held an 80% share and Southern Vectis 20% (later renaming it Badger Vectis) in order to launch an attack on Wilts & Dorset's Bournemouth and Poole areas where an opportunity was seen to further expand their activities. Unlike Badger's venture into Salisbury which was undertaken solely with minibuses, the Poole attack was to be launched with a combination of 7 new Iveco 49.10 minibuses, 14 Bristol RELLs and 2 dual purpose-bodied Leyland Leopards and in preparation six routes were registered, three of which included sections which competed directly with Wilts & Dorset. Although the use of the local operating name 'Poole Pandas' was considered, this was not pursued and when the services began on 6 September they were marketed under the Badgerline identity (Southern Vectis being a minority shareholder in the joint venture). The conventional buses, which were provided by both Badgerline and Southern Vectis and painted in Badgerline's green & yellow livery (mostly with green front panels) were crew operated and employed on services linking Turlin Moor, Poole, Bournemouth, Christchurch and Mudeford and Broadstone, Poole and Bournemouth while the minibuses were used on local services around Poole to Canford Heath and Bourne Estate and between Christchurch and Burton. Not having any premises of its own in its new area of operation, Badger Vectis reached agreement with Bournemouth Yellow Buses to stable its vehicles at the latter's Mallard Road depot in Bournemouth.

Although painted in Badgerline's green & yellow livery for the Badger Vectis operation, ECW-bodied Bristol RELL6G 40 (PDL492H) seen at Poole in October 1987 operating service 1 to Broadstone was actually owned by Southern Vectis, Badgerline's partner in this joint venture. (A.Gilmour)

Seeing the possibility of further expanding its coaching activities, during the summer Badgerline submitted a bid for NBC subsidiary Wessex of Bristol, although this proved unsuccessful with the company being purchased by its management. Meanwhile, an exodus of senior managers at Western National was witnessed during August following increased involvement in the company's affairs by Plympton Coach Lines managing director John Preece. Although it was obvious that Western National was experiencing some internal problems, these did not appear to be affecting Badgerline who continued to expand in other areas. Following the success of its first retail venture in Weston-super-Mare, Badger News opened its second shop in September at Mount Hill, Hanham, Bristol. Previously known as Hanham Mount Stores, this opened daily from 6.30am to 9.30pm for the sale of newspapers, convenience foods, fruit and vegetables, chemist sundries, hot and cold snacks and off-licence items as well as providing bus information and tickets.

Having gained a share of the bus market in Salisbury, Poole and Bournemouth, Badgerline turned its attention towards Portsmouth using its Quayshelfco 179 Limited company for its application for a new 46-vehicle operator's licence. In view of it quoting its operating bases as the Southampton CityBus depot at Portswood and a Ryder Truck Rentals depot at Hilsea, this appeared to indicate that this new attack was to be launched in association with Southampton CityBus who was at that time the subject of an attack by Southern Vectis, Badgerline's partner in Poole/Bournemouth. This indeed proved to be true with the new company, trading under the name 'Red Admiral',

Resting in Marlborough Street depot, Bristol are Roe-bodied Leyland *Olympian 9532 (NTC131Y) and ECW-bodied Bristol VRT 5544 (EWS752W), both of which were painted in Badgerline's Swift Link livery. (T.W.W.Knowles collection)*

Painted in Badgerline livery and carrying Mini Link fleet names is ECW- *bodied Bristol LH6L 466 (AFB597V) which was new to Bristol Omnibus Co. and had the last LH6L chassis to be built. (F.W.York)*

*Enroute to Portsea in March 1988, E948LAE was one of a fleet of Robin Hood-bodied Iveco 49.10s operated by Red Admiral, a company formed jointly by Badgerline and Southampton CityBus to operate services competing with those of Portsmouth City Transport. **(Travelscene)***

being owned by Badgerline and Southampton CityBus, each of whom held a 47.5% share and Alan Barrett (who was appointed as manager) holding the remaining 5%). Red Admiral began its operations on 11 December with a ten-minute headway service from Paulsgrove to Portsea via Portsmouth city centre which was operated by 15 new red and black-liveried Robin Hood-bodied Iveco 49.10s. Prior to this, however, Portsmouth City Council in November had unexpectedly taken the decision to sell its bus undertaking, sparking speculation as to whether Red Admiral might emerge as the main operator in the city rather than being merely a predator. Almost immediately, Portsmouth City Transport's employees formed a buyout team in an attempt to retain local ownership of the company, signalling a battle that was to last for several weeks before a victor eventually emerged. Obviously preparing for a future expansion of its services, the newly-formed Red Admiral purchased five Routemaster double deckers from London Buses at the end of October and placed them into store at Hilsea pending a decision on their use.

Further expanding with the purchase in December of Wessex Continental Travel of Plymouth and Portsmouth, a company who operated a range of over 20 continental holidays, Badgerline also made an offer for Cambridge-based Premier Travel Group, although this broke down with the emergence of a management bid for the travel side by Premier's two directors, leaving only the bus and coach business to be disposed of. In the event, a bid by Cambus for the company was rejected following resistance by driving staff and Premier was ultimately purchased by an alternative management buy-out team backed by Alan Stephenson and Giles Fearnley who had earlier purchased West Yorkshire Road Car Co. Ltd, from the NBC.

During the year, Badgerline had added a number of new Iveco 49.10 minibuses to its fleet in addition to its new Volvos and had introduced a new coach/dual purpose livery using diagonal white, yellow and green bands. Repainting had continued within the bus fleet to eliminate the former NBC leaf green and white scheme and by the end of the year only three Bristol REs still retained these colours, two of which were dispatched on long-term loan to the Bristol & Weston Health Authority for staff transportation duties whilst the other was loaned in July to Poole Bay Services in Dorset. 15 Bristol RELLs were transferred to Badger Vectis which also operated 6 of Southern Vectis's buses of this type which had been repainted into Badgerline livery whilst also joining the Bournemouth-based fleet were 6 Robin Hood-bodied Iveco 49.10s, a pair of Badgerline's full-height ex.London Country Bristol VRTs and a trio of leased ex.Greater Manchester Daimler Fleetlines.

Passing one of Charlies Cars Freight Rover Sherpa minibuses in Bournemouth in November 1987 whilst on long term loan for operation on Badger Vectis duties is Greater Manchester Park Royal-bodied Leyland Atlantean WBN965L which had been given full Badgerline livery. (Travelscene)

Acquired by Bristol Omnibus from London Country in 1980, full-height ECW-bodied Bristol VRT PPH470R is seen here operating a Badger Vectis service in Poole in September 1987 carrying fleet number 70 and sporting an additional Badgerline fleet name vinyl above its front wheel arch. (A.Gilmour)

An unusual vehicle transferred to Badgerline upon its separation from Bristol Omnibus Co. was ECW-bodied Bristol LH6L WE108 (KHU323P) which had been converted into a towing wagon in March 1984. It is seen here in its new role at Marlborough Street depot, Bristol. (F.W.York)

1988

As one door closed, another one opened however, and on 4 January Badgerline introduced its first minibus services in Hampshire under contract to Hampshire County Council. Serving rural areas around Fordingbridge where a new outstation had been opened for Badgerline's Salisbury operation, the new routes ran from Fordingbridge to Salisbury, Cranborne and Ringwood.

Despite expanding its activities throughout 1987, Badgerline continued to maintain its interests in its original territory and in addition to placing the 36 new Volvo B10Ms in service as mentioned earlier, it added to these a further 4 Van Hool-bodied Volvo B10M coaches and a quantity of new Robin Hood-bodied Iveco 49.10 minibuses. Additionally it acquired 11 Robin Hood-bodied Iveco 49.10s from Western National to support its Badger Vectis operations at Poole and moved its headquarters to a new location at Badger Manor, Edingworth, Weston-super-Mare.

After providing a network of emergency services in Plymouth during late January/early February 1988 when staff of Plymouth Citybus took strike action, Western National after having an offer to purchase the municipal company turned down, took the decision to register twenty services in the city which were designed to compete directly with Citybus. Planned to commence on 19 March, this action led to Citybus immediately registering four services out of Plymouth into traditional Western National territory and looking towards Cornwall as another area of retaliation. Thus, it appeared, another new bus war was about to break out! Meanwhile, in order to trim its costs, Badger Vectis converted its Poole area operations to one person operation at the end of January and replaced its Bristol REs with minibuses which were of adequate size to carry the number of intending passengers. Back in its home territory, Badgerline suddenly found that rather than being the predator, it was now facing new competition itself when Bakers Coaches of Weston-super-Mare moved into local bus operation and purchased a pair of Carlyle-bodied Iveco minibuses with a view to obtaining some local tendered work. Additionally Bakers launched a new 'Commutacoach' service between Weston and Bristol which competed with existing Badgerline services. For the 1988 season, Badgerline introduced an all-day ticket for its Roman City open-top tour at Bath which was to run daily from April to September, allowing passengers to hop on and off the bus at any of the twelve stops enroute and additionally introduced extra evening journeys on Mondays to Fridays. Back in Portsmouth on 4 March Red Admiral started its second route (from The Hard to Eastney with hail and ride facilities around Eastney), again using minibuses rather than the Routemasters which continued to remain in store.

Looking for expansion, Western National purchased the 33-vehicle business of Cornwall's largest independent operator Grenville Motors of Troon at the end of February, following it with the purchase of 31-vehicle Robert Risk of Plymouth in March. Whilst Grenville Motors concentrated largely on inter-urban bus services in the Camborne, Falmouth and Penryn areas but also ran a handful of excursions and tours, Risk whose fleet mainly comprised Ivecos, Fiats and Ford Transits but also contained a pair of Quests, a Dodge and a Bedford CF specialised in minibus and small coach contract and private hire work and also operated 'Flight Link' services between Bristol, Plymouth and Exeter airports. Conversely, Grenville's fleet was largely made up of full-size Bedford buses and coaches although it also featured a pair of Bristol LHS6Ls, 2 Leyland Atlanteans, an Albion Nimbus, an MAN coach, 4 Leyland Leopards and a Volvo B10M. Under their new ownership, both companies were to operate as separate entities and retain their existing identities, although it was planned to expand the Risk business into Cornwall at an early date. Meanwhile, Badgerline itself also gained further expansion when it

Seen in Plymouth in October 1988 displaying a Ferrybus fleet name on its cove panels is Western National 2886 (GOL414N), a Leyland National acquired from Midland Red East in 1983. (J.Whitmore)

Still wearing the livery and names of Grenville of Camborne from whom it was acquired by Western National in March 1988, Plaxton-bodied Leyland Leopard SUR284R had gained its new owner's fleet number 2451 by the time it was photographed here. (T.W.W.Knowles)

Amongst the vehicles taken over by Western National with the business of Grenville of Camborne was MAN coach SOI1552 which was given fleet number 2238 by its new owner. (Travelscene)

Western National subsidiary Roberts of Plymouth operated a number of Fiat minicoaches, one of which - Harwin-bodied 79.10 type 553 (LFR293X) is seen in 1990 at its parent's Laira Bridge depot at Plymouth. (T.W.W.Knowles)

Acquired with the business of Robert Risk of Plymouth in March 1988, Williams-bodied Ford Transit E683XVU was given fleet number 524 by its new owner, Western National but retained its former owner's livery and fleet names. (T.W.W.Knowles)

purchased Manchester-based National Travelworld Limited from the National Bus Company on 24 March, giving it 80 ABTA-approved travel agencies around Britain together with around 50 more owned by third parties but using the National Travelworld name under licence. Simultaneous with this acquisition, on 25 March Badgerline registered a new company under the title of Quayshelfco 215 Limited, renaming this Badgerline Buses Limited on 6 May.

Continuing to examine its traditional area of operation and seeking to improve services where needs arose, on 3 March Badgerline introduced a new express route (numbered X22) between Weston-super-Mare and Bristol via North Worle and seven days later began a new Saturdays only direct service from Weston-super-Mare to London. Later, on the 28th of the month it revised and improved its Minilink services in Trowbridge and Warminster and was successful in gaining a school contract some distance away from its established territory at Chepstow for which it outstationed a solitary bus at the National Welsh depot in that town.

After its period of growing success, Badgerline suffered its first setback when, on 27 March following mounting losses, it gave the required 42-days notice to withdraw all its services in Salisbury and its Badger Vectis routes in Poole and Bournemouth. Upon learning of these moves, however, the drivers at the 32-bus Badger Vecits base at Bournemouth staged a mass exodus and as a consequence the company was unable to maintain its operations and after informing the Traffic Commissioner of its predicament ceased running on 31 March after which Badgerline acquired the 20% stake held in the company by Southern Vectis in exchange for its shareholding in Vectis's Vikki Osborne holiday company. The Salisbury services, however, continued to operate until 7 May when these too were abandoned and the 25 minibuses employed upon them transferred elsewhere in the company. The response by Wilts & Dorset to Badgerline's attacks had proved too much for the Weston-based predator who admitted that it had not expected such retaliation from what it had believed to be an under-financed company. In Plymouth

Looking smart in its new Western National livery, coach-seated ECW-bodied Leyland Olympian 1800 (A750VAF) prepares to leave Plymouth bus station on the 84 service to Tavistock in June 1988. (J.Whitmore)

where Western National and Citybus were continuing their battle, a war of words had also been launched with each of the two operators claiming success in their latest moves, although in reality to date there appeared to be no winner. Western National's vocal managing director John Preece repeated that his strategy was to hasten Citybus's demise, predicting that its future would be a 'giant closing down sale' while Citybus retaliated by starting competing services in Plymstock and Saltash, both previously only served by Western National. And so the war continued ...... Meanwhile, to further increase its fleet Western National revised its livery from blue and white with red, yellow and blue bands to one of blue and cream relieved by two red bands.

REUNIFICATION IN BRISTOL

Undaunted by the failure of its attacks on Wilts & Dorset, Badgerline (Holdings) Ltd. still sought further expansion and made an offer to Midland Red West Holdings for the purchase of its business interests. These comprised Midland Red West and Midland Red Coaches which the company's management had purchased from the National Bus Company on 22 December 1986 and Bristol Omnibus Company which had been bought from the NBC by Midland Red West on 18 September 1987. If accepted, this would reunite Badgerline with Bristol Omnibus Company from which it had been separated on 1 January 1986. Despite attracting the attention of the Office of Fair Trading, the purchase of Midland Red West Holdings was completed on 26 April and the first sign of new ownership followed immediately when all tickets became fully inter-available between Badgerline and Bristol City Line services. It was, however, made clear from the start that the newly-acquired companies would continue to operate as separate entities with their own management teams, liveries and fleet names and that outwardly, there would be little change. Confirming this, a new-style Bristol City Line network map entitled 'The Overground Bus Map' which had been designed before the takeover was launched without modification early in May while similarly Midland Red West had introduced its new minibus service network in Hereford branded 'Hereford Hopper' on 23 April. For the latter, Midland Red West placed 28 new Reeve Burgess-bodied Mercedes Benz 609Ds in service painted in an attractive yellow, green and orange livery, and except for three all were given individual names such as Walter de Lacy, Nell Gwynne and On and Offa. Prior to Midland Red West's change of ownership it had successfully bid for a number of tendered services in Birmingham, some of which were weekday night routes, and these commenced operation on 1 May.

Almost before the ink had dried on the above events, Red Admiral on 13 May launched two more minibus services in Portsmouth using the vehicles surplus from the Salisbury closure. These linked Waterlooville with Southsea and Portsmouth and in addition, during early April Red Admiral had also gained three Hampshire County Council tendered operations in the Portsmouth area. Although the former London Routemasters were still owned, they continued to remain in store due to a strong favourable reaction to the minibuses.

As far as its fleets were concerned, Badgerline continued its investment in new vehicles with the purchase of 24 Optare StarRider midibuses, four of which were fitted with coach-type seating. Initially these were allocated to the company's Bristol and Weston-super-Mare depots where they ousted several Bristol REs, although the

Amongst the vehicles transferred to Midland Red West upon its formation in 1981 was Marshall-bodied Leyland Leopard 341 (GJW41N) which had gained the company's post-NBC livery by the time it was photographed here.

New to Midland Red Coaches in July 1982, Leyland Leopard 1053 was originally fitted with Willowbrook bodywork and registered LOA843X. Severely damaged in an accident when only four months old its chassis was rebuilt in 1984, re-registered Q553UOC, and fitted with a new Plaxton Paramount 3200 body. Seen at Digbeth depot, Birmingham in 1989 it had by that time been repainted into the all-red Midland Red Coaches livery of Midland Red West. (J.Whitmore)

Adorned with ReddiLink fleet names and painted in a red, yellow & orange livery for use on Redditch town services, Midland Red West Robin Hood-bodied Mercedes Benz L608D 1390 (C390RUY) stands in its home town bus station in July 1989. (J.Whitmore)

Acquired by Bristol Omnibus Co. from United Counties, Leyland National 1472 (ERP558T) shows off its new City Line Overground livery as it loads in Bristol Centre in February 1989. (Travelscene)

Unusually, Bristol Omnibus Co. Leyland National 1465 (HEU119N) was converted from single to dual-door layout in 1984 and is seen here in its new form operating service 8 to Clifton Zoo in City B Line livery. (Travelscene)

Painted in Bristol Omnibus Co's new red, blue & yellow City Line livery, open-top dual-door ECW-bodied Bristol VRT 5044 (LEU269P) was given City Tourer lettering for operation on the Bristol City Tour. (Travelscene)

Seen in the centre of Bristol, the electronic destination display on Bristol Omnibus Co's City Line Overground-liveried Roe-bodied Leyland Olympian 9537 (NTC136Y) appears to be causing problems and shows lavonlouth instead of Avonmouth. (K.A.Jenkinson)

latter were given a reprieve to continue in service until the end of the summer season in order to provide extra capacity where this was required. Bristol City Line gained a number of new Dormobile-bodied Iveco 49.10s ordered prior to the acquisition of the company by Badgerline Holdings whilst similarly Midland Red West received 28 new Reeve Burgess-bodied Mercedes Benz 609D minibuses mentioned earlier. Western National also purchased a number of new buses and coaches including 6 Leyland Lynx for use in the Plymouth bus war, 2 Neoplan Skyliner double deck coaches and 3 Duple 425 single deck coaches.

Preparing for the future, Badgerline Holdings underwent an amount of restructuring on 6 May when it formed four subsidiaries Badgerline Buses Ltd., Badger Retail Ltd., Badgerline Properties Ltd. and The Bristol Bus Station/South Bus Station Co. Ltd. Of these, Badgerline Buses Ltd. comprised Badgerline, Midland Red West, Bristol City Line and Midland Red Coaches and was placed under the executive directorship of Ken Mills while Badger Retail Ltd. controlled the company's travel and retail interests and was under the executive directorship of Douglas Ross. Both Mills and Ross had moved across from Midland Red West where the former was managing director and the latter financial director. Badgerline Properties Ltd. was set up as a management company for the group's properties including the National Travelworld agencies whereas The Bristol Bus Station/South Bus Station Co. Ltd. was formed to run the Marlborough Street, Bristol and Manvers Street, Bath bus stations on an arms length basis. A further company established by Badgerline was Dolsett Estates in which it had an 80% stake (the remaining 20% being held by a property company) and was a vehicle for a possible joint redevelopment of the Marlborough Street site at Bristol which was at that time under consideration.

In an attempt to improve its profitability, National Travelworld closed ten of its agencies at the beginning of May and renamed the remainder Badger Travel while at the same time Badgerline appointed Primesight Bus Advertising to manage the sale of advertising on both the interior and exterior of its buses in Bristol, Bath and Weston-super-Mare. Coinciding with these moves was called to a public inquiry before the Traffic Commissioner on 7 June to explain why it had been unable to fulfil the required 42 days notice period for its abandonment of its Badger Vectis operations in Poole/Bournemouth. The outcome of this inquiry was that the Traffic Commissioner placed a ban on Badgerline from registering any new services in the Poole/Bournemouth area, although he stopped short of imposing his discretionary 20% fuel tax penalty on the company. As a result of its withdrawal from Salisbury, Badgerline's Hampshire County Council contracted services in the Fordingbridge area were put out to re-tender and were won by Mayburys of Cranborne, thus ending Badger's foray into Hampshire. Across in Plymouth, common

One of six Leyland Lynxes purchased by Western National in 1988, 202 (E202BOD) awaits its passengers in Plymouth in June of that year. (J.Whitmore)

sense began to prevail when talks were opened between Western National and Plymouth Citybus in an attempt to bring to an end the un-necessary war between the two companies which had cost both dearly. As a sign of good faith, Western National deferred the start of further competitive services from 29 May to 29 June while Citybus put on hold its new service to Torpoint which it had intended to start on 22 May, although it registered a new service to Ivybridge to commence on 19 June. In the meantime, Portsmouth City Transport with whom Red Admiral were competing agreed the sale of its undertaking to a consortium of employees and Southampton CityBus early in June, bringing speculation as to the future of Red Admiral in which Southampton CityBus had a shareholding. All was revealed later that month when Badgerline sold its stake in Red Admiral to Southampton CityBus and thus completed its disengagement from the newly established operations outside its traditional territory. Alan Barrett, manager of Red Admiral retained his small stake in the company' however, and remained with it under its new ownership.

In a move to consolidate its coaching and leisure interests, Badgerline Holdings' Wessex Continental Travel subsidiary was integrated with Roman City early in June. Under this reorganisation, Wessex vacated its Plymouth headquarters and transferred its counter reservations to the Badger Travel chain. Wessex Continental's 1989 programme which mainly comprised extended tours to several parts of mainland Europe such as Spain, Austria and West Germany was now to be operated alongside Roman City's similar programme and as such would give Badger Leisure greater buying power of overseas hotel block bookings etc. Although Western National would provide many of the vehicles for the Wessex Continental tours, Deeble of Darley Ford would also continue to be a major contractor as it had been in the past. Having completed its consolidation, Badgerline on 1 October sold its Roman City and Wessex Continental Travel holiday operations to Bristol-based former NBC subsidiary Wessex National to allow it to concentrate more fully on its bus operations. Badgerline's stake in Roman City Travel was not, however, included in the deal and its two agency shops still remained within Badgerline Leisure's portfolio. Prior to these changes, on 13 July Western National had taken over at short notice the Devon County Council-subsidised service 627 from Berry Pomeroy to Torquay which had been operated by Total Travel until its sudden demise.

Although few inter-fleet transfers had taken place to date between Badgerline's various operating companies, 4 of its Bristol REs previously employed on the Badger Vectis services in Poole and Bournemouth were transferred to Western National for use on the former Grenville Motors service from Falmouth to Penryn while the Blue Bus fleet name and livery was resurrected in Penzance to identify the former Harvey's service to Mousehole which had been taken over with the Grenville purchase. This was applied to a trio of Bristol LHSs whereas the ex.Badgerline REs retained their former owner's colours. Amongst the other vehicles to move between companies were 12 of Badgerline's Robin Hood-bodied Iveco 49.10s made surplus following the withdrawal from Salisbury which were transferred to Bristol City Line, 3 Badgerline VRTs which were dispatched to join Western National and 3 VRTs together with a Mercedes Benz L608D which were transferred from Bristol City Line to Midland Red West to whom the VRTs had been on loan since the latter months of 1987. In addition, Western National also acquired a Leyland Leopard coach from Midland Red West and purchased 2 Bristol LHSs from United at Darlington while similarly Western National exchanged 3 of its Leyland Nationals with United from whom it received a trio of Bristol LHSs. Bristol Omnibus Co. who acquired 6 secondhand Leyland Nationals - 2 from Milton Keynes Citybus, 3 from East Kent and 1 from West Yorkshire relaunched itself in August under the new title 'Overground' and introduced an attractive new livery of yellow, red and blue although it was not until October that the new fleet name began to be applied to the fleet or the new colour scheme began to make a significant appearance.

Early in September, Badgerline gained a controlling interest in Western National when it purchased the 41% stake held by John Preece and Ashley Taylor who both then left the company by mutual consent. Taking the place of John Preece as managing director was Keith Athers, former managing director of Badger Vectis. Meanwhile,

Painted in a white & red livery and additionally lettered V.I.P.Executive, Western National's Duple 425 2242 (E218CFJ) is seen in Swansea whilst undertaking a private hire duty. (K.A.Jenkinson)

Repainted into a blue & cream livery and given Blue Bus fleet names for operation on the former Harveys of Mousehole service, Western National's rare Wadham Stringer-bodied Bristol LHS6L 1565 (KRL444W) was acquired with the business of Grenville of Camborne. (J.L.Hobbs)

Western National had won a large number of school contracts in the Plymouth area which had previously been operated by Citybus and in order to provide sufficient vehicles to maintain these from the start of the new school term on 6 September it was found necessary to hire in no less than 29 double deckers and 7 single deckers from other operators. Amongst these were 9 East Lancs-bodied Leyland Atlanteans from Hyndburn Transport, 4 Atlanteans from Southampton CityBus, 4 Atlanteans from Portsmouth CityBus, 4 from Rotherham & District, 4 Bristol VRTs from Badgerline, 3 Dennis Dominators from a west country dealer and 4 Leyland Nationals and 3 Leyland Leopards from Midland Red West.

Resting in Plymouth bus station whilst working a tour to Newquay in June 1988, Badgerline's Van Hool Alizee-bodied Volvo B10M 2503 (D503GHY) wore National Holidays livery together with its owner's fleet name over its front wheel arch. (J.Whitmore)

The peace talks at Plymouth finally achieved success at the end of September when both Western National and Plymouth Citybus reduced their fleets and replaced their competing services with a new simplified route network starting on 6 November. Under this acquiescence, in addition to both companies deregistering their competing services Western National was to take over two minibus workings on Citybus's cross-city service from The Ham to Mount Gould and in exchange was to pass back to Citybus some of its recently-won schools contracts. This left Western National with 10% more city mileage than it had had prior to the protracted war and yet enabled it to withdraw 25 of its vehicles from Plymouth and thus return most of its hired buses to their rightful owners. Similarly, Plymouth Citybus was able to reduce its fleet by 35 vehicles. Unfortunately, as a result of neither company registering the agreement running from 6 November to 12 June 1989 restricting competition with the other, both Western National and Citybus were called before the Restrictive Practices Court in the autumn of 1989. Western National also gained an amount of success following a new round of Devon County Council tendering in November when it won three services in the Torbay area which had previously been operated by Devon Services and Burtons Coaches and five radiating from Newton Abbot for which it was necessary to open a new outstation on Totnes Industrial Estate. A month later on 24 December, Devon General withdrew from the X80 Torquay to Plymouth route upon which it had operated jointly with Western National, thus leaving the Badgerline subsidiary with its full control.

Following its earlier success in Birmingham, Midland Red West gained several more tendered services in the Kitts Green area of the city and in West Bromwich with effect from 5 September and for their operation hired 17 Robin Hood-bodied Iveco 49.10 minibuses from Badgerline, although these were replaced in mid-October with new Iveco 49.10s. At around this same time, the last of Midland Red West's coaches to wear the company's old white, red and black livery (Plaxton-bodied Leyland Leopard 1077) was repainted all-over white whilst in December, to celebrate its 20th birthday, Badgerline unexpectedly repainted Bristol RELL 1092 (new in 1968) into Tilling green and cream as a nice reminder of the pre-NBC era. Prior to this, Bristol Omnibus Co. reversed previous policies and in September began rebuilding its newer Leyland Nationals from dual to single door layout whilst leaving the fleet were the Bristol VRTs which had been stored unused since 1986 when they were converted to left hand drive configuration for an American customer who later cancelled its order. Further depleting City Line's Bristol VRT fleet, 10 buses of this type were transferred to Badgerline while in their place came several Leyland Nationals acquired from companies outside the Badgerline Group.

Having recently been acquired from Badgerline and still wearing that company's livery, Robin Hood-bodied Iveco 49.10 1922 (E922KEU) had, however, gained Midland Red West fleet names by the time it was photographed at Castle Bromwich in the spring of 1989. (J.Whitmore)

Adorned with both Guide Friday fleet names and that of its owner Badgerline, 1975 vintage open-top Bristol VRT 8615 (JHW107P) was given an attractive cream and two-tone green livery for operation on the Bath City Tour upon which it is seen here. (N.Furness)

1989

Having satisfactorily sorted out its problems in Plymouth, Badgerline now awaited the outcome of the long-awaited Monopoly and Mergers Commission's report on its acquisition of Midland Red West Holdings. This was issued in March 1989 concluding that four out of the six members of the MMC panel found that the takeover 'may be expected to operate against the public interest'. although conceding that there had been no material loss of competition in commercial services as a result of the takeover, the report identified serious 'detriments' to competition in the provision of tendered services in Avon where both Badgerline and Bristol City Line operated. Thus Badgerline was given six months in which to deal with the adverse effects of the merger by way of undertakings to clear up the contracts situation and was warned that if agreement could not be reached with the Director General of Fair Trading within this period of time, an enforced sale might be sought. As a consequence Badgerline agreed to accept undertakings relating to the tendering of local authority supported services.

Following the sale of Roman City and Wessex Continental during the previous year, Badgerline moved further away from the leisure market in May when it sold off its chain of over 70 Badger Travel shops (formerly National Travelworld) to Co-operative Travel Care. Denying that the business had been sold because the returns were 'not as high as originally anticipated', Badgerline stated that its reason was purely a result of competition in the travel business getting fiercer. In its rationalised form, Badger Travel's revenue from its 10% agency commission was around £3.5 million, giving the chain a gross turnover in the region of £35 million. Prior to disposing of its travel shops, following an approach by Stratford-upon-Avon based open-top tours specialist Guide Friday who was keen to expand its operations to Avon, Badgerline agreed in March to a new joint venture between the two companies related to its established Bath Tour. Under the agreement, Badgerline was to provide the vehicles for the Tour while Guide Friday's contribution was the replacement of the previous taped commentary by on-board guides which, it was believed, would enhance the tour and attract greater patronage. For the new arrangement, Badgerline rather than submit to full Guide Friday livery instead modified the colour scheme of the buses employed on this operation to feature a dark green skirt and lime green between decks band with the remainder being cream. Both Badgerline and Guide Friday fleet names were applied.

Another bus repainted into a non-standard livery was Bath's Bristol VRT 5531 which, to commemorate the 85th anniversary of the start of electric tram services by Bath Electric Tramways was repainted into the original dark blue and white livery with maroon skirt and

Badgerline Bristol VRT 5531 (EWS739W) was painted in a special light blue & cream livery in 1989 to commemorate 50 years since the passing of Bath's electric trams. (P.T.Stokes)

During 1989/90 Bristol Omnibus Co. standardised on the Leyland Lynx for all its new conventional-size single deckers. One of the 1990 delivery - 1640 (H640YHT) is seen at the University of West of England painted in its owner's attractive red, blue & yellow City Line Overland livery. (K.A.Jenkinson)

Midland Red West purchased 8 new tri-axle Talbot Pullmans in 1990 for operation on the West Midlands PTE (Centro)-contracted service to Aston University for which they were painted in a green & yellow livery and given Quickstep fleet names. (J.Whitmore)

wheels used by that company. Meanwhile, Badgerline's Leyland Royal Tiger Doyen 2401 still retained its Roman City livery and was operated under contract to Wessex National for its operations under this banner. On the service front, on 28 May Badgerline reorganised its Bath minibus service 14 and upgraded it to 'big bus' status as routes 14, 14A and 14B. Due to the restricted nature of the roads in the Wansdyde Estate, however, it was necessary to operate the new 14A with four short B-series Leyland Nationals which were more easily able to negotiate this housing conurbation. By the late summer the loan of the 2 Bristol RELLs to the Bristol and Weston Area Health Authority ceased and the two buses concerned - 1313/5 - both had their red fronts (applied for the Health Authority) replaced by standard fleet colours prior to their re-entry to normal service.

The flow of new vehicles to Badgerline's various operating companies continued during 1989 with 33 Leyland Lynxes and 20 Dormobile-bodied Iveco 49.10s entering service with Bristol City Line and 10 all-Leyland Olympians being taken into stock by Badgerline at Bath, two of which were fitted with coach-type seating. The City Line Lynxes which incorporated a number of additional facilities to aid the elderly and less able bodied as well as featuring side and rear route number apertures were put to use from Muller Road depot during June and July on the 71 service between Filton and Bristol as well as on some services operated from Winterstoke Road depot.

Still wearing Red Admiral livery but having gained Midland Red West fleet names, Robin Hood-bodied Iveco 49.10 1951 (E951LAE) seen here at Digbeth depot in October 1989 began life with Badgerline three years earlier. (J.Whitmore)

Acquired by Badgerline from G&G, Leamington Spa in 1989, coach-seated East Lancs-bodied Leyland Olympian 5000 (C28EUH) carried its new owner's dual-purpose livery of white, yellow & green with a black skirt when seen leaving Bristol for Weston-super-Mare in August 1992. (T.S.Blackman)

Transferred between members of the group were 5 Leyland National 2s which moved from Midland Red West to Badgerline, 9 Robin Hood-bodied Iveco 49.10s which were permanently transferred to Midland Red West from Badgerline following a period of extended loan and 3 Leyland National Is which joined Midland Red West from Western National together with 2 Reeve Burgess-bodied Mercedes Benz L608Ds. Additionally, several secondhand minibuses were purchased for Midland Red West from companies outside the group with 9 Reeve Burgess-bodied Mercedes Benz L608D being obtained from Southdown and 4 Robin Hood-bodied Iveco 49.10s from Red Admiral while Badgerline somewhat surprisingly purchased a pair of coach-seated East Lancs-bodied Leyland Olympians from G & G, Leamington Spa, both of which had started life with Inter Valley Link in 1985. Midland Red West painted its newly-acquired Ivecos into its yellow and green livery for operation at Kidderminster and yellow and blue for use at Worcester although one of the latter's allocation received a cream and brown scheme to commemorate Worcester's Charter Year (1189 - 1989). City Line also acquired 11 Iveco 49.10s from Red Admiral to enable it to further reduce its once large fleet of Ford Transits. On the debit side, Western National also withdrew a large number of vehicles (including all its remaining Leyland Atlanteans and all but one of its Leyland Nationals) during the year, placing the majority of them in store for possible further use should the need arise.

Showing off its red & yellow Midland Express livery. Midland Red West Plaxton-bodied Leyland Leopard 668 (RDA668R) stands outside Evesham depot in August 1988. (K.A.Jenkinson)

A NEW DECADE AND A NEW VISION

1990

1990 began with the announcement that a new company had been set up under the title of Badgerline Holdings Light Rail to operate a new transit system in Bristol promoted by a consortium called Advanced Transportation for Avon. Headed by former People's Provincial managing director James Freeman who had been involved with ATA since 1988 when the consortium approached the Gosport-based operator with a view to it running the proposed Bristol light rail system, the new Badgerline company was not, however, involved in the promotion or financing of this new venture. Unfortunately, the new company's plans took an early knock when early in February it was unable to come to an agreement with ATA following Bristol City Council's vote against the second phase of the Metro putting the whole future of the £190 million LRT scheme in doubt. After a period of standing-off, Badgerline resumed its negotiations with ATA at the end of March in the belief that the scheme would eventually make the desired progress. Meanwhile, on 28 January Western National ended its agreement with Plymouth Citybus to honour each other's season tickets in the city following a survey which showed that many more City Rider tickets issued by Citybus had been used on Western National buses compared to the number of WN Commuter Cards used on Citybus vehicles. The only exception to the suspension were the council-supported services operated by both companies.

February brought a massive expansion when, on the 16th Badgerline Holdings purchased all the bus and coach interests of United Welsh Services Ltd., and in doing so increased its total fleet strength to over 2,000 vehicles. The deal included South Wales Transport Ltd.; A.E. & F.R.Brewer Ltd.; United Welsh Coaches Ltd. and a 67% stake in Port Talbot-based Skillplace Training Ltd. but not the group's freehold bus stations at the Quadrant, Swansea and Oystermouth, its four Travelwise Wales Ltd. travel agencies or its computerised holiday reservations business. Serving a large part of south and south-west Wales, this new acquisition took Badgerline into areas where it had previously not had a presence and in addition to adding 350 buses and coaches to its combined fleet it also gave it a further 9 depots and 5 outstations. South Wales Transport used several local identity fleet names on its vehicles including City Mini for its minibuses in Swansea, Sospan Link in Llanelli and Cleddau Minis in Haverfordwest, although all shared the company's standard livery. One of the first moves made by South Wales Transport's new owner was the hire of a Neath-bodied 1947 Leyland PS1 which had been restored in the livery of its original owner, Llynfi of Maesteg. This was used during the summer season on The Swansea Tour on behalf of Swansea City Council, an operation aimed primarily at tourists to the area.

Further south, in March Western National took over from Devon Services a trio of routes radiating from Totnes while in the Plymouth area a pair of the company's Bristol VRTs were specially adapted for the less mobile and put to work on Easybus services 7A, 10, 11, 48 and 84. Following the withdrawal of its unique Albion Nimbus which had latterly acted as a reserve vehicle for the former Harvey's Penzance to Mousehole service, the usual vehicles employed on this route, Bristol LHSs 1557/65/6 received a revised 'Blue Bus' livery which used a darker shade of blue with a cream waistband.

Less than two months after it had entered Wales, Badgerline moved eastwards across England to Essex and further expanded its portfolio by purchasing Gurna Holdings Ltd. on 12 April. This gave it control of yet another former NBC company, Eastern National Ltd. as well as the dormant Westcliff-on-Sea Motor Services Ltd., Coastal Red Ltd. and Class 1 Travel. With a fleet of some 470 vehicles and operations in Essex and parts of Hertfordshire, Eastern National also ran a number of London Transport contracted services on the eastern fringe of the capital and as such this gave Badgerline an excellent platform upon which to build in the future, should it wish to do so. Almost immediately, plans were drawn up by Badgerline to divide its newly acquired company into two separate units, each of which would

Still painted in corporate NBC poppy red & white livery when seen in Swansea in April 1990, South Wales Transport Bristol VRT 959E (WTH959T) in keeping with the rest of the fleet carried its offside fleet name in the Welsh language. (M.Currie)

Transferred from South Wales Transport to Brewers in August 1992, Leyland National 790 (OEP790R) is seen at Swansea bus station still wearing its former owner's green, orange & red livery to which ***Brewers fleet names had been added. (Travelscene)***

South Wales Transport fitted a number of its minibuses with roof-mounted advertising boards in order to increase its revenue. One such vehicle, Robin Hood-bodied Mercedes Benz L608D 239 (D239LCY) is seen thus equipped at The Quadrant bus station, Swansea. ***(Travelscene)***

Wearing an all-over yellow livery, Skillplace's ex.Eastern National ECW-bodied Bristol LH6L 55 (WEX931S) makes its way through Swansea whilst performing its designated duty as a driver training vehicle. (Travelscene)

Painted in the dual purpose version of Eastern National's attractive yellow & green livery, Alexander-bodied Leyland Tiger 1114 (HHJ375Y) awaits its Maldon-bound passengers at Colchester bus station. (D.W.Rhodes)

Eastern National 4007 (C407HJN), a coach-seated ECW-bodied Leyland Olympian dating from 1986, hurries along snow-lined roads near Ramsey on its way from Colchester to Harwich. (M.J.Collins)

operate as separate entities and on 6 June Badgerline South Limited was renamed Thamesway Limited which took over Eastern National's south Essex and Greater London operations together with all the LRT contracted services on 29 July from depots at Brentwood, Basildon, Hadleigh, Southend, Walthamstow and Ponders End. Initially, Thamesway whose fleet comprised some 253 buses and coaches, a large proportion of which were minibuses, initially retained its predecessor's livery to which only new fleet name vinyls were applied, leaving Eastern National with only 215 vehicles and depots at Braintree, Chelmsford, Colchester, Clacton, Harwich and Walton-on-the-Naze.

Still interested in the Avon Light Rail Transit system in Bristol, Badgerline took a 10% stake in Advanced Transport for Avon at the beginning of May making it the first bus company in the private sector to buy into a proposed LRT system in Britain. Under the agreement reached between the two parties, Badgerline was to be responsible for the day-to-day running of the new system when it eventually became operational. Less successful, however, was the bid submitted by Badgerline Holdings for Scottish Bus Group subsidiary Eastern Scottish which in the event was purchased by its management, thus denting its expansion plans to north of the border.

Fleet replacement and upgrading continued to be a priority and during the early summer Midland Red West replaced a number of its elderly Leyland Nationals at Digbeth (Birmingham) and Redditch with 50 new Leyland Lynxes, the company's first new conventional size buses since 1983. New Lynxes were also received by Badgerline and Bristol City Line while new Mercedes mini/midibuses were added to the fleets of Eastern National, Thamesway, South Wales Transport and Western National. The only new double deckers to enter service were 4 all-Leyland Olympians with Thamesway while United Welsh Coaches received 4 new Plaxton Paramount 3500-bodied Volvo B10M coaches. Amongst the vehicles cascaded between the group's subsidiaries to satisfy their immediate needs were two open-top double deckers which moved from Bristol City Line to Badgerline, 10 Bristol VRTs and a pair of Leyland Tiger coaches which migrated

Traversing St.Edwards Way, Romford on the 551 service to Ilford, former Eastern National Leyland National 1912 (DAR134T) had yet to be repainted into the colours of its new owner, recently formed Thamesway, whose fleet names were, however, carried on its cove panels. (D.W.Rhodes)

from South Wales to join Western National who also gained a Bristol VRT and 2 Ford Transit minibuses from Badgerline and a closed-top Bristol VRT which left City Line for pastures new with Badgerline. As a consequence of these moves, Western National virtually eliminated full-size single deckers from its fleet (except for its coaches) and following the arrival of its new Mercedes midis and secondhand Bristol VRTs, only its 6 Leyland Lynxes and a handful of Bristol LHSs remained active. To add variety, 2 of Midland Red West's Leyland Tigers were repainted into full Shearings livery for use on tours contracted by the Wigan-based operator while Bristol City Line repainted one of its open-top Bristol VRTs into the old Bristol tramcar colours of dark blue with a white waistband for operation on the Bristol City Tour and towards the end of the year Thamesway adopted a new livery comprising yellow and maroon.

Despite its huge success, Badgerline's open-top tour of Bath which was now run in conjunction with Guide Friday came under criticism from local residents and particularly those on Widcombe Hill which the tour buses climbed every 10 minutes. After lengthy discussions between the parties concerned, Badgerline offered a compromise by promising to halve the number of buses on that particular section of the route from the start of the 1991 season. With the number of passengers carried having trebled since 1988, nine open-top double deckers were now used on this increasingly popular service. Meanwhile, during the mid summer Badgerline lettered two of its Leyland Nationals (3036/8) for the Lansdowne park and ride service which soon began to prove popular although sadly did little to reduce traffic congestion in the city centre.

Purchased new by Eastern National in 1989, Reeve Burgess-bodied Mercedes Benz 811D 0800 (F800RHK) carried a 'Woodford Hoppa' local identity name on its side panels in addition to London Transport roundels for operation an LRT contracted service. It was, however, transferred to the newly created Thamesway company in July 1990 where it retained the same fleet number. (Travelscene)

Seen at Southend on Sea bus station painted in Thamesway's original yellow & maroon livery is Leyland Lynx 1424 (F424MJN). (D.W.Rhodes)

Continuing its expansion, Badgerline through its Brewers subidiary purchased the business of DLJ Private Hire of Maesteg in June together with that company's 15 vehicles, all of which were immediately withdrawn and offered for sale. Going shopping again on 22 June, Badgerline purchased former NBC Bristol-based coaching subsidiary Wessex of Bristol Ltd. together with its subsidiaries Wessex National Ltd.; Wessex Travel Services Ltd. and Wessex Educational Travel Services Ltd. Although specialising in National Express contracted work from its leasehold site in the St.Phillips area of Bristol, Wessex also undertook private hire work, excursions, extended tours, and also operated a shuttle service between Bristol city centre and Bristol Airport upon which it used an 18-seat Carlyle-bodied Freight Rover Sherpa painted in National Express livery. With a modern 33-coach fleet, Wessex National was viewed as a company which would compliment Badgerline's other operations and could be further developed in the fullness of time. Following this a month later Western National purchased the 7-vehicle Sunset Coaches of Penzance, further strengthening its position in Cornwall. Soon after the latter transaction had been completed, Western National was split into two divisions during August, the new Cornwall division being responsible for Camborne, Newquay, Penzance, St.Austell and Truro depots and the Devon division for the operations from Plymouth, Callington, Dartmouth, Tavistock, Torpoint and Totnes depots. At around this same time Western National introduced a colour-coded vehicle allocation system under which a different background colour was given to the fleet number plates of all its vehicles to signify their home depot (Camborne - red; Truro - blue; Newquay - cream and Penzance - silver etc.).

After announcing a pre-tax profit of £2,866,000 (despite the National Audit Office having clawed back £3.25 million from Badgerline following its sale of two properties) on a turnover of £71,170,000 for the year ending 31 December 1989 compared to a profit of £1,222,000 on a turnover of £52,249,000 in the previous twelve months.

Following a new round of tenders in Dyfed, South Wales Transport came under fire from several local independent operators who accused it of deliberately undercutting them in a bid to gain more

The oldest bus in the Badgerline fleet is 1940 open-top ECW-bodied Bristol K5G 8583 (GHT127) which is now employed on the Bath City Tour and sports both its owner's and Guide Friday fleet names. (J.Whitmore)

Having arrived at Plymouth bus station on a National Express duty, the driver of Wessex MCW Metroliner 222 (B222VHW) takes instructions from the local regulator before parking up for a well-earned rest. (A.Watkins)

Painted in corporate National Express livery and operated on the airlink service to Bristol Airport, Wessex Carlyle-bodied Freight Rover Sherpa D141NON leaves Marlborough Street bus station, Bristol with only one passenger onboard. (B.T.Channon)

work. When the new tenders came into force on 2 September Davies Bros. of Pencader lost around 90% of its contracted routes to the Badgerline subsidiary who, it was alleged, put in bids that were more than 25% lower than its nearest competitor. Whilst others were quick to criticise South Wales Transport over this matter, Badgerline had commissioned a £100,000 study aimed at helping public transport in Bristol and reducing traffic congestion in the city. Under the title 'Jam today, jam tomorrow?' it suggested 14 changes to Bristol's traffic system which it believed would ease buses through some of the worst choked areas. Of those surveyed, 91% thought that steps should be taken to make bus travel quicker and more efficient while 63% favoured more bus lanes and 62% thought there should be restrictions placed on car access to the city.

1991

The start of the new year witnessed the arrival of the first of Thamesway's 80 new Reeve Burgess-bodied 23-seat Mercedes Benz 709Ds, more than half of which were put into service at Southend where a major revision of the former Eastern National services resulted in the wholesale replacement of Bristol VRTs and Leyland Nationals by the new minis . In addition to increasing frequencies on existing services, several new routes were introduced which penetrated areas which had previously never enjoyed a bus service or were over roads served by other operators. Such was the success of this escalation of its operations that it was not long before several local companies such as Southend Transport, TV Taxis and Stephenson of Rochford lodged complaints with the Office of Fair Trading in the hope that it would order an inquiry. As the 'war' continued, Southend Transport whose routes had been flooded by Thamesway retaliated by putting on extra buses and also starting operations on several services that had previously been exclusive to the Badgerline subsidiary. Following these moves, Thamesway somewhat surprisingly announced in August that it was to close its Southend depot on 8 September and transfer its operations to its Hadleigh depot some six miles away, from where it would continue to maintain its Southend service network, albeit with reduced frequencies. While it continued to strengthen its position in parts of south-east Essex, Thamesway nevertheless withdrew its 400 service from Southend to London on the grounds that it was no longer profitable and that several sections of the route were covered by other existing services. Having found that its minibuses in Southend had been favourably received by passengers and that they had enabled the company to introduce services which were more able to penetrate housing estates etc., Thamesway on 8 July similarly replaced all its conventional buses in and around Basildon with minibuses. Earlier in the summer, Wessex had sold its Roman City division to Berkeley Coaches and immediately afterwards replaced the fleet name on its Roman City-liveried coaches with Wessex of Bristol lettering.

Not long into 1990, the first three projects suggested by Badgerline following its 'Jam today, Jam tomorrow?' campaign were put in place by Avon County Council with the fourth being implemented in April, proving the value of the survey. However, although the company's fortunes appeared to be improving in Bristol, this was not so in Bath where its plans to relocate its depot to Weston Island ground to a sudden halt following a decision made by Bath City Council to refuse planning permission for the redevelopment of Badgerline's current depot in London Road. As the move was only possible if the London Road site was able to be sold, it now seemed that the move would be unable to take place.

Meanwhile, despite assurances given to residents on certain parts of the route covered by the Bath open-top service, Badgerline still found itself in trouble and after Avon County Council decided at a meeting early in August to flout the 1985 Transport Act and contradict government policy by introducing a licensing system for the tour buses, Badgerline decided to call for a public inquiry. Regardless of the County Council limiting the service to five buses per hour (3 licences to Badgerline and 2 to Ryans Coaches who had also operated on the route for several years), both operators decided that in their view normal deregulated rules continued to apply and thus signalled their intention to continue their normal workings. As for most of the season Badgerline only ran two buses per hour anyhow, it appeared that the Council had contradicted its own intentions! Earlier City Line had invited Guide Friday to participate in its established open-top Bristol bus tour in order to gain the benefits of the latter's expertise in this type of operation. Running from mid-July to September and using two buses (one from each of its operators), City Line repainted its contribution, a Bristol VRT, into Guide Friday colours in order to maximise its marketing resources.

On the first day of September, large scale service revisions were implemented by Badgerline and City Line and in addition to a general reduction in frequencies, all seasonal services were suspended and several tendered routes were lost to other operators. Amongst these were the 303 Woolaston to Chepstow which was gained by Grindle of Cinderford, the 649 (Bristol - Keynsham) which passed to Eagle

Coaches and the 666 (Radstock - Bristol) and 766 (Bath - Clutton) which were won by Clapton Coaches. Eastern National was more fortunate in the tendering process, however, gaining several Suffolk County Council tenders for Monday to Saturday evening services which penetrated deep into Eastern Counties territory around Ipswich. Additionally, a new approach road at Stansted Airport enabled Eastern National to introduce a combined service every 15 minutes on its routes between Bishops Stortford and the Airport as well as reducing the mileage by seven miles. More unusual, however, was the provision by Eastern National of four of its Leyland Nationals for airside use at Stansted Airport from 28 October. For this purpose they were fitted with amber flashing lights and were licensed by the British Airports Authority who employed two of them each day between 6.00am and midnight to ferry passengers between the terminal building and aircraft. Following the above changes, Wessex found itself affected by the introduction of the National Express winter timetable on 27 October when it lost its operations on the services from Leeds to Coventry (310), Weymouth to Grimsby (772), Plymouth to Banbury (747) and the Bristol Airport Shuttle (731). In their place, however, it gained workings on the Leeds - Liverpool (361), London to Bradford (561) and Weymouth to Worcester (772) services as well as on Fridays and Sundays on the 308 between Cambridge and Birmingham, thus taking its coaches to places where they had previously not been familiar. Partly due to these changes and the arrival of three new Plaxton Expressliner-bodied Volvo B10Ms, Wessex reduced its double deck fleet to just two vehicles - an MCW Metroliner and a Scania. Western National also gained some expansion when in October it won four Devon County Council contracts for services radiating from Newton Abbot which had previously been operated by Devon Services. In the meantime, a new study had been commissioned jointly by Badgerline, ATA and Bristol City Council to review the options for the proposed Avon Transit route through Bristol city centre following rejection of the City Centre Bill by the House of Lords select committee.

On a happier note, Badgerline Holdings was able to announce increased profits for the year ended 31 December 1990 which were £1.29 million compared with £1.17 million in the previous year. This was achieved largely as a result of its three acquisitions although interest charges of £6.3 million on debts incurred by this buying spree had almost wiped out the company's £7.1 million trading profit. Increased fuel costs had also taken their toll, although in this area prices had now thankfully stabalised at a more reasonable level.

***Resting at Peterborough bus park, Eastern National Plaxton** Paramount 3200-bodied Leyland Tiger 1131 (C131HJN) displays the original Highwayman livery prior to its modification in 1991. (K.A.Jenkinson)*

Demonstrating its capabilities in Portsmouth and Bristol was this Belgian diesel/electric three-unit articulated bus which appropriately carried GLT lettering on its front panel. (T.W.W.Knowles)

As a consequence of the original plans for a light-rail system in Bristol still being in a state of flux, Badgerline Rapid Transit began working on an alternative plan which involved the construction of a guided busway and would use Belgian diesel/electric articulated buses. These dual-mode vehicles would function as diesel-powered buses in the suburbs but would follow a single central guideway in inner-city areas and where space was available would draw electric power from overhead wires. Although more expensive than conventional guided busways, the proposed Guided Light Transit system would be far cheaper than the original rapid light transit concept which was now facing several difficulties. A north-south core route in Bristol was proposed on which 29 articulated vehicles, each able to carry 175 passengers, would be used. In comparing costs it was stated that this type of system could be made available for £26.8 million whereas a conventional guided busway would be £17.4 million and a rapid light transit system £96 million. In order to demonstrate the type of vehicle which would be used, GLT who had now opened an office at 3, Haymarket Walk in Bristol, temporarily imported an example from Belgium which ran a number of free trips in Bristol city centre for the public. In addition to these moves, Badgerline also registered an interest in running privatised rail services when these became available and wrote to the Secretary of State for Transport indicating this and thus signalling its intention to further diversify. As part of a general rationalisation plan, Badger Retail sold six of its shops towards the end of the year, these being the least profitable in the chain.

Fleet changes continued throughout the year and in addition to taking delivery of numerous new vehicles (many of which were Mercedes Benz minibuses), the purchase of secondhand buses continued albeit only in small numbers. Amongst the latter were a trio of Alexander-bodied Leyland Leopards which were acquired by Thamesway from Kelvin Central Buses for driver training duties and retained their former owner's livery to which Thamesway fleet name vinyls were added. More unusual, however, was the repurchase by Western National of 2 of its former Marshall-bodied Bristol LH6Ls from Guernseybus as replacements for its ex.Crosville Bristol FS6G and East Kent AEC Regent V driver training buses. Towards the end of the year Bristol Omnibus Co. withdrew the last of its Leyland Nationals and placed them in store and for evaluation purposes borrowed an Ikarus-bodied DAF SB220 bus which it operated in service for a brief time on various routes in Bristol. Liveries also came under examination and after Eastern National revised its Highwayman colour scheme to incorporate more green round the windows and skirt, Bristol Omnibus Co. in March eliminated its old CityRider scheme of dark red with a yellow rear separated by a forward-inclined blue band in favour of the new yellow-based Overground livery.

WINNERS AND LOSERS

1992

As doubts grew about ATA's proposals, Badgerline Rapid Transit revealed plans to run guided light transit vehicles in the Bradley Stoke, Stoke Gifford and Filton areas of Bristol, an operation which could be undertaken at half the cost of a light rail transit system. Leaflets explaining the latest proposals were distributed to residents in those areas and in addition, two public meetings were arranged to enable meaningful discussion to take place. The vehicles used on the new GLT would be diesel-electric articulated single deckers possibly using a new energy storage system as an alternative to external electric power lines. Meanwhile, Avon County Council and Badgerline commissioned a feasibility study as part of the Bristol integrated transport and environment initiative (Brites), basing this initially on the proposed route from Hartcliffe to Cribbs Causeway. This was designed to produce travel demand forecasts plus economic and financial appraisals and evaluations against objectives set during Brites. Upon the abolition of the 120-year old Tramways Act and its replacement with the Road and Works Act, however, Badgerline took the decision to postpone its deposition of a Parliamentary Bill to operate a guided light transit system in Avon until the following year as it now appeared possible for promoters of rapid transit schemes to obtain an order under the new legislation. In the event ATA went into liquidation in March.

Existing operations also featured heavily in the news soon after the new year had begun, with several changes being implemented in Bath on 20 January when the X4 was truncated to run between Bath and Warminster and no longer ran into Bristol and the 264/265 routes (Bath to Trowbridge) which were completely split at Winsley from where the section to Bath was passed to Arrow Coaches under a Wiltshire County Council contract. Meanwhile, the uncertainty of the future of the ailing National Welsh company led Brewers to introduce a number of vehicles on the National Welsh timings on the services from Bridgend to Llynfi Valley and on the X5 between Swansea and Hirwaun from 13 January and on further services in the Bridgend area from 17 February. On the latter date, South Wales Transport also introduced workings on National Welsh's X2 service between Porthcawl and Cardiff and upon hearing of these registrations, National Welsh retaliated by starting operations on SWT's Swansea - Cardiff Shuttle for two weeks prior to Christmas 1991. Pursuing its objective to establish a sound commercial base to ensure that, should National Welsh collapse, passengers would still have a reliable public transport network at their disposal, South Wales Transport also registered a number of services in the Rhondda Valley which required around 30 minibuses. Prior to Brewers and SWT beginning their new operations, however, Brewers on 6 January purchased Morris of Pencoed's services from Bridgend to Coity while on 10 February South Wales Transport took over the operation of the GM Coaches services between Bridgend and Porthcawl. No vehicles were involved in either of these deals and as a result both Brewers and SWT acquired additional buses from other Badgerline subsidiaries as well as from Southern National.

Meanwhile, in March Eastern National restructured a number of its faretables. lowering fares on several services including that from Colchester to Chelmsford upon which it introduced its Master Saver ticket. This offered a maximum fare of £2.50 return, representing a

With a large smiling badger logo on its side panels and a London Transport Service vinyl in its cab side window, Thamesway Plaxton Pointer-bodied Dennis Dart 916 (K916CVW) passes Kings Cross railway station whilst working London Transport contracted service 214 to Parliament Hill Fields. (K.A.Jenkinson)

Amongst the coaches initially used on Thamesway's new City Saver commuter service between Southend and London was Duple Caribbean-bodied Leyland Tiger 509 (MKH893A). Acquired from South Wales Transport with whom it had originally been registered RCY117Y, it had been repainted into its new owner's orange & yellow City Saver livery and had been extensively lettered for the service by the time it was photographed at Aldgate bus station, London. (B.Bell)

Lettered for the Swansea to Cardiff Shuttle service and seen at The Quadrant bus station, Swansea, is United Welsh Coaches 121 (MKH48A), a Duple Caribbean-bodied Leyland Tiger which was originally registered RCY121Y. (Travelscene)

Collecting its Southend-bound passengers at London's Aldgate bus station is Thamesway 509 (MKH893A), a Duple Carribean-bodied Leyland Tiger which joined the fleet from South Wales Transport. Originally registered RCY117Y, it is painted in City Saver orange & cream livery to which is added a mass of promotional lettering and, behind its rear wheel arch, a smiling badger logo. (B.Bell)

30% discount while a new credit card-size season tickets with photograph was also launched. Additionally, Essex Ranger all-day tickets were re-introduced with an adult fare of £4.50 (40p less than the previous similar ticket) and a family variant offered at £9.00 (representing a saving of 80p). Thamesway meanwhile suffered mixed fortunes when, on 2 March, it lost its LRT contracts for services 20, 167, 235 and 275 to Grey Green and coupled with the loss of LRT contracted service 359, these caused the closure of the company's Walthamstow depot. On a brighter note, however, the LRT contract for the D8 (Stratford - Isle of Dogs) and 214 (Parliament Hill Fields - Liverpool Street Station) services was gained, the latter commencing on 15 August to give the company a presence in central London for the first time other than on its express routes from Essex.

Another victim of change through the retendering process was Badgerline who on 5 May lost six Avon County Council-supported services in Bath and Bristol to other operators (including City Line) but compensated for this by winning eleven in Bath, Bristol and Weston-super-Mare. Additionally, its commercial services on the Bath/Keynsham corridor were replaced by a new network and all the Summer Special services were reintroduced except for the 371 (Bristol - Cheddar). For its additional services, Badgerline needed to marginally increase its fleet and to achieve this acquired nine Bristol VRTs from Thamesway, made surplus by the loss of the LRT contracts mentioned above. City Line was slightly more fortunate than Badgerline, losing only three services under Avon County Council's round of retendering and gaining one. Midland Red West also lost out when it failed to retain its Wolverhampton area tendered services and additionally took the decision to withdraw from National Express contracted work.

On the vehicle front, joining the City Line fleet at around this time was an Alexander-bodied Mercedes Benz 608D minibus acquired from Kelvin Scottish as a replacement for its own Mercedes Benz L608D 7479 which had sadly been destroyed by fire in February and a Leyland Lynx which was loaned to the company by its manufacturer to cover for the Olympians which were returning to Leyland for attention to bodywork corrosion. In the meantime, Badgerline began to revise its green and yellow livery by the addition of a large badger to the lower side panels of single and double deckers alike, leaving no doubt as to their ownership. More of Thamesway's surplus Bristol VRTs were cascaded to Western National who gained ten while also joining the company were two new Plaxton Expressliner-bodied Volvo B10Ms purchased as replacements for a pair of double deck MCW Metroliners and two Plaxton 3500-bodied Volvo B10Ms acquired from Wallace Arnold for the private hire fleet. Later in the year, South Wales Transport evaluated two new types of vehicle, borrowing an Optare Delta-bodied DAF SB220 in August and a Plaxton Verde-bodied Dennis Lance in October, the latter having previously undertaken similar duties with Badgerline and although the Lance led to an order being placed, the Optare-DAF failed to generate more than a minority of interest.

Later in the summer, Thamesway launched a new service from Southend to London on 6 July which it was stated was in response to the growing British Rail commuter rebellion which was sick of the unreliable 'misery line' upon which cancellations were common place. However, the new service branded 'City Saver' also competed directly with Southend Transport's X1 route and immediately drew a reaction from the latter who reported the Badgerline subsidiary to the Office of Fair Trading for running uneconomic services, claiming that its new London operation was just another part of its ongoing assault against the municipal operator. Justifying its new route, Thamesway stated that its aim was to undercut British Rail and not Southend Transport, although it was conceded that its fares were cheaper than those charged by Southend. Having a peak vehicle requirement of nine single deck coaches, most of these were initially hired from other Badgerline subsidiaries until permanent additional coaches could be obtained. Amongst the fares charged on the new City Saver service was a £3 daily return and a £65 monthly ticket which was almost half the £139 cost of a British Rail monthly ticket, and in addition was also valid for travel on all Thamesway's commercial bus services. It was not until August 1993 that the Office of Fair Trading announced its findings on the Southend saga, but when it did, Thamesway was cleared of acting in an uncompetitive manner.

Returning to the subject of guided light transit, on 9 March Badgerline Rapid Transit proudly announced its Avon Gorge Expressway project which was an innovative way of tackling the peak hour congestion problems. The new Expressway would use the redundant British Rail single track line from Wapping Wharf near the centre of Bristol to Portishead and would utilise kerb guidance for its bus-based operation. Under this plan, existing Badgerline services from Portishead, Weston-super-Mare and Clevedon using the motorway would enter the busway at Portbury whilst those from Woodspring would join at Ashton whilst from Wapping Wharf to the city centre, buses would operate via existing roads. Additionally, a new park and ride site would be opened near junction 19 of the M5 motorway in an attempt to attract commuters from their cars and thus further reduce congestion and pollution within the city itself. Later, in June Badgerline Rapid Transit joined forces with People's Provincial and Gosport Ferry Limited to form a new company titled SeHants Overground who announced plans for a new guided light transit system linking Portsmouth, Portsea Hard, Gosport town centre, Brockhurst and Bridgemary with possible extensions to Southsea and Fareham. Under this plan, the route would be taken through a tunnel built under Gosport harbour. Indeed, such was Badgerline's expertise in the field of guided light transit that the system it had pioneered was now starting to attract interest from numerous other transport authorities including Leeds, Merseyside, Teesside, West Midlands, Belfast and Dublin.

Meanwhile, Badgerline's core activity of bus operation continued to flourish and in August it was announced that orders had been placed with Plaxton of Scarborough for no fewer than 396 new buses for delivery in 1993/4. These comprised 250 Beaver-bodied Mercedes minibuses, 69 Pointer-bodied Dennis Darts and 77 Verde-bodied Dennis Lances which were to be distributed amongst its various subsidiaries. Of these, 87 Mercedes Benz 709Ds, 21 Mercedes Benz 811Ds, 33 Dennis Darts and 26 Dennis Lances were scheduled for delivery in 1993 together with 22 Leyland Olympians while in addition, 30 Northern Counties-bodied Leyland Olympians had been ordered for delivery in the latter months of 1992 which, upon their arrival, would replace a similar number of City Line's Bristol VRTs at its Muller Road depot in Bristol. Although Badgerline had originally considered the Dennis Dominator for its new double deck order, it had turned instead to the Olympian due to it being more compatible with City Line's existing fleet. Despite not planning a corporate livery for all its subsidiaries, Badgerline, however, took the decision to feature a badger motif on all new group vehicles, positioning this in the vicinity of the rear wheel arch and later applied this to some older vehicles upon repaint.

Further restructuring aimed at concentrating all Badgeline's operations in the eastern part of its South Wales territory under one umbrella saw Brewers suddenly expand its activities during August. Coinciding with the transfer of its head office and engineering workshops from Maesteg to Port Talbot in September, it took over all

Built as a demonstrator, Leyland Lynx J916WVC was purchased by Brewers in 1992 and given fleet number 508. It is seen here carrying lettering for the Cymer to Penybont service along its cove panels. (B.Bell)

Western National purchased 15 new Carlyle-bodied Mercedes Benz 811Ds in 1991 to provide larger capacity buses on several of its services. One of these, 325 (H725HGL) is seen resting at Exeter in September 1992. (J.Whitmore)

South Wales Transport's local operations in Port Talbot (after which Maesteg was maintained as an outstation) and following the disbanding of United Welsh Coaches and the closure of its Gorseinon depot Brewers took over its activities as well. In the event, however, the United Welsh name and livery was retained after the transfer of its coaches to Port Talbot. As part of this reorganisation, a new company was formed under the title of Broch Cymru Ltd. (Badger Wales for the benefit on non-Welsh speakers) to which the Brewers operation was ultimately transferred.

As a consequence of service changes implemented by Badgerline on 28 September, the company's outstation at Yate was closed while in the Bradley Stoke area several City Line services were diverted to serve the newly-opened Tesco store. Earlier, in June, the Guided Light Transit demonstration vehicle had operated around Bradley Stoke for a brief time to enable the local population to sample the 'bus of the future'. Also started on 28 September by Brewers using new Leyland Lynxes were re-launched services 232/236 from Bridgend to Cymmer which were designed to compete with the re-opened British Rail Llynfi Valley line. Painted in a distinctive livery and sporting a small badger motif behind their rear wheel arch, these buses also featured route lettering on their cove panels.

Following the growing trend set by other operators, Midland Red West who had already imposed a smoking ban on all its minibuses and vehicles used on local authority contracted services extended this to the whole of its fleet in August following numerous complaints from anti-smoking passengers. Meanwhile, Thamesway's City Saver service from Southend to London had exceeded all its expectations and now operated every ten minutes at peak times and every hour throughout the remainder of the day. To meet this increased demand, more secondhand coaches were acquired (from Shearings of Wigan) whilst others were transferred from South Wales Transport and Western National. At the end of the year, a new annual ticket was introduced on this service at £730, this further angering Southend Transport whose comparable ticket on its X1 service to London was priced at £200 more. Indeed, Thamesway's success was not limited to its City Saver service but was also evident in other parts of its operating territory. In Basildon, patronage on its town services had increased by 15% during 1992 and almost all its services had been diverted to call at the railway station for the convenience of train passengers. The introduction of minibuses and the stability of fares were the two main factors in the increase, assisted of course by good publicity and the easy availability of local timetable leaflets.

Simultaneous with the entry into service on 10 December of Western National's 13 new Plaxton-bodied 31-seat Mercedes Benz 811Ds in and around Penzance the company withdrew the last of its Bristol LHSs which included the unique Wadham Stringer-bodied 1565 (KRL444W) and Marshall-bodied 1566 (PCV178R), thus bringing another era to an end. Prior to this, Western National had closed its Newquay depot and transferred its vehicles to St.Austell some fifteen miles away.

Before yet another year drew to a close, the Badgerline Group involved itself in a number of park and ride services in the run up to Christmas with Thamesway gaining the contract for an operation of this nature in Basildon, City Line in schemes linking Bedminster Down to Clifton and Broadmead and Canons Marsh to Wapping Wharf market and South Wales Transport from Landore and Brynmill to Swansea. Meanwhile, Badgerline evaluated a Mercedes Benz 0405 demonstrator in service from 14 to 22 December which ironically was fitted with guide wheels.

One of four Leyland Tiger coaches acquired by Thamesway from Bebb, Llantwit Fardre in 1993 for operation on the City Saver commuter service, Plaxton 321-bodied 519 (J48SNY) still had to receive its new orange & yellow colours and wore an all-white livery when seen at Lakeside bus station, Thurrock (D.W.Rhodes)

GOING PUBLIC

1993

The start of 1993 saw Avon County Council being forced into a position where it had to cut £1 million off its £4.6 million supported service budget for 1993/4 and to this end it circulated a list to all local operators showing the services to which it could no longer give financial support. Most of the cuts which were to be implemented on 8 May fell on urban routes, particularly in Bristol where City Line's loss appeared likely to be in the region of £150,000. Although the company studied the list carefully in order to see what could be saved by commercial registration, it felt that it would only be able to continue one or two on this basis, the remainder being too lightly loaded to be viable. At the same time that this news was announced, Bristol-based independent Arrowfleet suddenly called in the receiver and ceased trading, leaving Avon County Council to reallocate its contracts at a moment's notice. As an emergency measure four were awarded to City Line and two to Badgerline to commence on Monday 12 January, the remaining three passing to other local independent operators. In the meantime, Avon County Council launched its new plan which took the county's transport to the year 2013 and gave a substantial boost to the area's bus operators. Amongst the measures to be implemented were incentives to tackle congestion, pollution and road safety and also discourage car usage. To encourage the latter, it was suggested that new bus park-and-ride schemes should be introduced in Bristol, Bath and Weston-super-Mare, more bus priority lanes should be created, a concessionary fare scheme adopted for senior citizens and disabled people and a rapid transit system introduced in the greater Bristol area.

Thamesway again hit the headlines when towards the end of February it further cut several of its fares in Essex, introducing a £6 Savercard offering seven days almost unlimited travel in Brentwood and Harold Wood (inner zone) or £8 in Brentwood and Romford (outer zone) and a £2.50 Daysaver ticket for unlimited travel in Brentwood and Romford. Supporting this with a massive leaflet distribution throughout the areas concerned, it was hoped that this new lower cost travel opportunity would be a further incentive to persuade more people to leave their cars at home and use Thamesway's services. Across country in the south-west, Western National was busy replacing its Almex Timtronic ticketing system with more sophisticated computerised equipment in the form of Almex Eurofare and Microfare machines. The new system enabled drivers to transfer full ticket information from their machine at their local depot, this being collected automatically by main depot computers to enable the full details of the day's fares to be available for analysis by the following morning. In the meantime, following its reorganisation Brewers had introduced a new red and white livery for its expanded fleet, this replacing the blue and white, all-over white and South Wales Transport two-tone green which had previously adorned its vehicles.

Although plans for a light rail transit system in Bristol were still being pursued, early in 1993 Advanced Transport for Avon Ltd. had run into difficulties and had called in the receiver. This did not, however, rule out such a project in the future and the receiver put out to sealed tender the licence to take over the rights under the Avon Light Rail Transit Act of 1989 to construct, develop, maintain, use and operate the system. Initially six parties expressed interest, although it was to be some considerable time before the outcome was made known.

Despite the efforts by Guide Friday over the last two years to make the open-top bus tour of Bristol viable, its costs continued to exceed its revenue and thus it was reluctantly decided not to re-introduce it for the 1993 summer season. Much of the blame for its withdrawal was laid at the feet of Bristol City Tourism who offered the service no form of financial support, unlike other areas such as Birmingham and Cardiff who gave those city's tours total backing. Thus, after ten years of operation, the Bristol tour was laid to rest. No sooner had this decision been taken, local independent Ambassador Travel who had recently started a new city centre route in Bristol operating on a 20-minute frequency learned that Badgerline subsidiary Wessex was now planning to start a similar service in May, timing this five minutes earlier and operating it with Leyland Nationals carrying the fleet name 'Sky Blue'. As a result, Ambassador made a complaint to the Office of fair Trading over what it believed to be unfair competition and not in the public interest. Wessex, who was primarily a coach operator, in the meantime took delivery in June of eight new Plaxton Premiere-bodied Volvo B10Ms, five of which were painted in National Express corporate colours for use on its contracted express services, the remaining three being in Wessex's own livery.

Awaiting its departure to Hartcliffe on the X79 service is Wessex 707 (NFB599R), one of 6 Leyland Nationals transferred from Badgerline in 1994 for use in its Sky Blue fleet. (Travelscene)

Despite the battle between Southend Transport and Thamesway continuing, upon hearing that Southend Borough Council was poised to accept a bid for its public transport operations from British Bus, the undertakings executive directors who had failed in an earlier management/employee buy-out bid approached Badgerline to seek a more sensible approach to running services in the area.This led to the Borough Council quickly concluding its sale to British Bus in order to ensure that Thamesway did not gain part of its company. As one door closed, however, another one opened and in an attempt to increase patronage on its services South Wales Transport approached the Welsh Consumer Council with a request that it should set up independent consumer groups to monitor its operations. Under this scheme, panels of independent people would be assembled in Swansea, Neath, Pontardawe and Llanelli to assist the Badgerline subsidiary in assessing and improving its services. All the information collected would then be fed back to the bus operating company on a regular basis in order that action may be taken.

Despite its turnover being down by £1.8 million in 1992, Badgerline nevertheless recorded a record profit which was up by 32% before tax. Thamesway's long-running battle in Southend had proved extremely costly and in addition to having to cut fares in that area, Badgerline also suffered a loss of £535,000 on the sale of Thamesway's Southend depot and additionally had to close its

Drawing forward onto the X3 stand at Swansea bus station prior to commencing a journey to Maesteg is Brewers ECW-bodied Bristol VRT 981 (BEP981V) which began life in the South Wales Transport fleet. (Travelscene)

Seen in Birmingham operating service 94 to Chelmsley Wood is Frontline Buses all-red liveried 6276 (NOC726R), an East Lancs-bodied Daimler Fleetline which began life in 1977 with West Midlands PTE. (G.T.W.Carter)

Walthamstow base following the loss of a number of London Transport tendered routes. Although Eastern National was worst hit by the recession, Midland Red West also had to contend with tough trading conditions while South Wales Transport and Brewers Motor Services had both undergone substantial reorganisation. On the positive side, however, Western National, Badgerline and Bristol City Line all enjoyed a more successful trading year with the latter's trading base holding up particularly well thanks in part to the implementation of the bus priorities in Bristol suggested in the company's Jam Today, Jam Tomorrow campaign. The group's combined fleet now stood at 1914 vehicles and its turnover was £127.03 million.

Continuing its attempt to make bus travel easier and attract more passengers, early in June South Wales Transport launched a colour coding system for its services in the Swansea area. This new map which was of similar format to that used by London Underground was designed so that prospective customers could see at a glance which colour route they needed to reach their destination. A month after this innovative move, Eastern National changed its image by introducing a revised livery which whilst retaining the existing yellow, used a much brighter shade of green which was applied in changed proportions. Added to this was Badgerline's 'smiling badger' logo which was positioned on the skirt behind the rear wheel arch to each side of the body. The first buses to carry this new scheme were 16 new Plaxton Beaver-bodied Mercedes Benz 709Ds which were used to replace time-expired Leyland Nationals at Chelmsford, although it was not long before several older vehicles emerged from the paintshop in the new livery. Other new vehicles to be placed in service by the Badgerline Group during the first half of 1993 included 25 Plaxton Beaver-bodied Mercedes Benz 709D minibuses, 11 Plaxton Beaver-bodied Mercedes Benz 811D midis, 4 Northern Counties-bodied Volvo Olympians and 3 Plaxton Premiere-bodied Volvo B10M coaches with Western National; 2 Plaxton Premiere-bodied Dennis Javelins with United Welsh and 10 Plaxton Beaver-bodied Mercedes Benz 709Ds with Badgerline. Additionally, in May 4 of Brewers Leyland Nationals were transferred to Wessex for use on its new Sky Blue operation in Bristol while Brewers gained a variety of Leyland Leopards and Tigers from Western National, Badgerline, Midland Red West and South Wales Transport for its United Welsh Coaches unit. Wessex enhanced its National Express contract fleet with the purchase of 3 Plaxton Paramount-bodied Volvo B10Ms from Bebb of Llantwit Fardre in April and 2 similar coaches from Northumbria in July and Western National acquired a pair of coaches of this same combination from Wallace Arnold. Apart from the vehicles mentioned above, the remaining inter-fleet transfers mainly involved Badgerline who gained no fewer than 15 Mercedes Benz L608Ds from Western National, 8 Iveco 49.10s from Western National and Midland Red West and a couple of Bristol VRTs - one each from Western National and City Line.

Looking to the future, in June Badgerline appointed consultants to evaluate a plan to run guided buses along the Avon Gorge Expressway. If the company's calculations proved correct and the plans were believed to be viable, Badgerline stated that it would seek other private sector partners to assist in promoting the scheme which would involve a substantial element of park and ride. This new study followed the original inception of an Avon Gorge Expressway in 1992 along the largely unused single track railway line through this scenic area. If it went ahead, the guided busway would link Gordano, Bower Ashton and Wapping Wharf to provide a peak-hour express route for buses between Bristol city centre and the towns in south-west Avon. Meanwhile, the concept of revolutionary low-floor, low-emission buses continued to be explored and dubbed the Magnet Motor, a joint application for funding had been submitted to the EC by Volvo, Magnet Motor, Bath City Council and Badgerline. In the meantime, a German prototype of this type of bus was expected to arrive in Bath for evaluation in the not too distant future.

July 1993 witnessed the Badgerline Group gaining a small foothold in an area in which it had previously not had a presence when it purchased Frontline Enterprises Ltd. of Dordon near Tamworth. Trading under the title of Frontline Buses, this company had been born less than a year earlier when it took over the premises and some of the operations of the erstwhile Burman Travel and began a handful of local bus services, two of which ran from Chelmsley Wood to Birmingham city centre. On 24 December 1993, Frontline expanded its operations with the purchase of the small three-coach business of JGB Travel of Coseley near Wolverhampton, absorbing this into its own fleet at Dordon and soon afterwards revising its service network to concentrate on five routes radiating from Tamworth together with six schools services. Within days of its acquisition by Badgerline, its fleet was enhanced by the transfer of three Leyland Nationals from Eastern National, these being joined by a Ford Transit minibus from Thamesway in September and a new Plaxton Beaver-bodied Mercedes Benz 709D diverted from an Eastern National order to bring its total up to 16 vehicles. Whilst these events had been taking place, Western National had received delivery of the first Volvo Olympians to be built. Numbering four and fitted with coach-seated Northern Counties bodywork they were placed in service on 20 July on the X80 route between Torquay and Plymouth where, with their enhanced standard of comfort etc., they were welcomed by passengers and drivers alike. Sadly, rather than life beginning at 40, it came to an abrupt halt for South Wales Transport's well-loved 1953 open-top Bristol KSW5G double decker when it collided with a lamp post at Swansea on 17 August causing an amount of damage to its driver's cab. Acquired from Eastern National in 1974, this bus had been a familiar sight along the Gower coast each summer running a regular scheduled service, and it was at first wondered what its future may now hold. Happily, however, the damage caused in this accident was less serious that initially thought and during the winter months it was able to be repaired to enable it to resume its duties in the summer of 1994. Around the same time that

Joining the South Wales Transport fleet from Eastern National in 1974, open-top ECW-bodied Bristol KSW5G 500 (WNO484) is seen in May 1990 adorned with side posters for the Vintage Sea Front Service from Swansea to Limeslade. (Travelscene)

this unfortunate event took place, South Wales Transport installed new cash-counting systems at its Swansea, Neath, Llanelli and Pontardawe depots as part of a drive towards total quality management. Replacing arrangements where cash was handled through an all-night deposit safe and was susceptible to human error, the new De La Rue Systems machines immediately collated the total paid in by the driver and, if tallying with their ticket machine's total, issued a receipt to both the driver and management.

Reaching a new milestone in Badgerline's history, the Group announced in September that it was to seek a stock market listing in November and thus follow the successful flotations by National Express and Stagecoach. In taking this decision, it aimed to reduce debt, raise cash for investment and finance the expansion of its operations, all measures which would play an important role in the Group's development into the twenty-first century. Over 90% of Badgerline's shares were currently held by directors, present and former staff and their families and initially worth 3.3p each, the shares were now valued at £3.20 with independent sources claiming that they were likely to rise substantially on flotation. Issued on 27 October, the Group's pathfinder prospectus forecast a pre-tax profit of £12.6 million for the year ending 31 December 1993 and showed the combined fleet at 30 June 1993 standing at 2359 vehicles (395 double deckers, 831 single deckers and coaches, 1006 midibuses and 127 minibuses). When the full prospectus was published on 10 November, it showed the share price fixed for its flotation at £1.15 per share. A total of £47 million would be raised in the issue of which £31 million was placed with institutions and £16 million offered to the public. So popular with the public was this offer that it was 1.7 times over subscribed and thus it was necessary to scale down all the applications to ensure that all those who had showed faith in the Group gained a shareholding. Dealings on the London Stock Exchange commenced on Friday 26 November.

As the flotation plans were progressing, Eastern National fired the first shots in a new bus war when it registered three new services in Colchester which competed directly with routes operated by Colchester Borough Transport. Starting them on 4 October with 22 Mercedes Benz minibuses acquired from City Line, Badgerline and Western National, these linked a number of large housing estates and business parks to the city centre and operated at 10 or 15 minute intervals. As a consequence of this new intense competition, Colchester Borough Council decided to withdraw financial support from its loss-making transport undertaking and offer it for sale. This led to British Bus making a speedy approach and purchasing Colchester Borough Transport in mid-November, an action which gave Eastern National a competitor of greater might and one who had the necessary resources to repel the new challenger. One consequence of its increased activities in Colchester was the fact that Eastern National's depot in the town was unable to accommodate the additional minibuses and thus a new base was opened for these in the town at Haven Road.

As a result of recurring problems in the St.Pauls area of Bristol where a series of vicious attacks had taken place on City Line drivers in recent weeks, the company withdrew all evening services into the area in September after issuing several warnings of such measures, each of which had been unheeded. A total of 54 journeys per week were withdrawn and City Line announced that although this action was deeply regretted, it had no plans to resume these in the future. This was not the first time that City Line had been forced to withdraw services as a result of disturbances and it hoped that lessons may now be learned from the most recent suspension of operations and that it would not be necessary to extend such measures to other areas of the city. In complete contrast, Midland Red West began a new Fridays only late-night bus service in November when Whitbourne Parish Council, concerned at the lack of evening public transport in the area, offered to fund a journey leaving Worcester at 11.05pm to Rushwick, Broadwas, Bringsty, Whitbourne and Bromyard. Although finance was extremely limited and the Parish Council only had money available for a ten week trial period, Hereford & Worcester County Council offered to continue the support for one year and thus it was now left up to the local population to use this bus if it was to become more permanent. Back in Bristol, as part of Avon County Council's plan to reduce traffic congestion in the city centre, a Park and Ride site was opened at Brislington on 25 October from where transport into the centre was provided by City Line. Operated by 6 new Northern Counties Palatine II-bodied Volvo Olympians which were painted in a special silver and blue livery and adorned with lettering to promote the operation, the service ran every 12 minutes on Mondays to Fridays from 7.00am to 7.00pm and on Saturdays between 8.00am and 7.00pm with an increase to every 7/8 minutes at peak times. A return fare of £1.20 per person was charged and additionally a 10-journey weekly ticket was available at £5

Still seeking ways to improve the environment, Badgerline and Avon County Council submitted a joint bid to the Department of Transport at the end of October for a £16,000 grant to convert two double deck buses to run on liquefied petroleum gas which produced a cleaner exhaust gas with reduced emissions of soot, oxides, nitrogen and carbon dioxide. It was intended that the buses concerned would operate on service 14 in Bath and the X39 between Bath and Bristol and if the bid was successful, the trial would form part of a national experiment into the use of alternative fuel in buses. In the meantime, the flow of new buses to various Badgerline Group companies continued unabated with Eastern National receiving Plaxton Beaver-bodied Mercedes Benz 709Ds for use on Clacton's revised service network and the first two of a batch of Plaxton Pointer-bodied Dennis Darts, City Line gaining 26 Plaxton-bodied Mercedes Benz 709Ds and 20 Northern Counties-bodied Volvo Olympian double deckers, South Wales Transport 24 Plaxton Pointer-bodied Dennis Darts, 10 Plaxton Verde-bodied Dennis Lances and a Plaxton Premiere-bodied Volvo B10M coach and Badgerline 21 Plaxton-bodied Dennis Darts, 8 Plaxton Verde-bodied Dennis Lances and a Mercedes Benz 811D. Additionally 2 more new Plaxton-bodied Volvo B10M coaches were added to the Wessex fleet while Western National gained 4 coaches of this configuration and Thamesway received a solitary Northern Counties-bodied Volvo B6 which was first exhibited at the Coach & Bus Show at the National Exhibition Centre at Birmingham. Also joining the Wessex and Western National fleets were several Volvo B10M coaches acquired secondhand from Wallace Arnold and United Counties, none of which were more than four years of age. The arrival of such a large number of new vehicles since 1 August allowed numerous time-expired buses including City Line's sole surviving Bristol Lodekka to be withdrawn and sold whilst others were cascaded amongst the Group's various subsidiaries such as was now becoming customary. Not all these were on a permanent basis, however, as 4 of Badgerline's Leyland Nationals were sent on extended loan to Eastern National for use at

Carrying a Timecutter name on its side panels and a smiling badger logo behind its rear wheel arch, South Wales Transport Plaxton Verde-bodied Dennis Lance 818 (L818HCY) arrives at The Quadrant bus station, Swansea at the end of a journey on the express X5 service. (Travelscene)

Arriving at Templemeads railway station, Bristol is City Line 9654 (L654SEU), a Northern Counties-bodied Volvo Olympian painted in a special silver & blue livery for operation on the Bath Road park and ride service. (J.A.Godwin)

Colchester whilst similarly Brewers loaned a number of its surplus buses of this type to Thamesway who was facing a vehicle shortage at Southend on the run up to Christmas. Additionally, as Eastern National's fleet had expanded beyond its 221 operating discs several of its Leyland Nationals were 'sold' to Thamesway and then hired back!

As a result of the arrival of its new buses, South Wales Transport was able to revise its Swansea area services in November and introduce a number of new high-frequency midibus routes. Somewhat surprisingly, despite being 40-seaters the new Dennis Darts employed on the revamped town service network continued to sport the City Mini fleet names carried by their 25-seat predecessors while the new Dennis Lances which were used on rural services radiating from Swansea carried Time Cutter fleet names. Although South Wales Transport was enjoying increasing success in Swansea, its associated Brewers Motor Services was less than happy with Mid-Glamorgan County Council and complained to the Office of Fair Trading about the £3 million infrastructure grant it had made to British Rail in respect of its Maesteg to Bridgend railway line which competed with one of Brewer's main services. In addition to this upon which British Rail was offering a 50% fare discount, South Wales Transport complained that up to 12 routes connecting Neath, Port Talbot and Swansea would be affected by West Glamorgan County Council's plans to subsidise an hourly rail service between Neath and Swansea in 1994. Unfortunately, British Rail was immune from investigation by the OFT as a result of it being a nationalised company and thus the complaints were not acted upon. These moves, however, put a massive strain on both Brewers and South Wales Transport who incurred a substantial drop in revenue as a result of British Rail's activities.

Despite the government's U-turn on deregulation in London, Badgerline still maintained an interest in the London Buses companies when they were eventually offered to the private sector and stated that it had not been dissuaded from bidding for some of them. Indeed, it saw the capital as a further area of development for its activities and believed that it would be in a strong position to enter that arena having already gained experience through the London Transport services contracted to Thamesway.

1994

Following the sale of its Penzance depot and engineering workshops for redevelopment, these were finally closed in January when new facilities at Camborne were brought into use following their official opening by Sebastian Coe, M.P. The first month of the new year also witnessed an escalation of the bus war in Colchester when on 4 January Eastern National commencing operations on further Colchester Borough Transport services. Despite having recently been taken over by the British Bus group, the former municipal company on this occasion did not respond and instead continued to operate the revised network it had introduced on 1 November 1993. After some negotiation in March, however, it was agreed that from 25 April specific routes would be operated by one of the two companies concerned rather than by both and as a result Colchester Borough Transport withdrew from three of its main services and Eastern National from four. Although not connected with this move, Eastern National acquired a further number of Mercedes Benz L608Ds from Western National to enable it to eliminate the remainder of its Ford Transits and also gained a dual-door Bristol VRT from City Line for use at Colchester, this being the first bus of this configuration to be operated by the company.

Meanwhile, 1994 proved to be a year of massive expansion for the Badgerline Group who during the spring purchased two major operators in areas where it had not previously been represented in addition to strengthening its position to the south of Bristol with the acquisition of the services of a smaller independent company. The first of these was Butler Woodhouse Limited, the parent company of PMT Ltd, Crosville Ltd., S.Turner & Sons Ltd. and Mapleshore (trading as Stoniers) which was acquired on 11 March for £23 million. A former National Bus Company subsidiary, Stoke-on-Trent based PMT had been purchased by its management who had formed a new company for this purpose on 15 December 1986 under the title of Butler Woodhouse Ltd. Seeking expansion from the start, it began operations under the title Red Rider on Merseyside, the Wirral, in the West Midlands and in Leeds and gained an increased foothold on the Wirral in February 1992 when it purchased C & M Travel's local operations. Its sortie into Leeds was less successful, however, and was soon abandoned while its operations in the West Midlands were eventually sold to Stevensons of Spath. Still looking to further its interests, Butler Woodhouse purchased the Cheshire and Wirral operations of Crosville Motor Services - another former National Bus Company subsidiary - in January 1990 and followed this by acquiring a 22% stake in Rhondda Buses in South Wales. Although it had

Fitted with PMT Hanbridge-type bodywork, PMT Mercedes Benz 709D MMM453 (D453ERE) pictured at Hanley bus station wore its owner's green & yellow Hospitalslink livery. (K.A.Jenkinson)

Built as a demonstrator in 1988, PMT Knype-bodied Leyland Swift IWC318 (E342NFA) joined the PMT fleet later that year and is seen here at Newcastle bus station having completed a journey on a local service. (T.W.W.Knowles)

PMT 113 (YRE473Y), a 12-seat home-bodied Mercedes Benz 307D was part of its owner's Flexi fleet and is seen here appropriately lettered at Stoke depot.

***Despite it being several years since PMT had acquired the business of** Turners of Brown Edge, it still retained that independent's fleet name and livery on a small number of vehicles. Illustrating this is Plaxton-bodied Mercedes Benz 709D MMM431 (J431WFA) seen here in Hanley bus station on the 69 service to Brown Edge. (J.L.Hobbs)*

already established a presence in the Stockport area, it further expanded this in November 1993 when it purchased Greater Manchester area independent United Provincial Services Ltd. who traded as Pennine Blue. Conversely, however, in order to be able to concentrate more fully on its local bus interests, it sold its Paramount Leisure coaching operation to Leons of Stafford at the end of 1993 after already closing its bodybuilding subsidiary PMT Engineering Ltd. a year earlier. Having fostered the minibus concept over a wide part of its service network, it was not surprising that around half of its 500-strong fleet acquired by the Badgerline Group comprised small capacity vehicles, the bodies of many of which had been built by the company itself. Within days of joining the Weston-based Group, PMT's subsidiary Pennine Blue purchased the business a small, but nevertheless important, independent operator in North Staffordshire who in recent times had become a thorn in its side. This was G.V.Shaw of Werrington who traded as Moorland Rover with 16 minibuses running on routes in the heart of PMT territory. Unlike Stoniers which had been acquired on 28 February and whose name had been retained, Moorland Rover's services were immediately merged into the PMT network whilst its vehicles were withdrawn and placed in store pending disposal.

Badgerline's second major acquisition was that of Rider Holdings Ltd on 15 April for £38 million, a move which gave the Group control of a major part of West Yorkshire in addition to the historic city of York. Born from West Yorkshire PTE, Yorkshire Rider was purchased by its management and employees on 21 October 1988 and in the following year expanded with the purchase of the Bradford, Leeds and Otley depots and operations of former National Bus Company subsidiary West Yorkshire Road Car Co. Ltd. On 29 July 1990 it

*Illustrated earlier with Red Rider names, PMT Dormobile-bodied Mercedes Benz 709D MMM489 (K489CVT) is seen at Stockport bus station in August 1997 after receiving new corporate FirstBus-style **Pennine fleet names.** (K.S.E.Till)*

Painted in PMT's standard yellow & red livery but adorned with Crosville fleet names, ECW-bodied Leyland Olympian DOC156 (A156UDM) collects its Birkenhead-bound passengers at Chester bus exchange. (D.J.Stanier)

Acquired by PMT with the business of Pennine Blue and sporting 'Baby Blue' fleet names, Northern Counties-bodied Dodge S56 MRP537 (D848LND) which began life with GM Buses is seen leaving Ashton-under-Lyne bus station on a local journey to Hazelhurst in 1994. (K.A.Jenkinson)

Acquired by PMT with the business of Shaw, Werrington (Moorland Rover) but never operated by its new owner, Freight Rover Sherpas D757PTU and D746PTU await their fate in the yard of a Yorkshire breaker. (Travelscene)

One of eleven Roe-bodied Leyland Atlanteans purchased by Yorkshire Rider from Sovereign in 1989, all of which originated with London Country, Leeds District 6430 (KPJ261W) turns in to Bradford Transport Interchange at the end of its journey from Leeds. (K.A.Jenkinson)

Approaching Bradford Transport Interchange is Yorkshire Rider 1625 (EWW947Y), a Plaxton Paramount 3200-bodied Leyland Tiger which was acquired from West Yorkshire Road Car Co. Ltd. and is wearing its new owner's Gold Rider coaching livery. (K.A.Jenkinson)

further extended its territory when it acquired York City & District Travel together with Reynard Buses of York and in June 1992 it purchased the West Yorkshire operations of Pride of the Road. Seeking to compete strongly within its established area it took over Quickstep Travel of Leeds in November 1993 and on 9 April 1994 bought the local bus operations of Rhodes Coaches of Yeadon near Leeds which were placed under Quickstep's control. Thus, when it joined the Badgerline Group, Rider Holdings had a fleet of over 1,100 buses and coaches operating from depots in Leeds, Bradford, Huddersfield, Halifax, Todmorden, Kinsley and York. Divided into operating districts, Yorkshire Rider Leeds, Bradford, Halifax and Huddersfield all shared a common livery of cream and green as did Rider York whilst Quickstep Travel, which was maintained as a low-cost unit, retained its original cream and crimson colours. Rider's coaching operation was maintained under the Gold Rider name and

977 (SWW302R), one of the ECW-bodied Bristol VRTs inherited by Yorkshire Rider from West Yorkshire Road Car Co. Ltd. is seen in the fleet of Rider York passing the walls of this historic city. (K.A.Jenkinson)

For several years Yorkshire Rider maintained a vehicle in the livery of each of its predecessors. Representing Halifax Corporation was Roe-bodied Leyland Olympian 5096 (A96KUM) which wore that former undertaking's orange, green & cream colours and carried the legend 'Building on a great tradition' on its side panels. (K.A.Jenkinson)

Of the vehicles taken over by Quickstep Travel with the bus operations of Rhodes, Yeadon, only six saw service with the Yorkshire Rider Group. One of these was 23 (UOI4323) a Volvo B10M originally fitted with Van Hool coach bodywork which was given a new East Lancs body in December 1993. It is seen here in Canada Road, Rawdon after being repainted into its new owner's cream & crimson livery. (K.A.Jenkinson)

although the majority of its vehicles were painted in an oatmeal scheme with red and gold stripes, a number were adorned with National Express corporate livery for use on services contracted by that undertaking. Completing the trio of takeovers, in mid-April Badgerline acquired the stage carriage operations of Clapton Coaches of Radstock together with a number of that company's vehicles. Clapton Coaches' services covered a large area stretching from Portishead and Thornbury in the west to Devizes, Swindon and Salisbury in the east and around Radstock and Midsomer Norton several had competed vigorously with Badgerline. Of the vehicles acquired, five minis/midis were added to the Badgerline fleet whilst a Mercedes Benz 609D was dispatched to join Western National, two Willowbrook Warrior-bodied Leyland Leopards were cascaded to Frontline and the remainder offered for sale.

Whilst the above events were taking place, Badgerline had put in service 16 new Plaxton Verde-bodied Dennis Lances on some of its longer inter-town services radiating from Bristol whilst in the city itself its Wessex subsidiary's Sky Blue unit continued its battle against Ambassador Travel on services to Hartcliffe. Beginning a new service numbered X69 in April, its blue-liveried Leyland Nationals were timed to run two minutes ahead of Ambassador's planned X81 service which in the event was never started due to a lack of drivers. Offering a £12 six-weekly transferable ticket (which equated to 33p per day), Sky Blue had effectively halved Ambassador's revenue (the latter charging £1 return for its journey's between Bristol and Hartcliffe) as well as taking onboard some of Ambassador's drivers, and as a result had placed the latter in the position of being unable to introduce its new service. Further north, as a result of the delivery of 37 new Plaxton Verde-bodied Dennis Lances all of which were allocated to Digbeth depot, Midland Red West was able to cascade all that garage's Leyland Lynxes to Redditch and Kidderminster where they ousted mainly Leyland Nationals together with a few Leopards. Western National meanwhile closed its St.Ives outstation and reallocated its vehicles to Camborne.

Looking towards the future, in June Badgerline placed orders for new vehicles worth £60 million which it stated would replace almost 25% of its existing fleet during the next two years. Totalling 926 buses, these comprised 339 Plaxton Pointer-bodied Dennis Darts, 187 Plaxton Verde-bodied Dennis Lances, 317 Plaxton Beaver-bodied Mercedes Benz 709Ds, 50 Alexander Dash-bodied Dennis Darts and 33 Alexander Royale-bodied Volvo Olympians. Added to these were 53 buses (24 Dennis Darts, 21 Mercedes Benz 709Ds and 8 Optare Metroriders) in the course of delivery to PMT which had been ordered by that company prior to its acquisition by Badgerline. This massive order when completed would dramatically reduce the overall age of Badgerline's combined fleet and allow it to eliminate a great many of its non-standard and time-expired vehicles which it had inherited with the companies it had acquired. With new buses and coaches from the 1994 order now starting to arrive in quantity, it was possible to withdraw equally large numbers of older vehicles and included amongst these were Ford Transits of Badgerline, Eastern National and Thamesway; Leyland Nationals of Badgerline, Eastern National and Midland Red West and Leyland Leopards of Midland Red West. Although a few of these were cascaded amongst other Badgerline subsidiaries most were able to be sold to buyers outside the Group or were placed in reserve. An unusual visitor to Swansea at the beginning of August was London Buses recently refurbished Routemaster RML2735 which came to the city in connection with a wedding. Before its return to its rightful owner, it was, however, used by South Wales Transport on services 1, 2 and 3, attracting a great deal of attention in its bright red livery. Meanwhile South Wales open-top Bristol KSW was back in service on the Swansea to Oystermouth corridor following accident-damage repairs and Eastern National once again employed its two vintage open-top Bristol KSWs on Clacton sea front service 99 on Mondays to Fridays and Sundays from May until 2 September.

New to Clyde Coast Services, Ardrossan, Scott-bodied Mercedes Benz 609D F165XCS was acquired by Clapton Coaches of Radstock in 1990 and is seen here operating service 766 from Bath to Clutton.

Surprisingly fitted with a full destination display during its brief period of loan to South Wales Transport in August 1994, London Buses (CentreWest) Routemaster RML2735 (SMK735F) approaches Swansea city centre on service 1. Although not known at the time, CentreWest was to be purchased by FirstBus in 1996. (K.A.Jenkinson)

Laying over in Plymouth bus station after arriving on service 86 is Western National Plaxton Pointer-bodied Dennis Dart 412 (M412CCV) which carried its flags logo on its cove panels. (I.H.Winchester)

Having now addressed its fleet, Badgerline turned its attention towards its operations and on 29 May Midland Red West replaced its existing ticketing equipment with Wayfarer 2-type machines cascaded from City Line who had upgraded its system to Wayfarer 3. Prior to this, Eastern National had introduced a revised service network in Colchester which had increased its market share in the town as well as reducing unnecessary duplication of services while in July Thamesway launched a customer survey with advertisements in local newspapers which asked readers to fill in a simple questionnaire on aspects of local bus services. This, it was believed, would allow the company to know exactly what bus passengers - and potential passengers of course, expected from bus operators and would assist Thamesway in its future planning. On the penultimate day of July Eastern National ended its Country Car operation which was replaced by a minibus of Fargo Coachlines and at the same time its minibuses 601-30 had their 'Little Green Bus' vinyls removed. During the following month, after the arrival in Huddersfield on 1 August of Horwich-based Blue Bus who began competition with Yorkshire Rider by introducing a service from Huddersfield to Marsden and Dobcross, the Badgerline subsidiary quickly retaliated by upgrading its services along the Marsden corridor to Flagship status. Having already been introduced in Halifax, Bradford and York prior to the takeover of Rider Holdings by Badgerline, the Flagship services promised passengers a better quality of travel backed by money-back guarantees should the service fail to meet certain criteria. By upgrading the services concerned, running buses directly ahead of Blue Bus and reducing its maximum fare to 50p, Yorkshire Rider believed that it would soon see off its new competitor, although this proved to be a long way from reality and in the next few months Blue Bus strengthened its position and opened several more routes in direct competition to the incumbent operator in a war that was to continue for two years. This led to Rider launching a new service between Huddersfield and Golcar on 10 October which was marketed as the '300 Plus Bus'. For its operation, a number of Mercedes Benz L608D minibuses were acquired from Bristol City Line and rather than repaint them into Rider livery, they instead retained their City Line colours to which promotional logos were added in order to promote a 'special image'. Meanwhile, on 16 May following the revamping by National Express of its Leeds to Manchester service, six of Yorkshire Rider's Plaxton-bodied Volvo B10M coaches were repainted into 'Express Shuttle' livery for operation on this service. Despite a number of new buses being on order, Rider began a pilot project involving the rebuilding of

Retaining the yellow, red & blue colours of its previous owner Bristol City Line upon its transfer to Yorkshire Rider, Dormobile-bodied Mercedes Benz L608D 2011 (D540FAE) was lettered for the 300 Plus Bus service which ran in competition with Blue Bus in Huddersfield. (B.Newsome)

Seen leaving Bradford on National Express service 362 to Manchester, Yorkshire Rider's Express Shuttle-liveried Plaxton Paramount 3500-bodied Volvo B10M 1416 (D783SGB) had joined the fleet from Parks of Hamilton in 1988. (K.A.Jenkinson)

227
Grampian
EXACT FARE
XSA 227S

Grampian executive
Grampian executive
K3 GRT

Northampton
3 RECTORY FARM
POSH
CNH 52T

Alloa
BLUEBIRD
BLUEBIRD
B102 PKS

128 LONGNIDDRY
LOWLAND
BSF 765S

OBAN & DISTRICT

Mairs of Aberdeen
Mairs of Aberdeen
SCHOOL BUS
SCHOOL BUS
B490 CGN
D232 UHC

94 Montgomery Street
OLS 814T

South Queensferry 43
SMT Edinburgh
H477 OSC

50 Falkirk
Midland Bluebird
Midland Bluebird
ORS 208R

WSV 135

Just picked, just perfect.
cape
Fresh from the sun.
FREE ENTRY
OPEN
PLEASURE BEACH
75
FELIXSTOWE
GREAT YARMOUTH
Eastern Counties
GNG 709N

63. FALLIN
Midland Bluebird
Midland Bluebird
K473 EDT

94 CITY CENTRE
616
CityBus
DENNIS
H616 EJF

X94 NORWICH
Eastern Counties
Eastern Counties
H618 RAH

IAN GLASS
BEDFORD
C777 VSC

Excursion
Citycoach of Leicester
Citycoach of Leicester
B160 WRN

Seen on its first day in service, Rider York low-floor Alexander Strider-bodied Scania L113CRL 8404 (M404UUB) had yet to receive its fleet names. (K.A.Jenkinson)

one of the Leyland National Mk.I buses which had remained in store since its acquisition from Pride of the Road in June 1992 in order to give it a new lease of life. After removing its roof pod, replacing all its moulded sides with flat panels, equipping it with numerous DiPTAC features and fitting it with a Volvo engine, it eventually entered service in its rebuilt form at Huddersfield on 5 July. Although successful, it was felt that the high cost of its transformation could not be fully justified and thus no further vehicles were treated in this manner. Just as one project was abandoned, however, another took a further step forward when Rider's Alexander-bodied Scania N113CRB 8635 was dispatched to the German city of Essen for trials on its Wittenbergstrasse guided busway in preparation for the introduction of a similar system in Leeds. Much valuable experience was gained from its brief visit to mainland Europe and this set the scene for future developments in its native city. Continuing its programme of experiments, a Wright City Ranger-bodied Mercedes 0405 demonstrator was borrowed in July for use in Leeds and Huddersfield in connection with fuel trials and after these were completed the test equipment was fitted to one of Rider's Scania single deckers for continued evaluation. Soon afterwards, Rider York placed five new Alexander Strider-bodied Scania FlexCi low-floor single deckers in service on 15 August as the first step towards the upgrading of its fleet in this historic city and two months later, Rider York gained its first major park and ride contract when it successfully tendered for the new York City Council operation which was to commence in November from Grimston Bar to the city centre. Whilst the City Council took all of the revenue of the £1 per adult peak and 70p off-peak fare, it paid Rider York £112,000 for the operation of the service to June 1995 which was to be maintained by the company's two year old Ikarus-bodied DAF SB220s whose duties on York city services were to be taken over by Optare Delta-bodied DAF SB220s transferred from Yorkshire Rider at Leeds. Thamesway also became involved in a park and ride operation, albeit limited to the Christmas period, when Basildon Council again appointed the company to run the service as it had done in 1993.

After renumbering its Pennine Blue fleet into its own numbering scheme in March, PMT took the decision in August to fully absorb it and abandon its yellow and blue livery in favour of its own yellow and red and reflecting this, change its fleet name to 'Pennine'. Coinciding with this move, PMT entered into an agreement to exchange a number of routes with GM Buses South which competed with some

Photographs, page 34, top to bottom left :

Badgerline MCW Metrobus 6004 (DAE514W) on service 339 to Bath is overtaken by National Express-liveried Wessex Duple-bodied Leyland Leopard AFH190T. (F.W.York)

The first new buses purchased by Badgerline after privatisation came in 1987 and included 12 Alexander-bodied Volvo Citybuses. One of these, 5701 (D701GHY) is seen here painted in an all-over advertising livery for Badgerline subsidiary, Roman City Holidays.

Leaving Gloucester bus station for its Worcester home is Midland Red West Leyland National 547 (NOE547R). (Travelscene))

Painted in local Citybus livery, Midland Red West 1985 vintage Robin Hood-bodied Mercedes Benz L608D 1323 (C323PNP) leaves Worcester bus station on a town service. (J.L.Hobbs)

Top to bottom right :

Passing along High Street, Colchester on its way to Brightlingsea is Eastern National 3233 (LUA717V), an ECW-bodied Bristol VRT acquired from Yorkshire Rider. (D.W.Rhodes)

Seen passing Kings Cross railway station, London whilst working London Transport Buses contracted service 214 to Liverpool Street Station, Thamesway Plaxton Pointer-bodied Dennis Dart 902 (K902CVW) leaves no doubt as to its ownership with a large smiling badger logo on its side panels. (K.A.Jenkinson)

Displaying City Dart fleet names, Bristol Omnibus Co. Dormobile-bodied Mercedes Benz L608D 7508 (D508FAE) passes through Bristol city centre whilst working a local service. (T.S.Blackman)

The oldest vehicle in the fleet of Frontline Buses was former Kelvin Scottish Routemaster KVS601 (which began life with London Transport registered WLT408) seen here enroute to Chelmsley Wood on service 94. (R.G.Pope)

Photographs, page 35, top to bottom left :

Sporting United Welsh Coaches fleet names, Duple-bodied Leyland Leopard U193 (MKH486A, originally AFH191T) rests in Swansea while undertaking a private hire duty. (Travelscene)

Given a red front panel to signify that it is that it is operating on loan to Bristol & Weston Health Authority, Badgerline ECW-bodied Bristol RELL6L 1313 (LHT167L) is seen here carrying hospital workers into Bristol.

Arriving at Lakeside Shopping centre, Thurrock on its way from Southend to London on the S1 service is Thamesway City Saver-liveried Duple Carribean-bodied Leyland Tiger 510 (B336BGL) which was previously operated by Western National. (D.W.Rhodes)

Wearing a modified livery with blue lower deck panels and flags at between decks level is Western National coach-seated Northern Counties-bodied Volvo Olympian 801 (K801ORL). (J.A.Godwin)

Top to bottom right :

Entering Crewe bus station and carrying a Cheshire Bus notice on its front panel is PMT 772 (YBW488V), an ECW-bodied Bristol VRT acquired from Thames Transit in 1989. (K.A.Jenkinson)

Robin Hood-bodied Iveco 49.10 E947LAE of the jointly owned Badgerline/Southampton CityBus Red Admiral fleet heads through Portsmouth in March 1988. (Travelscene)

Painted in Brewers colours, ex.South Wales Transport Duple-bodied Leyland Leopard 116 (MKH690R, originally MCY116X) arrives in Swansea on a journey from Port Talbot. (Travelscene)

Painted in Cornwall Busways Hoppa livery, Western National Reeve Burgess-bodied Mercedes Bean L608D 68 (C683ECV) awaits its passengers at Newquay bus station in April 1991. (J.A.Godwin)

Wearing Wessex private hire livery, Plaxton Premiere-bodied Volvo B10M 138 (K650HT) rests in York whilst undertaking a holiday tour to the area. (Travelscene)

This page left :

Lettered on its side panels and in its windscreens for York's Grimston Bar park & ride service, Rider York Ikarus-bodied DAF SB220 1203 (J423NCP) collects its passengers in Piccadilly. (G.T.W.Carter)

Amongst the vehicles taken over with Durbins at Bristol was former Maidstone & District full-height ECW-bodied Bristol VRT WKO131S which is seen at City Line's Lawrence Hill depot in April 1997 after being repainted into the white & two-tone blue colours adopted for the Durbins fleet. (K.A.Jenkinson)

of those it had inherited with the Pennine Blue business and those it had transferred to that subsidiary from its disbanded Red Rider operation in the Stockport area. This led to GMBS pulling off the Ashton to Mossley, Carrbrook, Crow Hill and Dukinfield Circular services whilst in return PMT withdrew from Haughton Green and Wilmslow Road. Additionally, a small number of GMBS tendered services were also transferred to PMT whilst between Ashton and Hyde rationalisation resulted in fewer vehicles being employed by both companies. These moves, however, angered some of the other independent operators in the area who had previously worked harmoniously with Pennine Blue and ultimately led to more competition in this area rather than less. At around the same time it

New in 1988, South Wales Transport MCW Metrorider D186PWN initially carried its owner's predominantly white dual purpose livery with two-tone green and red relief as seen here when it was attending an open day at Cobham Bus Museum. (P.T.Stokes)

Next page, top to bottom left :

Grampian Transport Alexander-bodied Leyland Atlantean 227 (XSA227S) passes through the centre of Aberdeen on a school bus duty.

About to enter Greyfriars bus station in its home town is Northampton Transport Alexander-bodied Bristol VRT 52 (CNH52T) painted in Grampian-style livery. (P.Kay)

Travelling along Princes Street, Edinburgh on its way to Longniddry is Lowland 165 (BSF765S), a Leyland National inherited from Eastern Scottish in 1985. (P.T.Stokes)

Two of Mairs of Aberdeen's Mercedes Benz L608Ds, Robin Hood-bodied 714 (B490CGN) and Alexander-bodied 718 (D232UHC) rest at Dyce depot before undertaking their next their next school bus duty. (T.W.W.Knowles)

Top to bottom right :

Wearing the attractive green & gold Grampian Executive livery is Grampian Transport Jonckheere-bodied Volvo B10M 93 (K3GRT) seen here a long way from home at Poole Harbour. (J.A.Godwin)

Still painted in Midland Bluebird's old predominantly blue livery, Alexander-bodied MCW Metrobus 802 (B102PKS) was one of four such buses acquired from Kelvin Central Buses in 1990. (K.A.Jenkinson)

Seen wearing Midland Bluebird livery with Oban & District fleet names is Alexander-bodied Leyland Leopard CAS520W. (J.L.Hobbs)

Seen passing through Falkirk in March 1992 is Midland Bluebird Leyland National 14 (OLS814T). (Travelscene)

also announced that it was ultimately to close its head office and central repair workshops at Butler Street, Stoke-on-Trent once suitable new premises had been located, although in the event it was not until the following year that this move took place. Operationally, under a new round of retendering PMT gained five Cheshire County Council contracts in the Crewe area which had previously been maintained by Midland Red North, thus strengthening its position in this part of its territory and on 5 December purchased the local Wirral bus operations of Toppings of Wavertree. In addition to giving it two circular services running between Woodside and Woodchurch, this deal also included Toppings' four Leyland Lynx buses which joined its own eleven of this type and two which had been acquired from Westbus of Ashford in November 1993.

Further expansion was achieved on 14 October when Badgerline acquired the Bristol-based business of Durbin's Coaches, a company which operated 42 buses and coaches on schools contracts from depots at Almondsbury and Patchway, Bristol as well as undertaking an amount of private hire, tours and continental shuttle work. Included in the fleet were some Bristol VRT double deckers wearing their owner's 'Orange Bus' livery, Leyland, Bedford, Ford, Bova, DAF and Neoplan coaches and six Freight Rover Sherpa minibuses, almost all of which had been acquired secondhand. Rather than merge its new operation into that of City Line, it was decided to maintain it as a separate unit under the title of Durbin Travel for at least eighteen months and as a consequence, Roger Durbin, its former owner was appointed as managing director.

While Badgerline was enjoying success following the announcement of a rise in its pre-tax profits for the first six months of 1994 from £2.6 million to £5.4 million, it was beset with troubles in Essex where Eastern National staff at Chelmsford took strike action on 18 November following a long standing dispute dating back to 1992 resulting from the introduction of new minibus schedules and pay structures. In what had proved to be a long drawn out conflict, after dismissing 91 drivers the company found itself the subject of a 'dirty tricks' campaign with counterfeit notices being posted at bus stops informing passengers that they were not insured on the buses which were still able to operate. This, of course, was complete fiction, although misleading statements such as this did little to comfort passengers who were already experiencing a reduction in services as a result of the strike. Indeed, the situation became even more complicated when the sacked drivers threatened to plan a number of free bus services in the town! Although initially Eastern National was only able to operate around 25% of its services from its Chelmsford depot, within a couple of days it managed to maintain some 90% of its town services and 40% of the rest. This was achieved by bringing in drivers from South Wales, Bristol and PMT who were provided with hotel accommodation for the duration of their stay. In the meantime, Eastern National vacated its depot at South Street, Bishops Stortford and moved to new premises comprising an open yard at Anchor Street close to the town's bus/rail interchange. A new outstation was also opened by South Wales Transport at Ammanford while under a new round of West Glamorgan County Council tenders SWT lost its 37/38 services from Swansea to Oystermouth/Ty-coch to D-Coaches of Morriston.

Whilst Thamesway continued to withdraw and sell its time-expired Leyland Nationals and Ford Transits, South Wales Transport surprisingly rid itself of all its MCW Metroriders despite them being a mere seven years of age and Eastern National took out of service the

339 Bath
NATIONAL EXPRESS
DAE 514W

78A BRIGHTLINGSEA
EASTERN NATIONAL
LUA 717V

ROMAN CITY HOLIDAYS
You're sitting pretty with Roman City
D701 GHY

214
THAMESWAY
K902 CVW

373 WORCESTER
MIDLAND RED WEST
The suite shop.
NOE 547R

65 CENTRE
City Dart
D508 FAE

Citibus
C323 PNP

94
KVS 601

193 Private
UNITED Welsh COACHES
U193
UNITED Welsh COACHES
MKH 486A

34 HASLINGTON
FREE HOLIDAY INSURANCE
United
0782 577770
TRAVEL
Cheshire bus
YBW 488V

BRISTOL
MH 1313
Badgerline
LHT 167L

IVECO
E947 LAE

BREWERS

LONDON
SOUTHEND · BASILDON · LONDON
512
City SAVER
City SAVER
B336 BGL

TORQUAY
WESTERN NATIONAL
WESTERN NATIONAL
K801 ORL
VOLVO

JOHN SMITHS
Wessex of Bristol
Wessex of Bristol
VOLVO
K65 DHT

United Welsh Coaches Plaxton Premiere-bodied Dennis Javelin 172 (L6BMS) picks up its passengers at Redhill bus station in September 1994 while operating a tour on behalf of Ledger Travel. Looking immaculate, it sported a smiling badger logo on its rear side panel. (J.A.Godwin)

Passing through Chipping Sodbury on its way to Bristol whilst being evaluated by Badgerline is Optare Sigma-bodied MAN demonstrator M21UUA. (M.Lockyer)

last of its three Peugeot 7-seater cars which were originally purchased for the Countrycar operation in 1985. Brewers continued to receive Mercedes Benz 709D minibuses cascaded by sister company South Wales Transport in order to provide it with additional vehicles for its increased number of services while Frontline gained two Bristol VRTs together with a pair of Mercedes Benz L608Ds from City Line and two Leyland Nationals from Eastern National. Another recipient of redundant Eastern National Leyland Nationals was Yorkshire Rider who gained four in October. Soon after their arrival, Rider surprisingly introduced an experimental new livery which, in addition to cream, made use of several shades of green in a rather complicated scheme. Although this was never applied widely amongst the fleet, it was used on most new vehicles delivered in 1995 and ultimately became Kingfisher Huddersfield's new livery, of which more later. Despite this, however, Yorkshire Rider continued to pursue its policy of repainting a tiny handful of its buses in the livery of its predecessors under its 'Building on a Great Tradition' banner.

Earlier, on 1 October Badger Transit Developments had been re-launched with a wider remit including specific involvements in special fuel projects and a greater geographical spread following the Group's acquisitions in Yorkshire and the North Midlands earlier in the year. In addition to leading a project involving the conversion of a Dennis Dart vehicle for operation on compressed natural gas, the Leeds Guided Busway and Avon Gorge Expressway, following the wide experience it had gained in the planning of light rail systems, Badgerline Transit Developments was appointed on 22 November to act as consultant to West Yorkshire PTE and Leeds City Council for its £95 million Supertram scheme. Although detailed work right up to the placing of the contract for the design, build and operation of the route was to be overseen by Bob Tebb, Badgerline Transit Developments' northern director, this did not mean that the company would run the system when it was completed as at a later stage it would be necessary to invite a fresh round of tenders for this purpose. As well as these specific schemes, BTD was still investigating the concept of Guided Light Transit in addition to researching an all-electric vehicle for possible operation in Southend by Thamesway and overall continued to extend the capability of the Badgerline Group in public transport operation and develop new markets that bring in new profitable sectors.

Despite having placed large orders for new buses, the Badgerline Group nevertheless continued to evaluate new models as they were launched and during the second half of 1994 several were borrowed for in service trials. These comprised an Optare Sigma, Plaxton-bodied Dennis Dart with split level entrance step and a Berkhof-bodied Dennis Javelin coach which operated for Badgerline in September/October; a Volvo B6, Wright-bodied Mercedes Benz 811D and a Wright Urban Ranger-bodied Mercedes Benz 0405 which were evaluated by City Line in the early autumn, the latter passing onward to Midland Red West and a low-floor Wright-bodied Dennis Lance trialed by Western National in October.

Continuing its acquisition trail, Badgerline purchased the operations of Normans Coaches of Keynsham during the latter months of the

Previous page. top to bottom left :

Adorned with SMT Edinburgh fleet names, Midland Bluebird's ex.SMT Reeve Burgess-bodied Renault S75 1477 (H477OSC) leaves St.Andrew bus station, Edinburgh on a journey to South Queensferry. (K.A.Jenkinson)

Arriving at Buchanan bus station, Glasgow is Midland Bluebird Plaxton Paramount-bodied Leyland Tiger 1332 (WSV135, originally A332BSC) still painted in SMT livery. (K.A.Jenkinson)

Midland Bluebird 51 (K473EDT), an Alexander-bodied Mercedes Benz 0405 former demonstrator, rests in Stirling bus station before proceeding to Fallin on the 63 service. (C.Morrison)

Awaiting its Norwich-bound passengers at Peterborough bus station is Eastern Counties Duple-bodied Dennis Javelin 518 (H618RAH) painted in Grampian-style livery. (K.A.Jenkinson)

Wearing Grampian-style livery, Leicester CityBus Duple Laser-bodied Leyland Tiger 23 (B160WRN) which was acquired from Ribble in 1985 is seen at Albert Dock, Liverpool whilst working an excursion. As will be seen, it was adorned with Citycoach of Leicester fleet names. (K.A.Jenkinson)

Top to bottom right :

Still painted in the old blue livery of Midland Bluebird, Alexander-bodied Leyland Leopard MPE325 (ULS325T) stands alongside ex.Grampian Alexander-bodied Leyland Atlantean 708 (ORS208R) which still wore the colours of its former owner. (K.A.Jenkinson)

Wearing Eastern Counties predominantly red livery, ECW-bodied Bristol VRT VR143 heads towards Felixstowe on the 75 service with a T-shaped advert on its side panels and further advertising around its front destination screen. (P.Horrex)

Wearing the pre-Grampian style livery of maroon, yellow & ivory, Leicester CityBus East Lancs-bodied Dennis Falcon 616 (H616EJF) passes St.Margarets bus station on its way to Leicester city centre. (K.A.Jenkinson)

Amongst the vehicles acquired by Lowland with the Ian Glass business in 1991 was 625 (C877VSC), a Scott-bodied Bedford CFL 12-seat minicoach which is seen at Haddington depot in 1994 still wearing its original owner's livery. (K.A.Jenkinson)

Originally a coach in the fleet of Cumberland Motor Services, Frontline Buses Leyland Leopard 1904 (VRM602S) was fitted with a new Willowbrook Warrior bus body before entering service with the company in 1994. (P.T.Stokes)

Western National Plaxton Paramount-bodied Leyland Tiger 2208 (A532WRL) wore a white, red & grey livery when caught by the camera in Lynmouth, Devon whilst working a day tour from Plymouth. (K.A.Jenkinson)

A unique vehicle in the Thamesway fleet is Northern Counties-bodied Volvo B6 601 (L601MWC) which features a split level entrance and is seen here at Lakeside bus station, Thurrock. (D.W.Rhodes)

A unique vehicle in the Thamesway fleet is Northern Counties-bodied Volvo B6 601 (L601MWC) which features a split level entrance and is seen here at Lakeside bus station, Thurrock. (D.W.Rhodes)

year, inheriting the Keynsham town services which were marketed as 'Merry-go-Round' in the process while Brewers acquired the local bus services of Llynfi of Maesteg although in neither deal were any vehicles involved. Additionally Badgerline acquired the local bus operations of Paulton-based Somerbus on 1 December together with three vehicles - a Northern Counties-bodied Renault S56 still in the livery of its previous owner, Heatons of Leigh; a Wright-bodied Mercedes Benz 709D and a Duple-bodied Bedford coach. Seven services were included in the deal, three of which were immediately reallocated to Marlborough Street depot with the other three passing to Weston-super-Mare. Immediately prior to this takeover, City Line expressed its dis-satisfaction at the latest traffic calming measures adopted by Avon County Council claiming that the installation of road humps on several of its routes was slowing buses to a crawl and causing neck and back injuries to passengers and drivers. Refuting this claim, the County Council justified its action by stating that the humps stopped accidents and were thus necessary, although this did little to appease City Line who countered by announcing that it would alter a number of its routes to avoid them and would consider withdrawing others completely where suitable diversions could not be found.

Sadly, as 1994 drew to a close a disastrous fire at Eastern National's Colchester depot on the morning of 26 December completely destroyed 10 buses and severely damaged a further 5 as well as doing a considerable amount of damage to the depot itself. This was, however, in no way connected with the strike at Chelmsford depot and a person of no fixed abode was subsequently remanded on a charge of criminal damage. Fortunately it was possible to quickly draft in buses from other Badgerline subsidiaries including City Line, South Wales Transport, Thamesway and Yorkshire Rider to enable a full compliment of services to be maintained.

Painted in Shearings Holidays livery for operation on that company's tours is Midland Red Coaches Duple 340-bodied Leyland Tiger 1020 (C985HOX) seen here resting at Digbeth depot, Birmingham. (J.Whitmore)

MOVING TOWARDS A NEW ERA

1995

The threat of a free bus service operated by the drivers sacked by Eastern National at Chelmsford became a reality during the first week of January 1995 when six 15-seat minibuses, four of which were lent by the Transport and General Workers Union, began a service in the town. Not exactly minibuses, but rather crewbuses, these immediately brought a response from Eastern National as to their legality on public services and strengthened the company's resolve not to reinstate the drivers who had been dismissed. Indeed, as a show of strength it sacked a further eight drivers who had been suspended since the start of the strike almost eight weeks earlier and drafted in staff from other depots in order to meet its full compliment of services. After introducing a pair of 29-seat Mercedes Benz midibuses to the free bus fleet at the beginning of March, the Transport and General Workers Union began to realise that the chance of any of the sacked drivers regaining their jobs was fast diminishing and that the only way forward was to start up a commercial bus service in order to maintain its attack on the Badgerline subsidiary. Although plans were made early in April to obtain an operators licence and thus enable service registrations to be made, these were put on hold after the Union and Eastern National agreed to preliminary talks at ACAS as a way forward towards resolving this unfortunate situation, but meanwhile the free bus service continued. Following several weeks of discussion with ACAS, agreement was reached whereby the sacked drivers voted 80% in favour of an improved offer by Eastern National and were free to apply for vacancies with the company although it was made clear that there would be no automatic reinstatement. Thus the dispute ended during the last week in June and as a consequence, operation of the free bus service ceased.

In January, Badgerline placed the sale of advertising space on all its group vehicles under the control of Metrobus Advertising of London, a national company who had a wide experience in this field. Additionally, Thamesway introduced a special promotion in conjunction with Kentucky Fried Chicken under which the company's bus tickets could be exchanged for a second meal free of charge when customers purchased one from any KFC outlet until the end of February. Additionally, Thamesway invited comment in the local press regarding its recently modified livery to of a garish pink and yellow which it believed gave its vehicles a brighter image. Further north, to assist it with its 1995 Network Review which involved the complete reorganisation of its bus services in North Staffordshire, PMT removed the seats from three of its withdrawn Freight Rover Sherpas in January to enable them to be used for storage space at its Stoke headquarters.

Continuing its fleet upgrading, 12 new Plaxton Premiere Expressliner-bodied Dennis Javelins were purchased early in 1995 for use on National Express diagrams, 7 of which were allocated to Badgerline for the Bath to London service and 5 to South Wales Transport for the Swansea - Cardiff - London route. Additionally, new buses were placed in service by most of the Groups subsidiaries and in the case of Yorkshire Rider, the first of fifty Alexander-bodied Dennis Darts began a massive replacement programme which was designed to upgrade the fleet and allow the withdrawal of a similar number of ageing Leyland Atlanteans and Fleetlines. Looking towards the future, Badgerline Developments demonstrated a left hand drive natural gas-powered Mercedes 0405 single deckers to in several towns and cities served by the Group's subsidiaries during March as part of its joint campaign with British Gas to persuade the Government to sponsor trials of buses using this type of fuel. Believing that gas propulsion would greatly reduce pollution, particularly in built-up areas, Badgerline stated that the present and indeed any future Government should accept its environmental responsibilities and support the testing of gas-powered vehicles on a

Drawing out of Birmingham's Bull Ring bus station at the start of its *journey to Kidderminster is Midland Red West Plaxton Pointer-bodied Dennis Dart 304 (N304XAB). (G.T.W.Carter)*

Heading past the University of West of England on its way to Kingswood is Bristol City Line Dormobile-bodied Iveco 49.10 7605 (F605PWS) which carries a smiling badger logo across its side windows towards the rear. (K.A.Jenkinson)

Painted in the complicated two-tone green & cream livery adopted by Yorkshire Rider initially for its new buses, Huddersfield district Plaxton Pointer-bodied Dennis Dart 3202 (M202VWW) leaves Halifax bus station on the limited stop X37 service to its home town. (K.A.Jenkinson)

One of a pair of Leyland Lynxes acquired by PMT from Westbus of Ashford in 1993, SLC850 (G936YRY) is allocated to the Crosville fleet and is seen here calling at Rock Ferry depot on its way to Birkenhead whilst working route 2. (L.J.Long)

Painted in United Welsh Coaches livery and fitted with ExpressWest fleet names, South Wales Transport Willowbrook-bodied Leyland Leopard 109 (LCY109X) arrives in Swansea after completing a local service. (Travelscene)

wider scale. Despite its thoughts on Government involvement, however, Badgerline Transit Developments went ahead with its plans and placed an order for what it believed was the first purpose-built natural gas-powered bus for Britain. A Dennis Dart with Plaxton Pointer bodywork, it was proposed to operate this in the CityLine fleet alongside its conventional Dennis Darts for long-term evaluation. Another vehicle obtained for in service trials was a Bova Futura demonstrator which was borrowed from its manufacturer by South Wales Transport in February for operation on its National Express contracted services. Not to be left out, Western National placed in service a low-floor Wright Pathfinder-bodied Dennis Lance SLF of London Buses for a short period of evaluation which resulted in an order being placed for a solitary example of this combination (with support from Devon County Council) for use on the DCC tendered service 183 from Plymouth to Okehampton.

Badgerline plc further strengthened its position in Cornwall when on 20 March its subsidiary Western National purchased the business of Thomas of Relubbus who traded as Brookside. In addition to providing the company with 15 additional vehicles (all but 2 of which were, however, immediately placed in store at Penzance and Camborne pending disposal), this deal gave Western National services from Penzance to Praa Sands, Lamorna Cove and Treneere, the latter having been lost by WN to Brookside under the tendering process in 1992. Mr.Thomas retained 2 coaches for his continuing weekly Mystery Tour and Penzance - Truro Shopper operations while his son took 4 coaches with which to start a new business. Meanwhile, Durbins of Bristol continued to use the fleet name James Jean on some of its coaches.

Preliminary results published in April showed that Badgerline plc had been successful in increasing both its turnover and profits during its first full year since its flotation in November 1993. Pre-tax profits of £16.7 million were more than double that shown for the previous year whilst turnover had grown from £113.7 million to £223.5 million, although around £84 million resulted from its acquisitions, particularly PMT and the Rider Group. Looking to the future, proposals were announced at the start of April for the merger of the Badgerline Group with Scottish-based GRT Holdings which, if it came to fruition would create the UK's second largest listed bus conglomerate with a stock market capitalisation of £265 million and a turnover in excess of £300 million. If the shareholders of both groups accepted the deal, the newly created company which was to be known as FirstBus plc would be registered in Scotland but would have its headquarters in Weston-super-Mare. Ending on a high note, Trevor Smallwood who had led Badgerline from the National Bus Company to the start of a new era was rewarded for his services to the passenger transport industry by being awarded the OBE, an honour he richly deserved.

Numerically the first of four Optare StarRider-bodied Mercedes Benz 811Ds transferred from Badgerline to Western National in 199, 327 (E807MOU) is seen in the yard of Laira Bridge, Plymouth depot still painted in its previous owner's yellow & green livery. (T.W.W.Knowles)

Grampian

Being a council-owned undertaking which until 1974 was known as Aberdeen Corporation Transport, Grampian Regional Transport had under the 1985 Transport Act to be re-formed as a free standing company which could no longer be subsidised by the city's ratepayers and as a consequence on 20 February 1986 it was registered (in Scotland) as Grampian Regional Transport Limited. Prior to this, the Regional Council had on 10 January 1986 registered two other companies - Aberdeen Transport Limited and Aberdeen Citybus Limited - in order to protect these names and prevent others from using them. Grampian's fleet at this time was largely made up of Alexander-bodied Leyland Atlanteans, the only exceptions being 20 Leyland Olympians, 7 Leyland Nationals, 4 ex.London Transport Bristol LH6Ls, a solitary Ford transit and a trio of Leyland Leopards. During 1986 5 Plaxton Paramount-bodied Leyland Tigers were purchased and under its new title, Grampian Regional Transport Ltd. began its operations on 26 October without significant change, with most of the residents of the Granite City being unaware of the event. As had become customary, free bus services were provided in the city at Hogmanay in an attempt to persuade revellers to leave their cars at home and this year they were sponsored by Crawfords Three Star Whisky.

New to Aberdeen Corporation in 1965, Alexander-bodied Daimler CVG6 325 (CRG325C) was the only half-cab double decker to remain in the Grampian fleet in 1986 and has now been given preserved status by the company.

Wearing Grampian's old livery of green & cream with an orange between decks band, dual-door Alexander-bodied Leyland Atlantean 176 (NRC176M) is seen in Aberdeen displaying exact fare lettering above its windscreens. (T.W.W.Knowles)

After establishing a service from Aberdeen to Ellon in 1986, Grampian Regional Transport in retaliation to Northern Scottish who since deregulation had increased its presence in Aberdeen sought to expand its rural network and on 27 April 1987 launched new services to Inverurie, Westhill, Newmachar and Banchory and one to Stonehaven via Portlethen which incorporated a Stonehaven town service. All these were similar to existing services maintained by Scottish Bus Group subsidiary Northern Scottish and as such this new move represented a significant increase in competition between the two operators. Additionally Grampian introduced electronic Farecards as well as promoting a number of travel schemes which included the exchange of bus tickets for saving stamps etc. To cope with these new services 4 Leyland Nationals and 6 Leyland

Passing through Aberdeen city centre on its way to Garthdee is Grampian Regional Transport dual-door Leyland National 73 (KSO73P) which displays an Exact Fare notice alongside its destination screen. (T.W.W.Knowles)

Seen at Buchanan bus station after completing a Stagecoach Caledonian Express journey from Edinburgh in December 1989, Grampian Transport MCW Metroliner 56 (TRS333) painted in Grampian Executive livery awaits its return to Aberdeen on a Scottish Citylink service. (M.Currie)

Atlanteans were relicensed whilst for the company's coaching fleet the first of its new MCW Metroliner hi-line single deckers was delivered, painted in a cream livery with two-tone green stripes and Grampian Executive fleet names and 2 coach-seated MCW Metrorider minis. Looking to the future, Grampian began a programme of evaluation in June which was to include several different types of vehicle, the first of which was a Newport Transport East Lancs-bodied Scania N112DR double decker which was used in service for a couple of weeks on a variety of routes. Following this came a Carlyle-bodied Freight Rover Sherpa, a Leyland Lynx demonstrator, a West Midlands Travel MCW Metrobus, a Go-Ahead Northern ECW-bodied Leyland Olympian, a Derby City Transport Northern Counties-bodied Volvo Citybus and a South Yorkshire Transport Alexander-bodied Dennis Dominator and after studying their performance and features etc., a decision was taken in October to place an order for 10 Alexander-bodied Leyland Olympians - eight to dual door bus configuration and 2 to single door layout with coach-type seating.

Having now had a chance to assess its new rural services, those to Stonehaven and Newmachar were withdrawn in August due to their unsatisfactory financial performance while the others proved to be more successful and were continued without any significant change. Later in the year, several changes were made to the company's city services with the withdrawal at the start of November of the 1A, 2A and the Braehead journeys on the 26 and the amalgamation of services 7 (Balgownie Drive - Holburn Junction) and 33 (Guild Street - Westhill). More changes took place on 14 December when the 16 service in Footdee was replaced by a new route numbered 28 from Holburn Junction to Footdee and the introduction of Aberdeen's first midibus route, an off-peak circular service in the Mastrick area known as the Sheddocksley Shopper. Prior to this, to celebrate the company's first year of trading, an open day was held on 8 November at its King Street depot where amongst the vehicles on display was one of South Yorkshire Transport's Leyland-DAB articulated single deckers - an omen for the future perhaps!

More important, however, was the purchase of the Bucksburn-based business of G.E.Mair Hire Services Ltd. on 6 December, this extending Grampian's coaching interests as well as providing it with additional contract services and a local bus route from Sea Beach to Leggart Avenue in Aberdeen. Mair's, who had started as a taxi operator in 1956 and diversified into minibus operation two years later, had a mixed fleet of some 20 vehicles which included Bedfords, Volvos, a Bova, a Duple 425 and some Mercedes Benz L508Ds plus a number of taxis, although the latter were not included in the deal and were to continue to be operated by their existing owner. Rather than merge its operations into those of Grampian Regional Transport it was decided to maintain Mair's as a subsidiary and repaint its vehicles into a new livery of dark red. New premises were obtained at Dyce from which the new subsidiary was to operate and space was additionally rented to Mair's for its retained taxi business. Almost immediately, Grampian hired its four Bristol LHSs to the Mair's operation for use on its local bus service and after a few months permanently transferred them to Dyce.

Transferred from Grampian to its Mairs subsidiary in 1988, former London Transport ECW-bodied Bristol LH6L KJD412P is seen painted in its new owner's white & red livery. (T.W.W.Knowles)

1988

With increased competition in Aberdeen following deregulation and the expectation that the government was poised to instruct municipal bus operators to sell their companies to the private sector, Grampian Regional Transport's management team headed by its managing director Moir Lockhead made an approach to the council in August 1988 to purchase the company. Favouring this move which also involved the company's employees, the Council agreed to give the management/employees the first option and not to place GRT on the open market. While talks between the two parties were progressing, Grampian and its subsidiary Mair's joined forces with Dundee-based Tayside Regional Transport to launch a new tours programme which included several European destinations. Marketed under the name of Goldcrest Tours, this new venture gave Grampian and Mair's a new field of operation which it hoped to build upon in future years although in the meantime Grampian Coaches continued to offer its own programme of continental tours. As far as its local bus operations were concerned, Grampian maintained its services almost exclusively with double deckers after unsuccessfully introducing minibuses soon after deregulation. In addition to taking delivery of its 10 new Leyland Olympians ordered during the previous year, Grampian also purchased a pair of Plaxton Paramount-bodied Leyland Tigers from Potteries Motor Traction to further enhance its fleet. For the Mairs operation, a secondhand Leyland Leopard and a Volvo B10M were purchased along with a new Volvo B10M, 2 New Toyota minicoaches and a pair of coach-seated Mercedes Benz 609Ds.

In preparation for its acquisition of Grampian Regional Transport, its management registered a new company on 25 October 1988 under the title of GRT Holdings Plc and on 18 January 1989, took control of Grampian Regional Transport Ltd. which became the first Scottish local authority operator to be sold to the private sector. Under the deal, the management team held a 51% stake in the

Formerly Grampian Transport 61, Alexander-bodied Leyland Leopard HSO61N was transferred to the Mairs fleet in 1989 and is seen here in cream & red livery with the fleet name style which incorporated a thistle logo above the letter 'I'. (T.W.W.Knowles)

Purchased new for the Mairs feet in 1988 is Caetano-bodied Toyota HB31 E182DBB seen here resting at Dyce depot wearing the company's maroon & gold livery. (T.W.W.Knowles)

company, its employees 33% and financial institutions 16%, although subject to satisfactory performance it was agreed that the employee stake would ultimately rise to 49%. With employees now having a vested interest in the future of the company, staff were encouraged to come up with their own ideas for improving all aspects of the business and several were soon implemented. Amongst them was an offer by driver Alan Greatbach who, after complaining of the standard of service offered by the company's canteen took over its running with the help of his wife. Such was the commitment by everyone concerned. A further innovation was brought about by Aberdeen's retailers association whose aim was to make city centre shopping easier and thus attract more customers. To this end, Grampian launched a scheme under the title 'Hop 'n Shop' under which buses running the length of Union Street were marked with a red circle and those travelling to the new Bon Accord Centre were adorned with a green square. Bus stops along the routes were similarly marked to provide full co-ordination with these moves proving highly successful from the outset. In an attempt to retain passenger loyalty, Grampian in November introduced a new free gifts scheme under the title of 'Grampian Gems' for all City-Ride and Farecard users (the latter, introduced by Grampian earlier in the year, was a stored-value card which worked in a similar way to Phonecards and was fed through an on-bus reader was the first such 5p card to be used on public transport in the UK). This involved collecting 'Grampstamps' which were given with the above types of ticket and could be redeemed for gifts at a later date. Additionally, during December the West End Shoppers' Association sponsored a Monday to Saturday shoppers service around the city centre and for its operation MCW Metrorider 32 was named Rudolph and decorated with eyes and a red nose. Leyland Olympian 121 was also decorated for the Christmas period for use on various of the company's services while free services sponsored by the Aberdeen Evening Express newspaper were provided at Hogmanay.

1989

Having now secured their company's future, its new owners soon began to look for further expansion and began talks with Banchory independent Kirkpatrick's which it saw as a valuable addition to its existing operations. After forming a new company under the title of Ricmore Limited on 18 May 1989, this was used for the purchase of Kirkpatricks on 6 July when it was renamed Kirkpatrick of Deeside Limited. Like Mair's, Kirkpatrick who operated 8 coaches (Fords, Bedfords, a Leyland Leopard and a Volvo B58) and 5 non-PSV Ford Transit minibuses was to be maintained as a separate subsidiary and continued to operate from its existing depot at Banchory. Prior to this acquisition, Grampian had modified Mair's livery to maroon and gold

Kirkpatrick of Deeside's Devon Conversions-bodied Mercedes Benz L307D 909 (D851VSS) stands outside Grampian's depot in Aberdeen in 1993. (T.W.W.Knowles)

Enjoying a brief break at Aberdeen's Guild Street bus station before starting its return journey to Fraserburgh is Grampian Transport's Plaxton Paramount-bodied Volvo B10M 44 (F104SSO) which was acquired from Alexanders and retained that operator's fleet names and all-white livery. (M.Currie)

Painted in corporate Stagecoach Caledonian Express livery, Grampian Transport MCW Metroliner 57 (542GRT) stands at St.Andrew bus station, Edinburgh before leaving for Newcastle-upon-Tyne on National Express service 372. ***(C.Morrison)***

for coaches and white and red for its stage carriage vehicles whilst its own Goldcrest-branded coaches were given an attractive green and gold colour scheme. Illustrating its commitment to charities, GRT had fitted all its vehicles with red noses for Comic Relief in February and many vehicles retained these for several weeks.

Once again a South Yorkshire Transport Leyland-DAB bendibus travelled north of the border for display at an open day at King Street depot on 7 May but on this occasion it was used in service for five days prior to its return to its rightful owner. This gave Grampian first-hand experience of operating articulated buses and no doubt led to the ultimate purchase of a bus of this type some years later. In July, another stranger appeared on the streets of Aberdeen when a Berks Bucks ECW-bodied Bristol VRT was borrowed for two weeks to demonstrate a number of DiPTAC features with which it was fitted. During its stay in Aberdeen it was used on services 6, 11, 15 and 23 and proved popular particularly amongst older passengers and those who were less able bodied. The only new vehicles purchased during the year were an MCW Metrorider and 2 Mercedes Benz 609D minicoaches for the Mairs fleet which also received several secondhand vehicles including 3 ex.Southdown Plaxton-bodied Leyland Leopards, 2 Mercedes Benz L608Ds and a Volvo B10M. Grampian also took into its own fleet 2 Plaxton-bodied Leopards acquired from Southdown. as well as dditionally Grampian hiring 4 Leyland Leopard coaches from Lothian Regional Transport in November and purchasing 4 Volvo B10Ms from the defunct Alexander (North East), of which more later. On the reverse side of the coin, during the second half of the year it loaned a number of its own buses to other operators who were needing additional vehicles for a variety of reasons. Amongst these were a pair of Leyland Atlanteans which were loaned to Inverness Traction and 2 Leyland Nationals which were borrowed by Tayside Regional Council whilst one of its Alexander-bodied Leopards was transferred to Mairs. One other change worthy of note was the repainting of MCW Metroliner 57 into the white and blue livery of Caledonian Express for operation by Mair's on a service under contract to that company.

After a period of consolidation, immediately following the collapse of Alexander (North East) in mid-November, Grampian took over its services between Aberdeen, Peterhead and Fraserburgh which Alexander has started in December 1988 and also acquired the company's Glenhire executive coach hire operation around which Alexander (North East) had been developed. This was to be continued by Grampian Transport from its Mair's Coaches base at Dyce and the Alexander name was to be retained on the coaches used on its former services. Almost immediately GRT Holdings again went on the acquisition trail and, deciding to diversify, in December it bought Aberdeen-based Autotruck who sold a wide range of bus, truck and trailer parts through outlets in Forfar, Inverness and Elgin. Ironically, one of its customers was its main competitor in Aberdeen, Northern Scottish, who for many years had purchased hydraulic and air brake parts from Autotruck. Although a new venture for GRT Holdings, it was thought that this new business would fit in well with its existing engineering operation and would bring further commercial strength to the company as a whole.

Grampian Transport borrowed one of Mainline's Leyland-DAB bendibuses on a couple of occasions before placing an order for its own vehicle of this configuration based on a Mercedes Benz 0405G chassis. Typifying the Mainline buses is 2004 (C104HDT) seen here in its native Sheffield at Meadowhall bus station. (Travelscene)

SCOTTISH BUS GROUP PRIVATISATION

1990

With the forthcoming sale of the Scottish Bus Group to the private sector looming on the horizon, GRT Holdings took more than a passing interest and submitted a bid for Lowland Scottish, the first SBG subsidiary to be placed on the market, at the end of February 1990. During the following month and before the outcome of this offer was made known, GRT Holdings also submitted a bid for Midland Scottish, this not breaching the sale rule that no two adjacent companies could be purchased by the same buyer. In addition to expressing a firm interest in this company, GRT also sought to gain further footholds in its native Scotland by offering to support management/employee buy-out teams (including Northern Scottish) who might find the raising of finance a major stumbling block. During its first seventeen months of trading, GRT Holdings was able to announce a profit of £1.4 million on a turnover of £16 million which was a credible performance particularly when considering that passenger numbers had fallen during this period on Aberdeen city services.

Although the news on 1 June that Lowland had been purchased by its management/employees was received with some disappointment, the mood changed fourteen days later to one of jubilation when it was learned by GRT Holdings that its bid of £8.5 million for Midland Scottish had been successful (beating those submitted by Proudmutual, Caldaire, Stagecoach and the SEBIL consortium) and thus it had achieved its aim of gaining control of at least one SBG subsidiary. It was not, however, until 28 September that the purchase was sealed although plans had already been put in motion to introduce a new livery based on that used by Grampian Transport but using blue instead of green. Additionally, a new-style Midland Bluebird fleet name was introduced with the 'I' of Bluebird surmounted with Grampian's thistle emblem. The acquisition of Midland Scottish included 282 vehicles, a staff of 772 and depots at Alloa, Balfron, Bannockburn, Larbert, Linlithgow and Oban. Almost before Grampian had a chance to evaluate its new company, however, disaster struck at Midland's Oban depot on 28 October when a fire caused by an electrical fault in the drivers mess room destroyed most of the office block, more than a third of the depot, and severely damaged several vehicles including a Duple-bodied Leyland Leopard which only a few days earlier had been repainted into the company's new livery. As a consequence of this incident a number of buses had to be immediately drafted into Oban from other depots to minimise the disruption to services in the area. October 28 also saw Grampian Transport add a fuel surcharge of around 8% to its bus fares as a result of the Gulf crisis. Despite costs having risen by over 50%, the company had postponed its fares rise for as long as possible but felt that it could not continue any longer without incurring substantial losses. Thus, 15p fares were increased to 17p, 80p fares went up to 85p and a monthly ticket rose from £24 to £26. At the start of the summer season Grampian added a number of secondhand coaches to its fleet when it acquired 2 Leyland Leopards, 3 Tigers and 3 Volvo B10Ms from Leicester CityBus; PMT; Rennies of Dunfermline; Roberts, Cefn Mawr; West Kingsdown Coaches and Hallmark of Luton while at this same time a new livery comprising cream with a red skirt and two grey bands was introduced for the Kirkpatrick fleet. These new arrivals allowed the hired Lothian Leopards to be returned to their rightful owner as well as enhancing Grampian's coaching fleet while 4 Atlanteans and Daimler CVG6 25 were dispatched to Peterhead for use on the former Alexander (North East) routes during the early summer. Additionally, Grampian refitted Alexander names to a number of its coaches operated on the services it had acquired from that company in November 1989 although the vehicles concerned retained their Grampian Express livery.

Painted in Midland Scottish pre-Grampian style blue & cream livery but having been given new fleet names incorporating a thistle emblem above the 'I' in Bluebird, Alexander-bodied Leyland Fleetline RF752 (LMS152W) is seen at Falkirk bus station in 1991. During the following year it was sold to Kelvin Central Buses in whose fleet it was numbered 1692. (K.A.Jenkinson)

Freshly repainted and looking immaculate, Midland Bluebird Alexander-bodied Leyland Leopard 268 (HSU301) seen enroute to Allandale was originally registered GLS268S. (Travelscene)

On hire to Midland Bluebird and standing in the yard of its Larbert depot alongside Mercedes Benz L608D 606 (C821SDY) is Leicester Citycoach Plaxton-bodied Leyland Leopard 16 (YFJ16Y). (C.Morrison)

Painted in an attractive cream and triple-tone blue livery and adorned with Grampian-style Midland Coaches fleet names, Duple Laser-bodied Leyland Tiger 132 (SSU837, originally B132PNS)) rests at Buchanan bus station, Glasgow before working a Scottish Citylink journey to Aberdeen. (S.K.Jenkinson)

1991

Kelvin Central Buses became the next SBG subsidiary to be offered for sale and although GRT Holdings initially expressed an interest, this quickly waned as a result of the increasing problems being experienced by the Bishopbriggs-based company. Instead, it turned its attention towards Northern Scottish whose headquarters were also in Aberdeen and which it was thought would add further strength to GRT's activities in northern Scotland. In the event its dream failed to materialise when it was prevented from bidding by the Secretary of State for Scotland who feared that if successful it would attract the attention of the Monopolies and Mergers Commission. Following this move Stagecoach was named as the preferred bidder and indeed became Northern's new owner on 27 March 1991.

Grampian Transport began its first minibus service in Aberdeen on 24 March using 6 Reeve Burgess-bodied Mercedes Benz 709Ds in place of double deckers on its inner-urban circular service, these carrying Beaver Bus as well as Grampian Transport fleet names, while an announcement was made that experimental peak-hour bus lanes would be put into operation in Union Street, the city's main thoroughfare for a twelve month period starting in October 1991 in an attempt to improve bus times on services using this busy corridor. In May a new local service was started in Peterhead which replaced a withdrawn Northern Scottish route in the Catto Drive area and later in the year on 24 November, a new frequent cross-city park and ride service was inaugurated from Woodhill House to Aberdeen Exhibition Centre. This was operated each Saturday until Christmas on behalf of Grampian Regional Council and sponsored by the Aberdeen Evening Express.

Prior to the above, Midland Bluebird made its first new vehicle purchase since joining the private sector when in February it took into its fleet a pair of Reeve Burgess Beaver-bodied Mercedes Benz 709Ds which it placed in service at Stirling on a route upon which competition from local operator Laird was being experienced. Additionally, Midland also purchased 8 Leyland Leopard coaches from Lothian Regional Transport in April, placing these in service still wearing the white and black livery of their previous owner while to assist its repainting programme several vehicles were dispatched to outside concerns for this purpose including W.Alexander, East Lancashire Coachbuilders and TiE of Kirkcaldy. During this process, the coaches previously adorned with Red Knight livery were transformed into Scottish Citylink colours while later in the year across in north-east Scotland Mair's livery was modified to GRT's corporate style using cream, maroon and red. As was to be expected, several vehicles were gained by Midland on temporary loan from Grampian to cover various requirements and included amongst their number were some Leyland Atlanteans which were used largely by Alloa and Larbert depots. Meanwhile, on 8 April Midland implemented a number of revisions to its service network particularly in the Stirling area, introduced a new Grangemouth circular service, and converted its services 90/91 into Falkirk inner and outer circle routes respectively. On 22 April further changes saw the withdrawal of service 16 (Tullibody - Clackmannan) and the conversion of the 36

The first new vehicles to join the Midland Bluebird fleet following its acquisition by GRT were two Reeve Burgess-bodied Mercedes Benz 709Ds, the first of which - 625 (H925PMS) is seen resting at Stirling bus station. (K.A.Jenkinson)

One of six Reeve Burgess-bodied Mercedes Benz 709D minibuses bought new by Grampian in 1991, 437 (H37USO) is seen in the suburbs of Aberdeen displaying Beaver Bus fleet names. (T.W.W.Knowles)

Soon after taking control of Midland Bluebird its new masters took the decision to abandon the company's Red Knight livery and fleet name and repaint the coaches concerned into corporate Scottish Citylink colours. Seen at St.Andrew bus station, Edinburgh still adorned with its Red Knight identity is Duple 340-bodied Leyland Tiger 142 (SSU857) which was originally registered D142HMS. (M.Currie)

Seen whilst on loan to Midland Bluebird is Grampian Transport Alexander-bodied Leyland Atlantean 202 (ORS202R). This bus was later permanently transferred to the Midland fleet in which it was given fleet number 702. (C.Morrison)

(Riverside - Stirling) to become tendered service 256. The latter ceased at the end of June, however, when a new contract was instead awarded by the Central Regional Council to Malcolm & Wright of Fallin for its provision. In north-east Scotland, following the cessation of the former Alexander (North East) operations in July, the coaches used were dispersed between GRT's various fleets whilst at this same time as a result of a number of service changes Grampian delicensed 10 of its Leyland Atlanteans and 7 Leyland Nationals. Meanwhile, Grampian once again undertook the evaluation of a number of different types of bus before placing any new orders and amongst those borrowed for this purpose were an unregistered Reeve Burgess Pointer-bodied Dennis Dart of Southampton Citybus and a London Buses Wright Handybus-bodied Dennis Dart in February and April respectively and an Optare Vecta-bodied MAN 11-180 demonstrator and Plaxton Verde-bodied Scania N113CRB in July. In the event none of these attracted orders from the Aberdeen-based company. Further changes during 1991 witnessed the withdrawal of the Leggart Avenue section of Mair's service 57 in August due to poor patronage and the closure by Midland of its Alloa depot in October as part of its rationalisation plan. Despite their absence in 1990, Christmas lights and/or greetings were fitted to the front of four Atlanteans and an Olympian during December and on both Christmas Day and New Year's Day a partially subsidised revised network of services were operated to various areas of the city.

1992

Grampian Transport started the new year in fine fashion when it placed an order for one of Mercedes Benz's new generation of articulated single deck buses which was to be supplied with kneeling suspension and equipped for use on guided busways. To be bodied by Walter Alexander Ltd. at Falkirk, this was seen as a flexible alternative to light rail transit schemes and one which would provide the company with the opportunity to examine its advantages in every day service. Following the closure of its own depot in Gairn Terrace, Aberdeen, despite being regarded as a competitor, Northern Scottish rented space at Grampian's King Street depot and moved its vehicles into their new home on 12 January. Six days earlier, Grampian surprisingly enhanced its service 14 (Footdee - Woodend) by adding hourly extra journeys between King Street and the expanding town of Kingswells, thus reintroducing a partially rural operation only a few months after it had withdrawn all of its services to and from the more far-flung areas of the Region. Following a decision to operate its 1992 holiday tours programme under the name of Grampian Coaches instead of Goldcrest, the 4 Volvo coaches which had carried the white, gold and red livery of the latter were repainted into standard Grampian colours. Although Grampian continued with its plans to enhance its normal service network, it still saw the leisure industry as one of importance and in addition to continuing to operate its traditional three-hour sightseeing tour of Aberdeen, on 7June it introduced a shorter hop-on, hop-off one-hour version using a recently-converted open-top Leyland Atlantean which had been painted into an all-over 'City in Bloom' theme livery designed by local primary school children. Also launched at this same time was a new Explorer ticket costing £3 for one day or £5 for two consecutive days which gave unlimited travel on the whole of Grampian's network. Prior to the above, following a survey carried out by a local newspaper, Grampian Transport on 11 March adopted a no smoking policy on all its buses.

Throughout the year, vehicles continued to be loaned in both directions between Grampian Transport, Midland, Mair's and Kirkpatricks and on some occasions the vehicles concerned received the fleet names of their new temporary operators. Additionally, during June an Alexander-bodied Dennis Lance demonstrator was used in a number of Aberdeen services by Grampian while Midland converted an ex.Grampian Atlantean to open-top format and repainted it into a striking red and yellow livery in May for operation on the Stirling District Council Heritage Tour. Illustrating its willingness to assist a fellow operator in difficulty, Grampian dispatched 4 of its Leyland

Grampian Transport open-top dual-door Alexander-bodied Leyland Atlantean 231 (YSO231T) painted in an all-over livery for operation on the Aberdeen city tour rests at the city's harbour in 1996. (T.W.W.Knowles)

Grampian Transport's Alexander-bodied Mercedes Benz 0405G bendibus 1 (K1GRT) wearing its owner's 'Advance' livery is seen in Aberdeen operating on route 2 to Auchinyell and carrying a red circle in its nearside windscreen to indicate the particular city centre shopping area it served. (C.Morrison)

One of several Alexander-bodied Mercedes Benz L608Ds acquired by Midland Bluebird from Northern Scottish in 1992, 606 (C821SDY) seen here after receiving its new owner's cream & two-tone blue livery started life with Hastings & District in 1986. (C.Morrison)

Preparing to leave Oban bus station on the Ganavan service is Oban & District's former Midland Bluebird Duple-bodied Leyland Leopard FSU319 which started life registered CFS111S. (J.L.Hobbs)

Amongst the vehicles sold by Midland Bluebird to Oban & District in 1992 was a pair of coach-seated Elme-bodied Freight Rover Sherpas, one of which - D602FLS - is seen in Oban operating a stage carriage service. (J.L.Hobbs)

Atlanteans to Glasgow in May together with a Midland Bluebird example to help Strathclyde Buses to maintain its services following the disastrous fire at its Larkfield depot in which 50 buses were destroyed. Amongst the new buses placed in service at the start of the year were 5 Alexander-bodied Mercedes Benz 709Ds which were allocated to Midland's Bannockburn and Larbert depots where they were later joined by a number of Alexander-bodied Mercedes Benz L608Ds acquired from Bluebird Northern. Meanwhile, Midland closed its Callander outstation during the spring, transferring its vehicles and operations to Bannockburn.

After a comparatively uneventful summer, Grampian hosted an open day at its King Street depot on 8 November to demonstrate the latest developments in public transport and as well as showing off real time passenger information systems it gave the company the opportunity to publicly launch its new Alexander-bodied Mercedes Benz 0405G bendibus. Painted in a revised livery of cream with two narrow stripes of gold and dark green, this also carried a 'GRT Advance SE' logo on each side of its body signifying the inclusion of air conditioning and double glazing in its specification. Following a 23% increase in its profits for the year ending 31 March during which its turnover increased to £31.3 million, GRT Holdings announced a £4.5 million order for new buses for Grampian Transport and Midland Bluebird, this comprising 36 single deckers (16 Scania N113s and 20 Mercedes Benz 0405s) and 18 Mercedes Benz 709D minibuses, of which all were to be bodied by Alexander. In the event, due to the Scottish coachbuilder being unable to meet the delivery schedule, the bodywork order for the Scanias and Mercedes 0405s was transferred to Wrights of Ballymena in Northern Ireland.

Following the changing of its name in October from Midland Scottish Ltd. to Midland Bluebird Ltd., during the following month as part of its ongoing rationalisation it sold a controlling interest in its Oban operations to Derek Stuart, a former senior official of Fife Scottish. Included in the deal was the company's new depot in the town at Soroba Lane, 15 buses (11 Leyland Leopards, 2 Tigers and 2 Freight Rover Sherpas) and all the company's services in the area. Following the sale, GRT's dormant company Aberdeen Bus Ltd. was renamed Oban and District Buses Ltd. on 1 March 1993. Back in Aberdeen, Christmas Day services were once again operated with a subsidy from Grampian Regional Council but unlike previous years, no sponsor could be found for the company's Hogmanay services and thus on this occasion a £1 flat fare was charged.

1993

After having been operated in service since mid-November, Grampian's Mercedes Benz bendibus was returned to Alexanders at Falkirk in January for various modifications and at this same time it was fitted with guide arms to enable it to be used on a short length of guided busway at some time in the future. Re-entering service in Aberdeen during February, it was two months later transferred to Midland Bluebird for a six week period, and after having its green stripes repainted blue and gaining Midland fleet names it took up its duties from Larbert depot on services 72 and 91 on 27 April. Meanwhile, a refurbishment programme got underway related to Grampian's 1984/5 Leyland Olympians which included the fitting of a new heating system, non-slip flooring and several other DiPTAC features and an alteration to the seating arrangement which eliminated the inward-facing seats. More unusually, Mercedes Benz 709D minibus 436 was experimentally converted to operate using more environmentally friendly rape seed as a fuel instead of diesel and to publicise this its normal Beaver Bus fleet name was replaced by Greener Beaver Bus. Despite its success in reducing pollution, rape seed proved to be problematic in technical terms and 436 was reconverted to diesel power later in the summer.

On 31 January several service changes were implemented in Aberdeen to further improve the city network particularly during the evening period and on Sundays. Later, at the start of May Grampian ceased to be a contractor to National Express and as a consequence Jonckheere-bodied Volvo B10M 89 lost its Caledonian Express livery in favour of Grampian Executive colours. Although Kirkpatrick began the operation of the Banchory - Pitlochry section of the Wednesdays and Fridays Heatherhopper network of tourist services from 11 June, it unfortunately lost the tendered Banchory - Alford service while Grampian converted its circular service 6, service 7 (Guild Street - Bridge of Don) and Sunday operations on service 5 (Girdleness Road - Denmore) from big-bus to minibus operation using its 9 new Alexander (Belfast)-bodied Mercedes Benz 709Ds which were fitted with Beaver Bus fleet names. On 26 August, celebrations took place to commemorate the 95th anniversary of Grampian Transport and its predecessors. Amongst these was a parade of old vehicles which was headed by the company's Walker-bodied Albion PMA28 single decker which had begun life with Aberdeen Corporation in 1930 and had been repurchased for preservation in 1988. Restored to its original livery etc., it was joined in the parade by Grampian's other preserved vehicles - a 1965 Daimler CVG6, a 1969 AEC Reliance and a 1971 AEC Swift.

EXPANSION OUTSIDE SCOTLAND

Following a period of consolidation and fleet upgrading, GRT Holdings who had for some considerable time been looking for further expansion turned its sights south of the border where several local authority owned companies were looking at sales to the private sector. Amongst these was Leicester CityBus in which Trent Motor Traction had a 6.41% shareholding. Although it placed its own 93.59% share on the market in April, under the terms it had agreed with Trent, the latter was to be accorded the privilege of matching the best bid should the company not be purchased by its management/employees, should it wish to do so. In the event, after viewing the bids that were ultimately received, it declined this invitation. During the period in which Leicester was considering the bids received for its company, Northampton Transport and Grimsby Cleethorpes Transport were also put up for sale by their respective Council owners and like Leicester, these also attracted the attention of GRT Holdings. Having submitted bids for all three companies, GRT settled down to await the outcome and in the meantime was delighted to announce that during the year ending 31 March 1993 its profits had risen by a further 10% on a turnover of £32 million. Following this, Grampian Transport had achieved BS5750 accreditation in August 1993 after two years hard work and it was confidently anticipated that its subsidiary Autotruck would similarly gain a BS5750 certificate in November. According to a survey undertaken by the Independent on Sunday newspaper GRT Holdings was now recognised as one of the UK's top 100 fastest-growing independent businesses, and although it was in 98th position it ranked 24th in the Middle Market Group of companies.

The first of GRT's new Wright Cityranger-bodied Mercedes Benz 0405s entered service in September with both Grampian Transport and Midland Bluebird and delivery was completed during the following month. Painted in GRT's new corporate Advance scheme incorporating a green (Grampian) or blue (Midland) lightening bolt flash along their side panels, the Grampian buses were fitted with double glazing, Sutrak climate control, low entrance steps and kneeling suspension in order to improve passenger standards. At around this same time, the appearance of the Mair's fleet was transformed by the introduction of new liveries which were applied in GRT corporate fashion with stage carriage vehicles being repainted cream with one maroon and two red stripes, coaches becoming metallic maroon with gold stripes and executive vehicles gold with one maroon and two red stripes. This, it was believed, would facilitate the easier transfer of vehicles between Mair's and Kirkpatrick whose livery was cream with one maroon, one red and one grey stripe.

After its period of waiting, it was announced that GRT Holdings had been successful in its bid for Northampton Corporation Transport Ltd. and would take control on 14 October while its offer for Grimsby Cleethorpes Transport had not been accepted and instead that company had been sold to Stagecoach. With a fleet of 56 vehicles, Northampton Transport had made a pre-tax profit of £888,000 on a turnover of £4.3 million in the year ending 31 March 1992, although since that date it had suffered from increasing competition from Stagecoach subsidiary United Counties, thus leaving its new owners with much work to do to return it to its former position. Initially the company retained its existing red & cream livery and like Midland Bluebird, was to be maintained as a separate entity. Soon after its purchase of Northampton Transport was completed, GRT Holdings began talks with United Counties in an attempt to end the fares and service war which had been raging between the two operators for several months and after much discussion, agreement was reached under which all additional journeys by both companies would cease and United Counties would gain a greater share of service 1 running between Dufton and Weston Flavell and operations on route 15 from the town centre to Bushlands Road. Following these moves, the GRT company returned its fares to their normal levels (having cut these during the period of attrition) and now looked forward to a period of stability.

Within the space of a little over three weeks, GRT Holdings learned that its bid of £7.4 million for Leicester City Transport Ltd., Leicester CityBus Ltd. and Leicester CountryBus Ltd. had also been successful and it took over control of these companies on 10 November. Unlike Northampton, however, where few changes had been implemented by its new owner, the Leicester undertaking immediately underwent an amount of reorganisation which included fares being rounded up by between 3% and 5% and the revision of its management structure. As part of the latter, all except one of the former Leicester directors left the company and Northampton's managing director Chris Mahony

New in 1993, Midland Bluebird Wright-bodied Mercedes Benz 0405 53 (L553GMS) shows off its Advance-style livery as it leaves Buchanan bus station, Glasgow on the 39 service to Stirling.

Painted in an all-white livery and carrying Bluebird Coaches fleet names, Midland Bluebird Plaxton-bodied Leyland Tiger 151 (WSU489) which joined the fleet from Grampian Transport in 1991 passes Buchanan bus station, Glasgow whilst operating a contract duty. (K.A.Jenkinson)

Amongst the vehicles operated by Northampton Transport were a number of Alexander-bodied Bristol VRTs, one of which - 37 (VRP37S) is seen at Greyfriars bus station, Northampton wearing pre-GRT style red & cream livery. (T.W.W.Knowles)

Painted in its owner's old maroon & cream livery, Leicester CityBus Northern Counties-bodied Renault S56 757 (J757MFP) seen picking up its passengers outside the Haymarket Centre was one of fifteen such buses purchased new between 1991 and 1993. (G.T.W.Carter)

Having gained GRT-style livery, Northampton Transport East Lancs-bodied Volvo D10M 101 (D101XNV) approaches Greyfriars bus station on an evening journey to Kings Heath. (Travelscene)

Freshly repainted in corporate GRT-style livery, Leicester Citybus Alexander-bodied MCW Metrobus 35 (AUT35Y) passes St.Margarets bus station on its way to the city centre terminus of route 14. (K.A.Jenkinson)

268 (PJF268M), one of Leicester Citybus's once large fleet of MCW Metropolitans approaches the city centre enroute to Oadby. (K.A.Jenkinson)

additionally took over this role at Leicester. Although it was stated that all the company's staff would join the established GRT Employee Share Ownership Plan as soon as the company returned to profit, it was realised that much work would be needed to reach this position. In common with Northampton, Leicester whose fleet comprised 217 vehicles including half a dozen coaches and had depots at Abbey Park Road, Leicester and Barton Road, Barlaston was also to continue to operate as a separate entity. Almost immediately, however, both Leicester and Northampton adopted a new common livery of cream with red and maroon bands applied in GRT's corporate style and incorporated the thistle emblem in their fleet names.

Back in its native Aberdeen, Grampian Transport on 6 November began a Christmas park and ride service between the city centre, a temporary parking area at Woodhill House, Altens and the Exhibition Centre. Branded 'City Quick" and operated by Leyland Atlanteans, this new operation unusually ran on Sundays as well as Saturdays, confirming Scotland's new shopping traditions and the fact that Sunday was no longer regarded as 'a day of rest'. Later in the month on the 23rd, Grampian brought its new Wayfarer 3 ticket machines into use and at the same time fitted new Farecard machines to its buses which printed the value left on the card itself rather than on the ticket as done previously. Midland Bluebird also began a new service on 29 November, this running hourly on Mondays to Saturdays between Linlithgow and the Gyle Shopping Centre in Edinburgh. Conversely, the newly-acquired Northampton Transport lost one of its services and part of another to United Counties and as a result found itself with a surplus of buses. These, however, soon found a new home when on the penultimate day of December 4 of its East Lancs-bodied Leyland Olympians were transferred to Grampian Transport who in turn dispatched 2 of its Atlanteans to Northampton for use mainly on schools duties. Northampton was also able to withdraw the last of its minibuses while in Leicester the end of an era was marked on Christmas Eve when Citybus withdrew the last of its once large fleet of MCW Metropolitans. As well as the Northampton Olympians another stranger to appear in Aberdeen, albeit only briefly, was one of Yorkshire Coastliner's Alexander Royale-bodied Volvo Olympian coaches which was borrowed by Grampian Transport for a week for evaluation. In the event, however, despite being given temporary fleet number 28 it only ran in service (on route 22 Mastrick - Heathryfold) for around a couple of hours and was for the remainder of its stay unused!

ACCEPTED IN LONDON

1994

Undoubtedly the major event of 1994 as far as GRT Holdings was concerned was its decision to seek listing on the London Stock Exchange. The flotation was aimed at reducing debt and raising money for organic growth and acquisition and although 13,711,440 of the shares were to be placed with city institutions, GRT staff were also to be given the opportunity to gain a stake in their company. After plans were drawn up during which time GRT Holdings changed its name to GRT Bus Group, a prospectus was launched on 23 April in which it was stated that the company was interested in bidding for at least three of the London Buses companies, the share price was set at 160p with trading expected to start on 5 May. With an increasing number of private investors trusting their money to 'green' and 'ethical' investment funds, the success of the flotation was obviously helped by GRT's continuing interest in environmental work. All the new vehicles due for delivery to the Group during 1995/6 were to be specified with Euro 2 engines whilst in Aberdeen, Grampian Transport had already been running one of its Mercedes Benz 709Ds on biodiesel (rape seed oil) for three months and planned to experimentally fit a catalytic converter to one of its Leyland Atlanteans. In the meantime, however, the GRT Bus Group continued to upgrade its fleet by placing the first of sixteen Wright-bodied Scania N113CRBs in service with Midland Bluebird at the beginning of May. Replacing elderly Leyland Leopards and Seddon Pennine VIIs on the 38 service from Edinburgh to Stirling, the new buses quickly settled in, looking superb in their attractive cream and blue GRT Advance-style livery. Two more of Northampton Transport's East Lancs-bodied Leyland Olympians migrated to Aberdeen early in the year to join their sisters in the Grampian Transport fleet while leaving the company were several Atlanteans which were transferred to Midland Bluebird. Although service changes at the start of the year had been minimal, on 4 January Midland Bluebird lost its Central Regional Council contracts in the Stirling/Balfron/Glasgow corridor to Goosecroft Coaches of Stirling under retendering. Refusing to accept defeat, however, Midland commercially registered certain journeys on the routes concerned in order to retain a presence.

Elsewhere in the GRT Holdings empire, Leicester CityBus closed its former Gibsons depot at Barlastone and transferred its operations to Abbey Road, Leicester and at around the same time took more of its Dennis Dominators out of service together with a number of Renault S56 minibuses. To replace the former, several MCW Metrobuses were acquired from Midland Bluebird while Grampian's bendibus and one of its Mercedes Benz 0405s were dispatched on loan to Leicester in April after having their green stripes repainted red and maroon. After around a month in the city, the 0405 also spent a few weeks in service with Northampton Transport before being returned to Aberdeen in August.

Signifying another successful year, the GRT Group's figures to the end of March 1994 showed that the company made an operating profit of £5.2 million based on a turnover which had grown from £7.9 million to £39.9 million, this having obviously been helped by the acquisition of Northampton Transport and Leicester CityBus. Looking to the future, the GRT Group placed orders for 62 new buses for delivery in 1995/6 of which 7 Mercedes Benz 711Ds and 25 dual-door Optare-bodied Mercedes Benz 0405s were for Grampian, 10 Wright-bodied Scania N113s and 7 Mercedes Benz 711Ds for Midland Bluebird, 10 single-door Optare-bodied Mercedes Benz 0405s for

With its destination screen blank and paper labels affixed to its windscreen to indicate its next journey to Edinburgh, Midland Bluebird Wright-bodied Scania N113CRB 564 (L564JLS) awaits its passengers at Falkirk bus station. (T.W.W.Knowles)

Typifying Midland Bluebird's once numerous Alexander-bodied Leyland Leopards is 297 (GMS297S) seen here at Falkirk bus station in March 1992. (K.A.Jenkinson)

Standing at Larbert depot alongside Midland Bluebird 723 (XSA223S), an Alexander-bodied Leyland Atlantean which joined the fleet from Grampian Transport, is a sister bus which was undergoing cannibalisation after briefly giving service to Midland. (C.Morrison)

Although only on loan to Leicester CityBus, Grampian Transport Wright Cityranger-bodied Mercedes Benz 0405 L506KSA was repainted into its temporary owner's GRT Advance-style cream & crimson livery and given fleet number 002 as seen here in May 1994. (P.T.Stokes)

Leicester and 3 low-floor Volvo B10Ls for Northampton. Operationally, Grampian Transport began to apply discreet A, B. C or D allocation letters to all its vehicles to indicate in which part of its King Street depot each should be parked in order to assist drivers to locate their bus more quickly.

Having now achieved plc status, the GRT Bus Group as it had stated in its prospectus, continued to seek further growth and to this end on 18 July purchased Eastern Counties Omnibus Co. Ltd. for £6.7 million. Having been purchased from the NBC by its management in 1986, Eastern Counties whose headquarters were in Norwich operated a large number of services in Norfolk and Suffolk and had itself expanded with its purchase of Rosemary of Terrington in 1993. Of its 370 strong fleet, however, only 74 (10 Olympians, 15 Dennis Javelins, 5 Dennis Lances, 4 Dennis Darts and 40 Mercedes Benz 609Ds) had been purchased new since 1987 and the remainder were largely Bristol VRTs, Leyland Nationals and Ford Transits and thus it would be necessary to invest a large amount in replacement vehicles at an early date in order to upgrade standards. Nevertheless, its strong profit growth and future potential made it an attractive addition to GRT's growing portfolio as well as giving it a presence in an area in which it had previously had no representation. No properties were, however, included in this deal as all were leased by Eastern Counties and thus the existing agreements were altered to allow GRT to continue their occupation for varying period of time.

Almost before it had settled in to its new operating territory, Eastern Counties found itself being threatened by the Sheffield-based Mainline Group who announced in September that it was to begin a number of town services in Ipswich later in the year. Although most of Eastern Counties services operated by its Ipswich depot radiated to urban areas outside the town, the company nevertheless feared that Mainline would abstract an amount of passengers sufficient to cause concern. To meet this new challenge, the GRT company immediately set about preparing registrations for a limited number of new urban services despite assurances given by Mainline that its new service network would pose no threat to Eastern Counties. Planning to start these in mid-November with eight vehicles running on services to three major housing estates, Eastern Counties was careful not to compete directly with the incumbent Ipswich Buses and to make its intentions known so as not to initiate yet another bus war. In the event, Mainline subsequently cancelled its plans to invade Ipswich

Leaving the Old Cattle Market bus station, Ipswich, at the start of its journey to Felixstowe Dock is Eastern Counties Northern Counties-bodied Dennis Lance LC36 (K736JAH) which still wore the red livery in which it was received new in 1993. (D.W.Rhodes)

Eastern Counties ex.East Kent Dormobile-bodied Ford Transit TH850 (D779NUD)) seen in Norwich operating a local service to North Thorpe carried advertising posters below and above its side windows in addition to sporting a City Line fleet name on its bonnet. (T.S.Blackman)

Wearing Eastern Counties predominantly cream dual purpose livery, coach-seated Northern Counties-bodied Leyland Olympian DD5 (F105AVG) prepares to leave Norwich bus station on the long run to Peterborough on service 794. (T.S.Blackman)

Passing along Crown Street, Ipswich is Eastern Counties Plaxton Pointer-bodied Volvo B6 VP93 (M593ANG) which had originally been ordered by Mainline for its planned invasion of Ipswich which, in the event, never took place. *(D.W.Rhodes)*

Painted in a cream livery with light green relief, SMT Alexander Srider-bodied Volvo B10B 1201 (L201KFS) leaves the gloom of St.Andrew bus station, Edinburgh on route 16 to Blackridge. ***(Travelscene)***

after encountering difficulties in obtaining its O-licence for its new operation and on 14 October sold the 10 Volvo B6s it had planned to use to the GRT subsidiary. Surprisingly, however, after receiving this news Eastern Counties still went ahead with its plans and launched its three new services, each of which operated on a 15 minute headway.

Turning its attention back across the border, the GRT Bus Group announced early in September that it had made an offer for the acquisition of SMT Omnibuses plc. who coincidentally also operated a fleet of around 370 buses and coaches, albeit in Edinburgh and the Lothians region of Scotland. Formerly a subsidiary of the Scottish Bus Group, Eastern Scottish as it was then known was purchased by its management in 1990 and soon afterwards reverted to its SMT title. Announcing that valid acceptances of its offer for SMT shares in respect of 96.4% of those issued had been received on 10 October, GRT thus beat British Bus who had also submitted a bid, and completed its acquisition. A typical former Scottish Bus Group fleet which contained Ailsa Volvo, and Leyland Fleetline, Olympian and Lion double deckers, Volvo B10M and Leyland Tiger coaches and Volvo B10B and Seddon Pennine VII single deck buses, SMT also operated a sizable number of Renault-Dodge S56 and MCW Metrorider minibuses particularly in Edinburgh. With depots in Edinburgh, Bathgate, Dalkeith, Musselburgh and Livingston, this further strengthened GRT's position in central Scotland and it now looked forward to significant efficiency improvements from its new SMT and existing Midland Bluebird companies whose operating territories bordered on to each other. Unfortunately, however, immediately prior to gaining SMT, Midland Bluebird had been forced to implement fare increases of up to 10p as a result of a 5-6% drop in passenger numbers over each of the previous two years although the price of its zonal tickets in Stirling and Falkirk and its commuter Capitalcards in Edinburgh were maintained at their existing levels. Similarly, Leicester CityBus increased its single fares by 5p on 27 November. The third increase by the GRT company in just over twelve months, this was claimed to be necessary to fund investment,

The Scottish Bus Group strongly favoured the Seddon Pennine VII during the 'seventies and early 'eighties and not surprisingly fitted most with Alexander bodywork. One such vehicle, SMT's coach-seated ZS896 (GSX896T) is seen at St.Andrew bus station, Edinburgh painted in the livery introduced by its owner upon privatisation. ***(Travelscene)***

Carrying City Sprinter fleet names for operation on local Edinburgh services and painted in pre-GRT style livery, SMT's Alexander-bodied Renault S56 MR466 (E466JSG) rests on the layover bay at St.Andrew ***bus station, Edinburgh.***

Two of SMT's ECW-bodied Leyland Fleetlines, OSG61V and GSC861T both still wear their pre-GRT style of green & cream livery. (K.A.Jenkinson)

Seen at St.Andrew bus station, Edinburgh whilst being evaluated by SMT is Optare Vecta-bodied MAN demonstrator J367BNW which was given temporary fleet number MO367. Showing local service number C23 in its destination screen, it carried a label in its windscreen to inform passengers that it was operating to East Pilton and Morningside. (P.T.Stokes)

improve the standard and cleanliness of vehicles and cover additional costs as a result of the autumn budget by the government. Meanwhile, coinciding with its purchase of SMT that company's already-planned service changes in Livingston were implemented on 10 October when several routes were diverted to serve new bus stops on Almondvale Boulevard.

After a delay of some eighteen months, Aberdeen's first permanent park and ride service was finally opened on 24 October. Running from the Bridge of Don Exhibition Centre car park to the city centre this was operated commercially by Grampian Transport using eight Wright-bodied Mercedes Benz 0405s painted in a special livery of cream with a green skirt merged with yellow, a large red 'ribbon', and fitted with removable magnetic panels bearing the legend 'City Quick'. Running approximately every seven minutes on Mondays to Fridays and every ten minutes on Saturdays when a second park and ride service was operated between Woodhill House and the city centre, the new City Quick operation had the blessing of the Scottish Office and Grampian Regional Council who had introduced a number of traffic management measures which were designed to ensure its success. Not long after their introduction to the new City Quick service, the buses concerned had their magnetic boards replaced by permanent vinyls. Prior to the above, Mair's together with new operator Cruden Bay Coaches won the contracts to operate a new night service network in Aberdeen which began on 27 August with routes from the city centre to Northfield, Summerhill, Mastrick, Tillydrone and Scatterburn. Additionally, in May Midland Bluebird had acquired two 'passenger-friendly' buses for use on the sponsored 'Castle Shuttle' service to Stirling Castle, one of which was a Talbot Freeway, the other a CVE Omni.

Continuing to look to the future, however, soon after it completed its purchase of SMT, the GRT Bus Group made a £2.17 million offer for Reiver Ventures Ltd., parent of Lowland Scottish Omnibuses, another former Scottish Bus Group subsidiary which had been bought by its management and employees in August 1990 during the SBG sell-off. Running around 160 vehicles from nine depots on services in the Borders Region and into Edinburgh, in addition to expanding through its purchase of Ian Glass of Haddington in 1991. Although the Ian Glass name and livery was retained on a number of vehicles, Lowland also had its own profitable coaching interests as well as providing commercial training and running a self-drive business. Unlike most of the other former SBG companies, Lowland's fleet was mainly single deck and although the Seddon Pennine VII predominated, a number of Leyland Tigers, Leyland Nationals, Dodge S56s, Optare MetroRiders, Bedford VAS5s and some Scania K113CRB coaches were included. Of the 17 double deckers, 6 were Leyland Olympians, 4 were Fleetlines and 3 each were Bristol VRTs and Dennis Dominators whilst the remaining example was a former Leyland Titan demonstrator inherited from Ian Glass. The other

One of 8 Optare MetroRiders purchased new by Lowland in 1994, 720 (L720JKS) is seen here wearing its original yellow & two-tone green livery. (C.Morrison)

Typifying the Lowland fleet is Alexander-bodied Seddon Pennine VII 37 (LSC937T) seen wearing its owner's attractive yellow & green livery at Haddington depot. (K.A.Jenkinson)

Standing in the yard of Lowland's Haddington depot are 960 (B160KSC), an Alexander-bodied Leyland Olympian inherited from Eastern Scottish in 1986 and painted in Lowland's yellow & green livery and 988 (VAO488Y), a Leyland Titan still wearing the colours of its former owner Ian Glass. (K.A.Jenkinson)

Still wearing the cream, turquoise & orange livery of their former owner Ian Glass, Lowland's Duple-bodied 626 (C700USC) and Van Hool-bodied 621 (ESX257) - both DAF MB200s - stand in the yard of Haddington depot. (K.A.Jenkinson)

Resting at Lowland's Haddington depot is all-white liveried Plaxton Paramount 3500-bodied Scania K113CRB 104 (C104TSH) carrying Ian Glass fleet names. (K.A.Jenkinson)

New to London Country, Plaxton Paramount-bodied Leyland Tiger 567 (B267KPF) was acquired by Lowland from Ian Glass in 1991. Seen here at Haddington depot after receiving its new owner's livery, its windscreen was adorned with a variety of stickers indicating that it was to be used on the limited stop service to Haymarket, Edinburgh and that Lothian Senior Citizens could travel for 20p. (K.A.Jenkinson)

former Ian Glass vehicles still in service were coaches of a variety of makes and types ranging from Bedfords to Dennis Javelins through DAF MB200s, a Fiat 60.10, an AEC Reliance and various Leyland models. After completing the usual formalities, acceptances were received from 96.5% of Reiver's shareholders and the company passed to its new owner early in November. Although initially few changes were made to the services operated by the two newly acquired companies, on 11 December SMT gained a bonus when Lothian Regional Transport discontinued all its services west of Gogar and Barnton in Edinburgh, citing commercial reasons including bus station charges at Livingston. Seeing the chance to increase its presence in the area, on the following day SMT doubled its service between Livingston and Bathgate and provided additional peak-time buses on three main corridors. Conversely, however, on 10 December it withdrew its Edinburgh City Sprinter minibus services C1, C11 and C27 from Hunter's Tyrst to Pennywell, Craigour and Leith respectively and the C23 service from St.Andrew Square to Morningside leaving Lothian Regional Transport free to serve these areas.

Prior to these moves, the GRT Bus Group who had gained full control of Lothian Transit on 7 November, further strengthened its position in Edinburgh when on the 27th of that month its new subsidiary acquired the operations of Edinburgh Transport, a company in which Stevensons of Uttoxeter was the major shareholder. Although no vehicles were included in the deal, the existing Edinburgh Transport fleet continued to be used until mid-December when it was replaced by Dodge and Renault minibuses hired from SMT whilst its services were registered to Lothian Transit on 16 January. Midland Bluebird also gained some minor expansion on 15 November when it was awarded the Central Regional Council contracts for the Sunday and evening journeys on the 208 (Balfron - Glasgow), 210 (Stirling - Glasgow) and 211 (Stirling to Balfron) services previously operated by Goosecroft Coaches.

Before the year ended, Lowland vacated its depot and office in Berwick-on-Tweed and instead shared a new 'bus shop' with Northumbria Motor Services in the town's main street. Following the closure of its depot the GRT subsidiary used the Department of Transport HGV training station in Berwick for the overnight parking of its vehicles. During the latter part of 1994 a number of fleet changes resulted in the appearance of unfamiliar vehicles with several of

Seen at Haddington working a journey to Edinburgh, Lowland Plaxton Supreme-bodied Seddon Pennine VII 422 (PSU322, originally LSC950T) was later transferred to Lothian Transit before returning to the Lowland fleet in 1996. (T.S.Blackman)

GRT's subsidiaries, not least the loan of one of Grampian Transport's Wright-bodied Mercedes Benz 0405s to Leicester CityBus and Northampton Transport and another to Eastern Counties for evaluation purposes. In the case of the latter, it was repainted into Eastern Counties livery before leaving Aberdeen, indicating that its loan was to be for an extended period. Having only been in Aberdeen for around a year, it was somewhat surprising when Grampian's six ex.Northampton East Lancs-bodied Leyland Olympians were all permanently transferred to SMT in December whilst in the run up to Christmas four of Grampian's Leyland Atlanteans and one of its Olympians were adorned with illuminated festive decorations.

LOOKING TOWARDS THE FUTURE

1995

After an extremely eventful year, it was wondered how 1995 might compare and whether or not further expansion might be achieved. Like Badgerline, GRT had also been investigating the feasibility of the guided busway concept and in partnership with Suffolk County Council, its subsidiary Eastern Counties had already involved itself in a £2 million project at Kesgrave on the outskirts of Ipswich. In connection with this, Eastern Counties had fitted guide wheels to its six new Plaxton Pointer-bodied Dennis Darts in preparation for the opening of the new Kesgrave guided busway on 30 January, although in the event it was brought into use a couple of weeks earlier on the 16th. In addition, the buses concerned were given 'Superoute 66' branding for operation on the commercial Eastern Counties service bearing this number which connected the communities of Kesgrave and Martlesham Heath with Ipswich railway station and the town centre. Further enhancing the scheme, London Underground-type real time passenger information was installed at selected bus stops and terminals, although this did not become fully operational until April. On the reverse side of the coin, however, following increased competition from Northumbria, Lowland Omnibuses withdrew its town services in Berwick-on-Tweed on 4 February with the loss of 10 jobs, although it continued to maintain its rural routes radiating from the border town.

In its home town of Aberdeen, Grampian Transport embroiled itself in a dispute with Grampian Regional Council in February after refusing to continue to participate in the region's 10p concessionary fare scheme following financial changes implemented by the Council which effectively reduced the payments made to operators. Being the only one of the 44 participating operators to take this stance, it was served with a compulsory participation notice by the Regional Council and thus had little option but to continue to work within the scheme while meetings were arranged to resolve the situation. Stating that the company would lose a sum well into six figures as a result of the revised payments, the company stated that fares may have to be increased overall and some services cut as a result, In addition, consideration was given to claiming additional resource payments from the Council in respect of other concessionary passengers such as children etc. As threatened, on 2 April Grampian Transport increased childrens fares from 50% to 75% of that of the equivalent adult fare, stating that whilst this move had been forced upon the company, it would reinstate child fares at their previous levels if the council reconsidered its decision on its concessionary fares payments. Meanwhile, Grampian Transport drew up an innovative plan which offered free travel on the King Street park and ride service in Aberdeen in a bid to attract new passengers. In exchange for employers spreading the word about the proposed scheme for which no starting date had yet been set, employees would be given a week's commuting free of charge. Before these plans could come to fruition, however, Grampian Transport was delighted to learn that despite user figures being below what had been hoped for, its park and ride contract was to be extended beyond its one-year trial period which was due to end in October and would now continue over the Christmas period and possibly beyond.

Following the trend set throughout the GRT Bus Group, Eastern Counties altered its livery to one of corporate styling using cream as its base colour with red bands and the thistle emblem replacing the dot above the letter 'I' in the 'Counties' part of its fleet name. Additionally the company received 14 Iveco 49.10 and a handful of Ford Transit minibuses cascaded by Leicester CityBus and also

An unusual acquisition by Eastern Counties in 1995 was ex.SMT Alexander-bodied Seddon Pennine VII 1841 (JSF909T) which is seen in its new owner's livery at Bury St.Edmunds depot. (M.H.A.Flynn)

Looking somewhat sorry for itself and with its headlights removed, Eastern Counties ex.Leicester CityBus Carlyle-bodied Iveco 49.10 F701MBC awaits its fate at Great Yarmouth depot still painted in the colours of its former owner. (M.H.A.Flynn)

borrowed one of Grampian Transport's Mercedes Benz 0405s for evaluation. Continuing the transfer of vehicles between different members of the GRT Group, Leicester CityBus dispatched 4 of its Dennis Dominators on loan to SMT while during February and March Grampian hired a 29-seat Keillor-bodied Iveco 59.12 from Rennie, Dunfermline for use on schools contracts.

After supporting the late night bus network in Aberdeen operated by Mair's since August 1994, Aberdeen City Centre Partnership announced that it could no longer provide finance for the routes concerned and as a consequence all were discontinued on 18 February. At this same time, Grampian made it known that it was to revise almost all of its services in Aberdeen in May when more Beaver Bus minibus routes would be introduced and some conventional services would be upgraded to SMT-style Diamond standard. In the event, a small number of routes were altered earlier than originally planned on 26 March when the 27 service from Guild Street to the Airport was truncated to operate at peak hours only to Kirkhill Industrial Estate and the Airport served by a new express service which ran via a more direct route. Lowland also revised a number of its services in the Lothian Region during March and at the same time took over the operation of Lothian Transit's 315/325 services from Edinburgh to Astley Ainslie Hospital. At Easter, Lothian Transit also withdrew its former Edinburgh Transport commercially-registered services 93/93A between South Gyle and Tranent.

Almost mirroring Badgerline, GRT had for some time been investigating the use of alternative fuels in order to reduce

Pictured whilst on loan to Midland Bluebird for in-service evaluation is low floor Northern Counties Palatine-bodied Scania L113CRL FlexCi demonstrator M113RNK. (C.Morrison)

Northampton Transport coach-seated Duple-bodied Volvo B10M 114 (G114ENV) emerges from the gloom of its home town bus station still painted in pre-GRT-style livery. (T.W.W.Knowles)

environmental pollution and in order to prove its commitment in this area it inspected a German natural gas powered low floor left hand drive Mercedes Benz 0405 and although it had planned to use this on its Marischal College - Hillhead service in Aberdeen during its brief stay, insurance difficulties prevented this. Later it displayed another left hand drive compressed natural gas powered low-floor Mercedes Benz demonstrator in Edinburgh early in March and before returning this bus to Hannover in Germany later in the month, it also exhibited it in Leicester and Norwich in an attempt to gain some tangible support from the local authorities, stating that it was seeking £150,000 worth of assistance before it would be prepared to place an order for six buses of this type (six being the critical number to justify the cost of British Gas installing the necessary fuelling equipment). Had it not been for the developments taking place soon afterwards, GRT might well have proceeded with this new venture, but as will be seen, these were overtaken by the events of the next few weeks! Meanwhile, in order to allow greater concentration to be devoted to its bus operations, GRT sold its Autotruck business to Partco subsidiary Woodhead RSR for around £800,000, the deal including its four commercial vehicle spares depots in Aberdeen, Dundee, Glasgow and Inverness.

Proving to be an extremely eventful month, March also witnessed the start of talks between the GRT Bus Group and Nottingham City Council which, it was hoped would result in Nottingham City Transport taking a shareholding in GRT in return for the latter gaining a 10% stake in the East Midland council-owned undertaking. Although these talks continued for some time, an agreement was never reached, however, and Nottingham City Transport remained totally owned by the City Council. Simultaneously, GRT stated that

Painted in a special livery for operation on the 27 service to Aberdeen Airport is Grampian 120 (B120MSO), an Alexander-bodied Leyland Olympian of 1985 vintage. (T.W.W.Knowles)

Displaying SMT Coaches fleet names and corporate GRT-style livery, Duple 340-bodied Leyland Tiger 345 (A15SMT, originally D345ESC) enjoys a break at Westfield depot. (K.A.Jenkinson)

***Having gained corporate GRT-style livery, Lowland Alexander-bodied** Leyland Olympian 952 (D902CSH) passes through St.Andrew Square, Edinburgh on its way to Balerno. (Travelscene)*

despite its earlier interest in ScotRail, it would be less keen to proceed if that division was franchised in its entirety, feeling that it should first be broken down into smaller units. In the meantime, GRT had entered an interest in all eight rail franchises to enable it to give itself time to examine each of them more closely. Across the border in Scotland, SMT closed its Bathgate depot on 12 March and split its allocation between its Livingston and Westfield depots and a new location at the Centrex Vehicle Training Centre at Deans (Livingston) and at the same time effected a number of service changes in the area. Under these, most routes were removed from Almondvale Boulevard in Livingston whilst several services were diverted back to St.Andrew bus station at Edinburgh from their stances on the north side of St.Andrew Square. Another depot closure was that of Mair's at Dyce on 2 April after which its vehicles were transferred to Grampian Transport's King Street premises and its legal address to 395 King Street, Aberdeen (although the lettering on its vehicles showed this as St.Peter Street, Aberdeen where the entrance was to the King Street offices!).

As planned, Grampian Transport launched its new customer-orientated 'Gold Service' in Aberdeen on 28 May on services 16 (Springhill - Faulds Gate/Cove) and 17 (Newhills - Faulds Gate). Similar in concept to the Diamond Services operated by SMT, Rainbow services operated by Trent and the Flagship services operated by Yorkshire Rider, Grampian's Gold Service utilised a team of dedicated drivers who had been trained in customer care, offered passengers a money-back guarantee if due to the company's fault their bus is more than 10 minutes late and promised operation by the latest buses - ten Optare-bodied Mercedes Benz 0405s. In addition to being double glazed and air conditioned, these vehicles which were built to GRT's 'Advance' specification carried 'Gold Service' lettering at the front of their cove panels as a further way of promoting this new operation. On the previous day, Bluebird Buses service 5 (Balnagask - City Centre) which competed with Grampian's route bearing the same number was discontinued and replaced by a new Grampian service numbered 5A, leaving Bluebird with only one remaining Aberdeen city service while a few weeks earlier a new Z Card had been introduced by Grampian which allowed unlimited travel in a specified zone around the city centre. This was designed to appeal to those who used the bus regularly but found the City Card too expensive because of the shortness of their journeys.

Following the arrival of some new Scania buses and coaches, Lowland altered its livery to one of GRT corporate styling using yellow with two-tone green bands as did SMT (using cream with green bands) and also received a number of secondhand double and single deckers transferred from SMT. More unusually, Lowland also gained the contract for the operation of a heritage coach - a recently refurbished Harrington Cavalier-bodied AEC Reliance - on behalf of Prestige Tours who retained ownership of the vehicle while more mundanely it introduced a new local service network in Hawick on 8 May. Of much greater importance, however, was the announcement which had been made at the start of April of a proposed merger between the GRT Bus Group and the Badgerline Group which, if brought to a conclusion would result in the formation of a new company under the title of FirstBus plc, of which more later.

Painted in the predominantly red Chieftain Tours livery, Lowland Plaxton 3500-bodied Scania K113CRB 101 (C101RSH) has just returned to Haddington depot after completing an extended tour duty. (K.A.Jenkinson)

FirstBus

June 16th 1995 signalled the start of a new era when, following the acceptance of their shareholders, Badgerline Holdings plc and the GRT Bus Group PLC merged together to form a new company under the title of FirstBus plc. Although the new company was incorporated in Scotland with its registered office and operational headquarters at 395 King Street, Aberdeen, its corporate headquarters were located at Strowlands, Edingworth Road, Edingworth, Weston-super-Mare thus confirming that it was a truly Anglo-Scottish group. Moving closer to the Stagecoach Group in terms of its combined fleet size with some 5,600 vehicles, FirstBus in addition to having a major presence in Scotland, also controlled several important areas of England and Wales through both its former Badgerline and GRT companies. To the travelling public, however, the only visual change to the buses of both former groups was the addition of window stickers adjacent to the entrance door and in the rear bulkhead which bore the new FirstBus logo and the legend 'Welcome to FirstBus' and the disappearance of the window labels carried previously which carried a smiling badger and the wording 'A Badgerline Group Company'.

Prior to the merger taking place, plans had been drawn up by Badgerline subsidiary Rider York to relocate to a new depot and already work had begun on a new site at James Street not far from the existing leasehold depot at Barbican Road which had been inherited from York City & District. Brought into use on 10 July, the new depot which had formerly been used by British Road Services and had been converted for its new role at a cost of over £1.5 million had in addition to modern engineering facilities, open-air parking space for 125 buses as well as easier access than the old premises. At this same time, Rider York's offices were moved to the new site from their home in Walmgate, thus bringing all the company's activities to a single base. Also already in the pipeline was the introduction by Badgerline of low-floor buses on Bath's city services. Given financial support by Avon County Council who additionally modified several bus stops to make them more suitable for the new vehicles, Badgerline had placed an order for six Wright Pathfinder 320-bodied Dennis Lance SLFs which incorporated a number of innovative features, one of which was the provision of space for up to eight baby buggies. Placed in service on 4 July, the new buses immediately attracted favourable comments from passengers and indicated that quality continued to be the key to attracting more people to leave their cars at home and use public transport. In addition to the Badgerline examples, Western National also took delivery of a new Wright Pathfinder-bodied Dennis Lance SLF on 13 July for operation on its 183 service from Plymouth to Okehampton which was supported by Devon County Council. North of the border Mair's of Aberdeen who had ceased local bus operation earlier in the year to allow greater concentration on its coaching and contract activities returned to the stage carriage scene on 26 June when it commenced operation of a subsidised service between Peterculter and Rob Roy caravan site previously maintained by Smith of Cruden Bay. A week later, it began a second supported summertime service from Holborn Junction to Sea Beach which had previously been operated by its parent Grampian Transport.

As a result of the closure of Stirling bus station on 9 July and its subsequent demolition, Midland Bluebird's services were diverted to temporary stands on the former Mairs Motors site close to Craigs Roundabout until a new facility was constructed within a new

Rider York Duple Dominant bus-bodied Leyland Tiger 1657 (EWR657Y) which was new to West Yorkshire PTE in 1983 and still wore Yorkshire Rider livery, travels along Station Road, York on its way to Bishopthorpe. (K.A.Jenkinson)

Western National's low-floor Wright Pathfinder-bodied Dennis Lance SLF221 (M221EAF) despite being lettered for the Devon County Council-supported 183 service from Plymouth to Okehampton was actually operating the 187 service when caught by the camera in Tavistock bus station on its third day in service (16 July 1995). Enjoying only a brief stay in Devon it was sold to Leeds City Link in 1996. (J.L.Hobbs)

Two of Mairs coaches, Van Hool Alizee-bodied Volvo B10M PSU629 (previously B229LSO and originally 737ABD) and Plaxton Supreme IV-bodied Leyland Leopard PSU630 (originally FDF272T) are seen at their owner's depot. In 1996, PSU630 was transferred to Northampton Transport. (M.Currie)

Amongst the last Bristol RELLs to remain in service with Badgerline was 1297 (EHU391K). Still painted in its operator's old livery, it rests at Wells a few weeks before its withdrawal from service. (J.L.Hobbs)

shopping complex close to the town's railway station, although in the event it was some eighteen months before the new terminal was brought into use. In Bristol, City Line closed its Kingswood depot on 8 July, its allocation being then transferred to Lawrence Hill whilst on the 29th of the month Badgerline bade farewell to the last of its well-loved Bristol RELLs, thus ending an era spanning more than thirty years during which time Bristol Omnibus Co. had operated 439 examples of this type. On their final day, all three survivors ran on all day service as duplicates on their usual haunts, the 126 (Wells - Weston-super-Mare), 160 (Wells - Shepton Mallet), 163 (Wells - Taunton), 173 (Wells - Bath) and 376 (Bristol - Yeovil). As all the above was taking place, Eastern National found itself facing new competition in Colchester as a result of the arrival of a new operator, Budget Busways in June. Running a fleet of Leyland Nationals, Budget registered a number of services which challenged those of the incumbent operator, although in the event this was to be short lived as the newcomer suddenly ceased trading in August.

The first expansion to be achieved by FirstBus since its creation took place north of the border when in July Midland Bluebird purchased the small but lucrative eight-coach business of Kings of Dunblane. Although its operations were immediately transferred to Midland's Bannockburn depot, the King's identity and livery were to be retained in order to maintain customer loyalty etc. Further north, Grampian Transport implemented a fares increase under which most prices rose by 5p, although those at the lowest and highest ends of the scale remained unchanged. In defence of its move, Grampian stated that this was necessary in order to be able to increase its investment in new vehicles and thus further enhance the quality of travel for residents of the granite city. At this same time, Midland Bluebird similarly increased its fares by 5p (those over £1 rising by 10p) in order to address rising operational costs whilst in an attempt to reduce its costs SMT withdrew several of its services in West Lothian with effect from 23 July including the Livingston town centre and Livingston to Bathgate routes. This placed increased pressure upon Lothian Regional Council, whose transport budget was already greatly overstretched, to find funds to ensure that at least some of the services were maintained under the tendering process. In South Wales, as a result of the re-timing of certain services Brewers outstation at Burrows Coaches, Nantymoel had its allocation reduced from three to two buses from 23 July while a week later on the ultimate day of the month six Mid-Glamorgan County Council tendered services in the Bridgend area were taken over by Brewers from Pathfinder of Brynna. In addition, a further Pathfinder service (Bridgend - Merthyr Mawr) which had been due to commence on that evening was instead started by Brewers.

Although purchased by Midland Bluebird in 1995, the fleet of Kings of Dunblane has retained its own identity and livery as illustrated by Plaxton Paramount 3500-bodied Leyland Tiger 164 (H838SLS) seen resting in Midland's Bannockburn depot in September 1997. (K.A.Jenkinson)

A further move towards rationalisation and cost reduction was made in July when the Rider Group moved out of its headquarters at Windsor House in the centre of Leeds (which was only around a year old and had been built to replace the former head office at Swinegate) to new premises close to the M62 motorway at Cleckheaton and which was more centrally located to the four Rider operating districts. Almost before the company had time to settle in its new home, disaster struck at Rider's large depot at Torre Road, Leeds when an arson attack on the evening of Sunday 23 July destroyed thirteen double deckers and caused damage to several others. Ironically, the seat of the fire was at identically the same point where eight double deckers had been destroyed in a similar attack in November 1984 and had it not been for the prompt action of the staff and the fire brigade, the 1995 toll would have undoubtedly been much higher. Fortunately, as the school holidays had reduced the depot's peak vehicle requirement and with the help of buses drafted in from other Rider depots, all the services operated by Torre Road on the following day were able to be fully maintained without the loss of a single journey.

Following the instruction given to Stagecoach by the Office of Fair Trading to divest itself of its 20% shareholding in South Yorkshire-

Preserved by Leicester Citybus but still occasionally used in service is its first Dennis Dominator, East Lancs-bodied 233 (UFP233S) which has been restored in the livery in which it was delivered new in 1977. (G.T.W.Carter)

One of Thamesway's new generation of orange & yellow-liveried City Saver coaches, Plaxton Premiere-bodied Volvo B10M 603 (N603APU) collects Southend-bound passengers at Lakeside bus station, Thurrock in September 1995. (D.W.Rhodes)

based Mainline, FirstBus began talks with the Mainline Partnership Ltd. in July which it was hoped would culminate in its purchase of Stagecoach's stake in the company. For a variety of reasons these negotiations proved to be somewhat protracted and it was not until January 1996 that they were brought to a conclusion as will be seen later. Meanwhile, in order to promote its CitySaver service between Southend and London, Thamesway in August offered those purchasing an adult or senior citizen day return ticket at the normal price the opportunity to take with them a companion for only 10p return. In addition, on 19 August the company introduced the first four of a £2 million fleet of nineteen new Plaxton Premiere 350-bodied Volvo B10Ms which incorporated reclining seats, lap belts, reading lamps and adjustable air vents for each passenger and were painted in a striking new orange and yellow livery. Continuing its investment in new vehicles, a further eight Plaxton Pointer-bodied Dennis Darts were placed in service by Eastern National in August, replacing time-expired Leyland Nationals on the 31 service from Maldon to Chelmsford. Perhaps more unusual, however, was the entry into service during the last week in July of four 9-seat Peugeot Boxers purchased by PMT for use by its Crosville unit on the Chester dial-a-ride network.

Painted in National Express Air Link livery for operation on the service between Marlborough Street bus station, Bristol and the city's airport is Wessex Talbot Pullman 145 (H201JHP) which joined the fleet from Midland Red West in 1995. (K.A.Jenkinson)

Still pursuing its reorganisation and expansion policies, September proved to be a month of great activity which started on the 1st with the restructuring of Rider Holdings. Although Rider York and Quickstep Travel were to continue unchanged, the four Yorkshire Rider districts were each to be given greater autonomy whilst remaining under a single umbrella. Each district would now have its own managing director and financial budget and would adopt its own trading name and thus Yorkshire Rider Bradford became Bradford Traveller, Halifax became Calderline, Huddersfield became Kingfisher and Leeds became Leeds City Link. Although it was believed that each would also adopt its own distinctive livery, in view of the consideration being given at that time to the introduction of a corporate colour scheme for the whole of the FirstBus Group, the new companies merely applied their new fleet names to Rider's existing cream and green scheme. Meanwhile, FirstBus's expansive plans continued to move forward first with the acquisition by Western National of the 26 vehicle business of Lidgey's Coaches of Tregony, Cornwall in September and on 1 October by Brewer's purchase of Cardiff City Transport's coaching unit and its local Vale Busline operations in the Vale of Glamorgan which it had recently taken over from Golden Coaches of Llandow. These comprised the evenings and Sunday Barry town circular, weekday Bridgend to Cardiff and Llantwit Major to Barry routes, Llantwit Major to Cardiff Express and the Sundays Cardiff - Bridgend - Porthcawl service plus a number of schools contracts. Although no buses were included in the deal, 4 of Cardiff's coaches (2 Leyland Tigers and 2 Scania K113s) were acquired and placed in the United Welsh Coaches fleet at Port Talbot. Also taken over at around this same time were a number of school contracts in the Carmarthen area from D-Coaches while Thamesway purchased Wickford-based District Bus from British Bus Group subsidiary Southend Transport. Included in this deal were District Bus's services (in the Basildon area), its depot at Shot Farm, Wickford and 11 minibuses plus 5 MCW Metroriders which were on loan from Northumbria. The latter were, however, quickly returned to their rightful owner following the arrival of 5 Mercedes Benz L608Ds from City Line. Perhaps of greater importance, however, was the purchase on 9 October of People's Provincial for £4.1 million. The history of the latter company who operated a fleet of 167 buses around Gosport, Fareham and Portsmouth dated back to 1882 when the Provincial Tramways Company Limited began a horse-tram service from Gosport Beach to Brockhurst. Operating under the fleet name Gosport and Fareham Omnibus Company since 1929 the company was sold to the National Bus Company on 1 January 1970 and was subsequently purchased by its management and employees on 8 May 1987. For this purpose, a new company was incorporated on 13 March 1987 under the title of Legibus 877 Limited which was

Having had its fleet names removed following Yorkshire Rider's division into six autonomous operating units, Calderline 5517 (FUM489Y) had yet to receive its new identity when seen leaving Halifax bus station on a journey to Heptonstall. An ECW-bodied Leyland Olympian, it had begun life with West Yorkshire Road Car Co. Ltd. (K.A.Jenkinson)

One of a number of ex.London Country Roe-bodied Leyland Atlanteans acquired by Yorkshire Rider from Sovereign in 1989, 6427 (KPJ255W) adorned with Leeds area fleet names stands outside Kirkstall Road depot. (K.A.Jenkinson).

***Having had the green area on its lower deck panels extended** rearwards to accommodate its new Kingfisher fleet name, Roe-bodied Leyland Atlantean 6338 (VWW338X) leaves Huddersfield bus station on Honley Circular service 315. (K.A.Jenkinson)*

*Wearing Yorkshire Rider's white Flagship livery, Kingfisher Plaxton Verde-bodied Dennis Lance 4002 (M402VWW) is seen leaving **Huddersfield bus station. (K.A.Jenkinson)***

***Until 1997 the only former Greater Manchester bus in the fleet of** Bradford Traveller was Northern Counties-bodied Leyland Atlantean 6423 (UNA800S) which was transferred from Leeds City Link and is seen here in Bridge Street, Bradford wearing pre-corporate FirstBus-style fleet names. (K.A.Jenkinson)*

One of the four vehicles taken over by South Wales Transport from Cardiff City Transport was Plaxton Paramount 3500-bodied Scania K113CRB F907DHB which is seen here whilst still wearing its former owner's livery. ***(D.P.B.Davies)***

Resting at Truro is Lidgey of Tregony's Duple-bodied Bedford YRQ CTF471J which had joined the fleet in 1975 from Davies of Penygraig. (T.W.W.Knowles)

Passing through Basildon on its way to Kathleen ferrier Crescent on service 105 is District Bus cream & red liveried Carlyle-bodied Freight Rover Sherpa E509TOV. (J.Podgorski)

Provincial's old green, cream & black livery is carried by 403 (AYR299T), a Leyland National acquired from London Buses in 1991 and seen here at Portsmouth. (T.W.W.Knowles)

Prior to its sale to FirstBus, Provincial added more cream to its livery as illustrated by Marshall-bodied Iveco 59.12 185 (M185XTR) pictured here at Fareham bus station. (F.W.York)

changed to People's Buses Co-ownership Limited on 29 April 1987. Ten months later on 11 February 1988, it incorporated a further company named People's Portsmouth Buses Limited to establish additional services in the Portsmouth area and this was also transferred to FirstBus ownership. In the meantime, back in the south-west Western National was busy reorganising its coaching interests under which its Roberts subsidiary was to be disbanded and merged with Plymouth Coaching to for a new unit, which under the title of Devon Coaching would be based in Plymouth. Under this plan, the Roberts livery was to be discontinued in favour of Western National's standard colours although the Roberts' manager, Robert Risk, was to remain with the company with responsibility for the new combined coaching operation.

Following the success of its CitySaver service from Southend to London, Thamesway introduced a CitySaver shopping express service in October linking Woodford Green, Chingford, Walthamstow and Ilford to the Lakeside Shopping Complex at Thurrock and the Eastgate Shopping Centre at Basildon. Maintained with orange and yellow-liveried coaches, this was an immediate success and produced much additional revenue for Thamesway. In the south-west as a result of the popularity of its summer Transmoor Link service from Exeter to Plymouth via Mortonhampstead, Western National took the decision to continue this on Saturdays throughout the winter

UVG Urban Star-bodied Dennis Dart demonstrator N604GRV makes its way to Southsea whilst on loan to Provincial whose fleet names and FirstBus logos it temporarily carried. (F.W.York)

Seen adorned with FirstBus logos and numbered 204 in the fleet of Northampton Transport, East Lancs-bodied Dennis Dominator F152MBC was acquired from Leicester Citybus in 1997. (G.T.W.Carter)

Midland Bluebird Optare Prisma-bodied Mercedes Benz 0405 70 (N70CSC) in SMT livery leaves St.Andrew bus station, Edinburgh on Diamond Service route D28 to Bathgate. (K.A.Jenkinson)

period, a move which proved to be fully justified by the loadings witnessed on most journeys. Sadly, however, as a result of the ever increasing number of attacks on bus drivers and passengers across the whole of Britain and the growing problem of on-bus vandalism, the time had now come where action was needed to curb such incidents. Thus, in an attempt to improve the safety on public transport Northampton Transport and Stagecoach subsidiary United Counties both agreed to carry uniformed police officers, special constables and traffic wardens free of charge on all their services for a trial period of six months while in Scotland SMT introduced a dedicated telephone line supported by on-bus advertising to report attacks on drivers and vandalism with a £200 reward for all resulting prosecutions. Additionally, in a move to improve the safety of women wishing to travel late at night, Grampian Transport added further night routes to its network in Aberdeen on 13 October. These operated from the city centre to Cults/Cutter and Summerhill/Sheddocksley/ Kingswells on Friday and Saturday nights with the last departure at 2.10am. A further initiative relating to evening travel was introduced by Eastern National on 4 September in the form of a Chelmsford Night Ranger ticket. Priced at £1 for a return journey anywhere within Chelmsford after 7.0pm, it was hoped that it would encourage a greater number of passengers to use the company's buses at times when they were generally only lightly loaded.

Still showing an interest in the government's rail privatisation programme, FirstBus committed itself to a 24.5% stake in Great Western Holdings, one of the bidders for the Great Western Trains franchise. The remaining shares in GWH were held by its management and employees (51%) and 3i (24.5%). Meanwhile, announcing the results for the six months ending 30 September 1995, FirstBus was able to report that its operating profit had risen by 23% to £19.4 million (before merger, restructuring and ESOP costs) whilst turnover had increased by 16% to £174 million. Early benefits of the merger of Badgerline and GRT had been achieved by merging several of the operating companies and the rationalisation of the professional services of the two original groups and it was stated that the second half of the year would see further actions to achieve lower staff costs by the implementation of improved working practices and productivity.

Throughout this momentous year, the flow of new vehicles had continued unabated with buses and coaches ordered prior to the formation of FirstBus assisting the new group to upgrade the fleets of many of its operating companies. Amongst these were Northampton Transport's three new low-floor Alexander Ultra-bodied Volvo B10Ls and the final ten of the thirty-five Optare Prisma-bodied Mercedes Benz 0405s ordered by GRT, the latter being allocated to SMT for

In 1995 Eastern Counties acquired four ECW-bodied Leyland Fleetlines from SMT, one of which - 346 (GSC856T) - is seen at Rosemary Coaches depot at Kings Lynn in November 1996 still painted in the green & cream livery of its former owner and still carrying its fleet name on its side panels. (M.H.A.Flynn)

Eastern Counties Plaxton Paramount 3200-bodied Leyland Tiger 24 (CSV303 originally A207SAE) seen sporting Rosemary Coaches fleet names at Kings Lynn depot was one of three coaches of this configuration acquired from Badgerline in 1996. Sneaking into the photograph is Rosemary Coaches ex.SMT ECW-bodied Leyland Fleetline 355 (GSC855T) still painted in the colours of its former owner. (M.H.A.Flynn)

Acquired from Northampton Transport and later cascaded to SMT, Grampian's East Lancs-bodied Leyland Olympian 137 (A82RRP) is seen at the King Street, Aberdeen depot of its intermediate owner. (B.Newsome)

operation on its 'Diamond' services between Bathgate, Livingston and Edinburgh. Painted in GRT Advance-style cream and green livery, they were given 'SMT Lothians' fleet names and were equipped with air conditioning etc. Apart from these new arrivals, a number of buses and coaches were transferred between companies to assist them with their immediate needs and included amongst these were several ex.Eastern National and City Line Mercedes Benz minibuses which joined Brewers, a number of ex.SMT Renault S56s and Daimler Fleetlines which were cascaded to Eastern Counties along with a pair of former Badgerline Leyland Tigers, and an ex.Eastern National Leyland National and six former Northampton Transport East Lancs-bodied Leyland Olympians which moved from Grampian to SMT at Edinburgh. In order to cover the short-term requirements of Eastern Counties who was experiencing some maintenance difficulties, the company in October hired a number of buses from Ipswich Buses and Great Yarmouth Transport while Rider York briefly gained a pair of Leyland Atlanteans on loan from Grampian and, more surprisingly, City Line received a Strathclyde Buses Volvo Olympian on 12 September to replace one of its own buses of this type which had been returned to Volvo for engineering purposes. During its stay in Bristol which lasted until 18 October, the Strathclyde double decker was used exclusively on the 48 service to Blackhorse. Providing even more variety to the FirstBus Group were several demonstrators which were obtained for evaluation in preparation for the placing of future orders. Amongst these were an Optare Metrorider and a low-floor Wright-bodied Scania L113CRL which were used by Midland Red West in July and September respectively and a Scania L113 which was trialed by PMT in October.

Still showing United Welsh Coaches fleet names on its front panel but having it covered by an advert on its upper deck side panels, Brewers ECW-bodied Bristol VRT 946 (HHK234X) originated with Eastern National and later served with Thamesway from whom it was acquired in 1991. (D.P.B.Davies)

One of 30 Northern Counties-bodied Leyland Olympians delivered to Bristol Omnibus Co. in 1993, City Line-liveried 9618 (K618LAE) picks up its passengers in Bristol Centre. (D.P.B.Davies)

Following the expiry of its lease at Digbeth garage in Birmingham, Midland Red West vacated the premises towards the end of October and although continuing to house 34 buses in the city centre at the Bull Ring bus station, it transferred all its maintenance work to Worcester depot. All its midibus operations in the Birmingham area had ceased following the loss of almost all its Centro contracts and as a consequence of the arrival of its new Plaxton Verde-bodied Dennis Lances, the company had been able to withdraw a large number of Leyland Nationals, many of which were quickly sold to West Midlands Travel. In the wake of the sudden cessation of D & N of Ystradgynlais on 10 October, South Wales Transport took over the operation of that company's three services with immediate effect but surprisingly sub-contracted the 66A (Gwys - Penycae) to local independent Long of Abercraf and the 68 (Coelbren - Ystradgynlais) to Silverline of Merthyr Tydfil. Meanwhile, a new bus only road link controlled by retractable bollards had been brought into use in Swansea between the University and Singleton Hospital and in order to use this, all the buses allocated to services 4, 16, 18C and 41-43 were fitted with sensor units to enable them to activate the bollards. Continuing its experiments designed to encourage greater use of its buses, Badgerline introduced a new marketing initiative in Bath on 13 November which, for a period of three months, offered reduced fares to regular users of four services radiating from the bus station to Ensleigh, Bathampton and Southdown. Under this scheme a card could be obtained which entitled an adult to travel at the child rate and also allow a return ticket to be purchased before 9.0am with a

Painted in a red & yellow livery for use on London Transport Mobility Bus contracts, Thamesway Marshall-bodied Dennis Dart SLF N854CPU rests in the yard of Basildon depot in April 1996. (K.A.Jenkinson)

Adorned with route branding for Thamesway's Premier 100 service from Lakeside Shopping Centre at Thurrock to Chelmsford, Plaxton Pointer-bodied Dennis Dart 971 (N971CPU) rests at Lakeside bus station in January 1996. (D.W.Rhodes)

The first of Bradford Traveller's experimental new liveries was applied to Roe-bodied Leyland Olympian 5084 (A84KUM). Utilising dark and light blue, this was less than pleasing and in the event 5084 remained unique for several months until it was repainted again into its owner's then new standard livery which, incidentally, has since been revised again. (K.A.Jenkinson)

reduction of up to half price. This new scheme co-incidentally began a week before local operator Ryans began its first commercial service in Bath which shadowed Badgerline's 10 and 11 routes from the bus station to Southdown using double deckers! Continuing to pursue its ongoing restructuring programme FirstBus reunited Badgerline and City Line under the Bristol Omnibus Company umbrella on 31 October, although both companies were to operate as separate units and use their existing fleet names and liveries.

Doors continued to open and close for Thamesway as the year neared its conclusion and on 11 November the District Bus operation was absorbed into the company's Basildon network with all the vehicles concerned being withdrawn except for two which remained at Basildon in Bristol City Line livery. Although the London Transport contract for the 307 (Barnet - Enfield) service was lost to Cowie Leaside, thus rendering the company's four all-Leyland Olympians surplus to requirements, a new London Transport Mobility contract was won and for this 4 new Marshall-bodied Dennis Darts painted in London Buses red livery and equipped with wheelchair lifts were purchased and allocated to Basildon depot. A further new service to be launched in December was that from Chelmsford to the Lakeside Shopping Complex at Thurrock. Running via Basildon and employing new dual-purpose seated Plaxton Pointer-bodied Dennis Darts, it was marketed under the title of 'Premiere 100' and was designed to provide passengers with a faster, better quality service than they had previously experienced. In the meantime, reflecting its ongoing rationalisation Thamesway closed its depot at Brentwood on 9 December although its yard continued to be used as an outstation for

New and old members of Leeds City Link's subsidiary Quickstep Travel's fleet, Plaxton Pointer-bodied Dennis Dart 3274 (N374JUM) painted in its operator's new livery passes old-liveried Leyland National 6 (PEV706R) in the Headrow, Leeds. (K.A.Jenkinson)

One of the first buses to gain Rider York's new livery was Leyland National 1343 (MNW130V) which originated with West Yorkshire Road Car Co. Fresh from the paintshop it is seen opposite York Railway station displaying only a route number on its destination screen. (K.A.Jenkinson)

10 minibuses as well as a store for withdrawn vehicles. In preparation for a move which was to take place in 1996 of which more later, Eastern National Ltd. changed its name to Essex Buses Ltd. on 1 December whilst at the same time a dormant FirstBus company, Class One Travel Ltd. was renamed Eastern National Ltd. in order to preserve its title.

After giving the subject of a corporate livery a great deal of consideration, FirstBus decided instead to allow all its operating companies to retain their own individual colour schemes and thus, after a period of waiting, Yorkshire Rider's subsidiaries were each at last able to break away from the current green and cream and 'go their own way'. Although Kingfisher decided to retain the Rider Group's somewhat complicated two-tone green and cream as its new standard in view of the large number of new single deckers and minibuses which it had received so painted in recent months and Rider York also was to keep its existing cream and green, albeit applied in a slightly modified layout, the other Rider companies introduced completely new schemes which were unveiled on 21 December. Calderline chose an attractive white, blue and yellow for all its vehicles whilst Bradford Traveller adopted blue as its base colour. After repainting a handful of buses into different variations of dark and light blue, it eventually settled on light blue with a dark blue skirt and red relief while Leeds City Link chose ivory with red and orange stripes. Despite Quickstep at first retaining its established ivory and crimson, it was not long before this was changed to Leeds City Link's new colours, albeit with Quickstep fleetnames.

COMMITMENT TO A CLEANER ENVIRONMENT

1996

The start of the new year witnessed the beginning of a new era in bus travel when on 3 January FirstBus launched Britain's first purpose-built compressed natural gas-powered bus following its commitment to a cleaner environment. Having already introduced four LPG-powered buses in Bath (two Bristol VRTs and two Leyland Olympians), Badgerline had already taken the decision to trial a CNG bus before it had merged with GRT to form FirstBus and it was thus no surprise that the new CNG-powered Dennis Dart was allocated to City Line at Bristol for evaluation. Fitted with a Plaxton Pointer body which had been modified to carry six gas canisters on its roof, it was painted in a special silver-grey livery and allocated to Lawrence Hill depot from which it was to operate alongside conventional diesel-powered Dennis Darts for comparison. Fuelled at the nearby British Gas fast-fill depot at Eastville, it was powered by a lean-burn Cummins B-series engine and cost £115,000 compared with £70,000 for an equivalent diesel-engined bus. As one innovative move took place, however, another one ended and at the same time that the new CNG-powered Dennis Dart entered service, FirstBus announced that it was not to purchase any further new air-conditioned buses in the foreseeable future. Introduced by GRT, air conditioning (on Optare Prisma-bodied Mercedes Benz 0405s) despite being problem free was seen as being expensive and in addition, customer surveys

Painted in a silver & grey livery, Bristol City Line's gas-powered Plaxton Pointer-bodied Dennis Dart 1548 (N548HAE) carries a rail-link vinyl above its front pillar in addition to wearing promotional lettering on its sides, front and the roof pod which conceals its gas cylinders. (S.R.Procter)

Seen in Swansea bus station soon after its acquisition by South Wales Transport from D-Coaches (Rees & Williams) in 1996, Alexander Dash-bodied Dennis Dart 399 (K82BWN) still wore the livery of its former owner. (D.P.B.Davies)

One of the former Leicester Citybus East Lancs-bodied Dennis Dominators acquired by South Wales Transport for onward sale to D-Coaches of Morriston, MUT262W still wearing the colours of its original owner is seen at D-Coaches depot immediately after its transfer. (S.R.Procter)

revealed that the additional cost was not perceived as adding significant customer benefit.

Continuing its search for expansion whenever the opportunity arose, on 6 January FirstBus through its subsidiary South Wales Transport purchased the Dyfed and Tawe Valley local bus operations of D-Coaches of Morriston, Swansea which included those operated in the Ammanford area using the Rees & Williams title. Under this deal, SWT gained nine DiPTAC equipped buses, Rees & Williams depot at Tycroes and its Dyfed County Council's Bws Dyfed contracts around Ammanford, Llanelli, Carmarthen and Llandeilo as well as some D-Coaches services in Swansea. Continuing to use the Rees & Williams name for its inherited operations in the Ammanford area, South Wales Transport passed 20 double deckers (including 10 Dennis Dominators acquired from Leicester CityBus for this purpose) to D-Coaches for use on the local authority contracts which it retained. From 19 February, however, all the Rees & Williams services were consolidated with existing SWT routes and as a consequence, SWT's Ammanford outstation was then closed and its former duties transferred to Tycroes depot. Prior to this move, Brewers expanded its operational area on 29 January when it took over the tendered Village Bus network in the Vale of Glamorgan from Shamrock Coaches. For its operation, two of Brewers' Mercedes Benz L608Ds were refurbished by South Glamorgan County Council at a cost of £15,000 which included the fitting of new floors, seats and heating systems and equipping to DiPTAC specification. Additionally each was installed with a mobile phone, this being necessary for the 'Divertabus' scheme which allowed passengers to request a pick-up point in advance. Painted in green and white 'Village Bus' livery, they operated a network of ten routes centred on Cowbridge and offered a Village Day Rider ticket at £2.70.

In Scotland, Grampian Transport expanded its Gold Service network on 14 January when it replaced double deckers on route 11 (Craigiebuckler - Golf Links) with new Alexander-bodied Dennis Darts. Also introduced on the same date was a new direct service (numbered X18) from Dyce to Airyhall while withdrawn were the 25 service from Culter to Tillydrone and the Airport Express route, the latter being replaced by an extension of service 27 (Guild Street to Kirkhill). Following quickly on the heels of these changes, a new peak-hour express route was started on 29 January from Broad Street to Sheddocksley numbered X44 while on 18 March operation commenced on the new express X45 between Broad Street and

Painted in Mainline's Eager Beavers minibus livery, Reeve Burgess-bodied Renault S56 334 (G334NWB) awaits its passengers in Pond Street, Sheffield before continuing its journey to Fishponds. (G.T.W.Carter)

Cove which was marketed as the Charleston City Express.

Following talks initiated more than six months earlier, FirstBus early in January completed its acquisition of Stagecoach's 20% equity stake in Mainline and thus gained an important foothold in South Yorkshire in and around Sheffield, Rotherham and Doncaster, an area where it had previously not had a presence. Meanwhile, as part of its ongoing restructuring programme, FirstBus announced that it was to reunite Eastern National and Thamesway under one umbrella as Essex Buses Ltd. on 1 March. Although both companies would continue to trade separately and retain their individual liveries and fleet names, the centralisation of administration etc. would enable a number of cost saving measures to be introduced and thus considerably reduce overheads. In many ways, this was returning the two companies to their position prior to July 1990 when Thamesway was created by Badgerline from Eastern National. Prior to this change taking place, Eastern National relocated its Bishops Stortford depot to the Causeway Business Centre on 21 January while a week later Eastern Counties renumbered its fleet into a scheme which omitted the prefix letters so long associated with this company.

Still regarding the environment as an extremely important issue for the future and after introducing LPG buses to Bath and a CNG bus to Bristol, FirstBus took another step forward early in February when it made the decision to use emission-cutting low-sulphur diesel for the whole of its 5,700 strong fleet and to this end signed a contract with Shell for its future supplies. One of the first bus operators in Britain to adopt this type of fuel, it also enabled the group to introduce catalytic exhaust treatment at an early date in order to further reduce pollution levels. In the meantime, however, Badgerline sold its two LPG-powered Bristol VRTs to Stratford-on-Avon based Guide Friday towards the end of 1995

After several years of working in harmony with Badgerline in Bath, local independent Streamline Buses finally agreed in late January to requests made to it by students at Bath University for a lower cost service from the University to the city centre in competition with Badgerline's route 18. Despite the FirstBus company quickly increasing its frequency and reducing its fares by around 40%, the

Yellow & red liveried Northern Counties-bodied Dennis Dart 402 (K402EDT) of Mainline is seen collecting its passengers in Sheffield. (T.G.W.Carter)

One of a number of Badger retail shops, this particular newsagent and tobacconist is located inside Marlborough Street bus station, Bristol. (K.A.Jenkinson)

Operating service 161 to Bradley Stoke, Durbin's freshly repainted ex.Bristol Omnibus Co. Dormobile-bodied Mercedes Benz L608D D501FAE passes through Bristol Centre. (Travelscene)

Wearing the white & two tone blue livery of Durbin Coaches, Plaxton Paramount 3500-bodied DAF MB200 8200 (SSU437) seen at Lawrence Hill depot had been registered from A985UFB in April 1993. (K.A.Jenkinson)

Following the merging of SMT with Midland Bluebird and Lowland, several Midland vehicles had SMT logos added as illustrated by this view which also shows Midland's bluebird emblem above the front wheel arch of an unidentified vehicle. (C.Morrison)

Resting at Midland Bluebird's Westfield (Edinburgh) depot are former Grampian Alexander-bodied Leyland Atlantean 744 (DSA244T) and ex.SMT Alexander-bodied Seddon Pennine VII 1608 (SSX608V), both of which carry SMT logos and cream & green livery. (K.A.Jenkinson)

students remained loyal to Streamline who found it necessary to add more buses to the route in order to meet the growing demand. With both companies claiming victory in this new bus war, it was Badgerline who was first to concede and scale down its operations, however, and withdraw some of its additional vehicles.

Following the merging of Badgerline and City Line a few months earlier, further rationalisation took place in the Bristol area on 3 February when Durbins' operations were fully integrated into Bristol Omnibus Company and its depot at Patchway was closed. As a consequence of this move, all Durbins' Freight Rover Sherpas were sold together with a number of the company's coaches leaving only 6 Bristol VRTs, 13 coaches and 2 minibuses to transfer to the company's new home at City Line's Lawrence Hill depot. Retaining Durbins as a low-cost private hire and schools contract unit, the 21 vehicles mentioned above kept their existing liveries and fleet name for this purpose and were immediately joined by Badgerline's two coach-seated East Lancs-bodied Leyland Olympians and a Plaxton Paramount-bodied Leyland Tiger coach from this same source.

As a result of the operators licence of Goosecroft Coaches being revoked by the traffic commissioner on 22 March, Midland Bluebird took over the operation of subsidised service 268 (Dollar - Tullibody) on the following day under emergency arrangements. Meanwhile, further north Grampian Transport was involved in a three-way vehicle exchange which related to vehicle evaluation and brought a Rider York Alexander Strider-bodied Scania L113CRL to Aberdeen on 10 March. Replacing it at York was one of Leeds City Link's Scania N113CRBs whose place was taken at Leeds by a Grampian Wright-bodied Mercedes Benz 0405 which was equipped with guide wheels for use on the Scott Hall Road guided busway. All three buses returned to their rightful owners during June. Another Grampian Transport bus to be dispatched to Leeds, albeit under different circumstances, was Gold Service Optare Prisma-bodied 537 (N537VSA) which after only 29 days in service was maliciously badly damaged by fire by one of its passengers in Union Street, Aberdeen on 25 March and as a result was returned to Optare who replaced its interior. A further change in Scotland saw Lowland absorb Lothian Transit on 1 April, close its Newtongrange garage, and on the same day take over the Dalkeith and Musselburgh depots of SMT, closing its own former Ian Glass depot at Haddington and moving its head office from Galashiels to Dalkeith. SMT's other premises at Westfield (Edinburgh), Almondvale and Centrex (Livingston) passed to Midland Bluebird and although the company's livery and fleetname was to be retained for all its former operations, SMT now no longer existed as a separate entity thus ending 90 years of history. In the event, however, it was not until June that the legal lettering and operators discs on the vehicles concerned were altered to reflect their new ownership.

***One of a pair of Ford Transits acquired by Lowland from Grieve of** Hawick in 1994, coach-seated Deansgate-bodied 1749 (H649USH) painted in an all-white livery rests at Dalkeith depot in September 1997. (K.A.Jenkinson)*

*Parked in St.Andrew bus station, Edinburgh is Lowland 389 (BSS76 originally A678DSF), a Jonckheere Jubilee-bodied Leyland Tiger acquired with the Ian Glass business in 1991 and still wearing that **operator's fleet names (in FirstBus corporate style) and livery. (K.A.Jenkinson)***

Although all these changes related to FirstBus's Scottish subsidiaries, Western National also made news on 31 March when a major enhancement of its Sunday services throughout Cornwall was implemented, restoring numerous long-lost links and together with several new services the whole was operated as an interconnecting network. Prior to this, Western National had introduced a new service between Truro and St.Mawes which used the King Harry Ferry for the first time ever.

Continually looking for further expansion, FirstBus added two more companies to its growing portfolio on 2 April when it purchased GM Buses North and Portsmouth Transit, the first giving it a major foothold in an area where it had previously not had a presence, the second strengthening its position on the south coast. The acquisition of GM Buses North which had been purchased from Greater Manchester PTA by its management and employees in 1994 came only two weeks after its sister company, GM Buses South had been bought by Stagecoach and thus the former giant PTE undertaking (which had been divided into two separate units on 13 December 1993) had now passed to the ownership of Britain's two main bus operating groups. Adding 950 buses to FirstBus's combined fleet, GM Buses North had extensive operations not only in the northern and western suburbs of Manchester but also in Oldham, Bury, Rochdale, Wigan and Atherton with routes stretching out as far as Liverpool and Todmorden which were maintained from six depots. Conversely, Portsmouth Transit had been born on 17 January 1991 from Portsmouth Citybus and parts of Southdown and was set up by Harry Blundred following an instruction to Stagecoach from the Office of Fair Trading in 1990 to divest itself of its Portsmouth operations. Adopting the title Red Admiral for its Portsmouth city operations and Blue Admiral for its 'country' services radiating from Fareham. Portsmouth Transit ran a fleet of around 150 minibuses, a number of which were unusually of dual-door layout. As may be recalled, the Red Admiral name was, however, first used by Badgerline when it began operations with new Iveco minibuses on services in the Portsmouth area in 1987 which it ultimately sold to Portsmouth Corporation. In view of the fact that both Blue Admiral and Red Admiral operated several services which were adjacent to or

*Added to Western National's fleet in the spring of 1995 was ECW-bodied Leyland Leopard ANA93Y which is seen here at Tavistock outstation still wearing the red & white livery of its previous owner, **Brewers. (J.L.Hobbs)***

***Transferred to Lowland from Midland Bluebird in 1996, all-white** liveried Alexander-bodied Leyland Leopard 1698 (SSC108P) seen at Dalkeith depot in September 1997 is fitted with a centre door and wheelchair lift for the carriage of disabled passengers. (K.A.Jenkinson)*

*Still wearing the yellow & green livery of its former owner Eastern National from whom it was acquired in 1994, Western National Reeve Burgess-bodied Mercedes Benz L608D 164 (C214HJN) had gained lettering for the Ivybridge - Modbury - Bigbury service when caught **by the camera during the following year. (J.L.Hobbs)***

Painted in pre-FirstBus GM Buses North orange, black & white livery and sporting that operator's old-style logos, Leyland National 201 (ABA26T) rests in Wigan bus station in January 1996. (K.S.E.Till)

competed with those of Provincial, it came as no great surprise when it was announced that the three operations were ultimately to be merged under the Provincial name and their different liveries replaced by a new cream and red scheme. Although Transit's depots at Hilsea and Fort Wallington were both included in the deal, the latter was to be closed on 26 March but would be retained for use as a paint shop and for the storage of withdrawn vehicles. The merger eventually took place on 26 May when Blue Admiral and Red Admiral ceased to exist as separate companies. The rationalisation of services which coincided with this move rendered a large number of the minibuses acquired with the Admiral fleets surplus to requirements and all the remaining Ford Transits - 40 in total - were immediately sold to Southern National whilst 10 Iveco 49.10s were placed in store. As a

Painted in the livery of Red Admiral is Carlyle-bodied Mercedes Benz 811D H171GTA which was new in 1991. (J.Whitmore)

Seen displaying Blue Admiral fleet names is D641NOD, a 16-seat Mellor-bodied Ford Transit. (J.Whitmore)

Painted in a special yellow, black & white livery for operation on 'Quality Choice' services in and around Wigan is GM Buses North low-floor Northern Counties-bodied Volvo B6 1058 (M258NVM) seen here at Wigan depot. (B.Newsome)

consequence of its service revisions, the enlarged Provincial soon found itself in dire need of additional full-size single deckers and to satisfy its requirements in July gained 18 Leyland Nationals from Strathclyde Buses subsidiary Kelvin Central Buses. Several of these were immediately pressed into service still wearing their former operator's livery and it was not until later in the year that all had been transformed to fully reflect their new ownership.

By now, although having discounted plans to introduce a unified livery for all its bus operating companies, FirstBus had instead adopted a corporate style of fleet name which was to be endorsed with the group's logo and applied universally. This was, however, at first only affixed to vehicles upon repaint and thus was introduced slowly. In May, GM Buses North took the decision to strengthen its orange branding and changed its identity to Greater Manchester and adding blue lines to its new overall orange livery. This, it was believed, would make its buses easier to recognise against those of Stagecoach-owned GM Buses South which at that time shared a livery similar to that of the FirstBus company.

The flow of new buses continued during the first six months of the year and amongst these were a pair of Alexander Sprint-bodied 25-seat Mercedes Benz 711Ds equipped to DiPTAC standards for Eastern Counties. Making their debut in February at Lowestoft on Suffolk County Council contracted services, these were a welcome replacement for the company's first-generation minibuses previously employed on these duties. Following these in March was the first of ten low-floor Plaxton Pointer-bodied Dennis Dart SLFs purchased for Thamesway's use in and around Southend while in May Midland Red West placed a similar vehicle in service which was equipped to carry two wheelchairs when required. This was though to be the first super low-floor bus to be operated in a Midlands rural area and was operated on a different route each day in Shropshire and Worcestershire. As a consequence of the arrival of new buses throughout the FirstBus group, a number of older vehicles were

Having a Provincial fleet name and FirstBus logo added to its Red *Admiral livery of red & white with a blue band, Carlyle-bodied Mercedes Benz 811D 388 (H179GTA) seen at Southsea in June 1996 was later renumbered 809. (T.S.Blackman)*

Acquired by Provincial from Kelvin in 1996 and still wearing its previous owner's red & cream livery, Leyland National 407 (MDS864V) is seen heading to Southampton soon after its entry into service in its new home. (F.W.York)

Passing Bolton bus station and still painted in the old GM Buses North orange livery, Northern Counties-bodied Leyland Atlantean 4459 (SND459X) had, however, gained new FirstBus Greater Manchester fleet name vinyls on its sides and front panel. (K.A.Jenkinson)

One of Greater Manchester's new low-floor buses, Northern Counties-bodied Volvo B6 1054 (M254NVM) shows off its owner's new deep orange livery to which blue bands have been added at floor level and below its windows. (K.S.E.Till)

transferred between companies to meet their particular demand and amongst these were Brewers who received Mercedes Benz minis and Leyland Tigers from Western National, Quickstep and Yorkshire Rider; Eastern National who gained a quantity of Bristol VRTs from Yorkshire Rider and Western National whose fleet was enhanced with Leyland Tigers, a Lynx, some Bristol VRTs and Mercedes Benz L608Ds cascaded by Yorkshire Rider, Brewers, Midland Red West, Durbins, Badgerline and Eastern National. PMT increased its minibus fleet with some Mercedes Benz L608Ds from Bradford Traveller and Leyland Leopards from Calderline and Midland Red West while Midland Bluebird inherited 20 Leyland Atlanteans from Grampian and Eastern Counties received Leyland Tigers and Olympians, Mercedes Benz L608Ds and Bristol VRTs from a number of sources including Eastern National, Yorkshire Rider, Badgerline, Thamesway, Midland Red West and Northampton Transport. Additionally, at around the start of the year Eastern Counties had, in order to overcome shortages in its operating fleet, continued to hire a number of single deck vehicles from Ipswich Buses and Great Yarmouth Transport, the former being mainly Dennis Falcons, the latter twenty-two year-old ECW-bodied AEC Swifts as well as using its own open-top Bristol VRT (VR353) in single deck mode with its upper deck sealed off! To meet the needs of thirteen newly-acquired schools contracts, Northampton Transport acquired a varied selection of secondhand buses and coaches amongst which were 2 Leyland Tigers and 5 Leopards from FirstBus's various Scottish subsidiaries and 3 Dennis Dominators, a Leopard and a Tiger from Leicester CityBus whilst Leicester acquired 7 Alexander-bodied Leyland Tiger buses from Timeline. The latter were initially placed in service in the livery of their former owner, albeit with their front end in Leicester colours, pending their repainting into fleet livery. Apart from its fleet changes, discussions aimed at increasing its on-bus advertising revenue were held between FirstBus and Buspak which resulted in the latter being awarded the responsibility for all the advertising contracts at City Line and PMT whose combined fleets exceeded 800 vehicles.

Despite Badgerline having taken more than a passing interest in several light rail transit schemes earlier in the decade, it was becoming increasingly obvious that FirstBus favoured bus guideways rather than light rail schemes. This was highlighted in an address given by Moir Lockhead to the Chartered Institute of Transport at

Resting close to Shrewsbury bus station is Midland Red West low-floor Plaxton Pointer-bodied Dennis Dart SLF 341 (N341EUY) which was purchased for operation on Shropshire County Council tendered services. As will be seen, it carried promotional Super low-floor bus lettering on its side panels. (M.H.A.Flynn)

Unique in the FirstBus fleet, Brewers Van Hool A600 506 (G841PNW) was acquired from Yorkshire Rider who had never operated it since gaining it with the business of Rhodes of Yeadon in April 1994. (S.R.Procter)

Having recently arrived from Yorkshire Rider, ECW-bodied Bristol VRT WWY122S was immediately pressed into service by its new owner Eastern Counties still wearing Rider's cream & green livery and fleet numbers. It is seen here at Bury ***St.Edmunds in April 1996. (M.H.A.Flynn)***

Ipswich in March when he stated that 'in terms of value for money, light rail schemes could be classed as fairly expensive, especially when compared to lower-cost operations such as guided busways'. He went on to illustrate that in the case of the Sheffield SuperTram, this served only 3-4% of the population whereas buses served 100%.

Although FirstBus's core business continued to be local bus operation, a number of its subsidiaries still maintained an interest in the leisure market with excursions and tours etc. One of the most prolific in this field was Midland Red Coaches who operated a 17-strong fleet from Midland Red West's Redditch depot. In preparation for the 1996 season a major refurbishment programme was put in hand under which 10 of the company's coaches were to be re-panelled, re-upholstered and re-painted into a new all-red livery. In addition to its customary extended holiday tour programme, new destinations were added to the Isle of Man and North Devon as a result of popular demand whilst several new day tours were also offered. Taking another step forward in leisure travel, following an approach by some employees of Eastern Counties the company agreed that there was an opening in the market for a tourist service in Norwich and its surrounds operated by double deck buses and to this end approached Stratford-on-Avon based Guide Friday, a specialist in this field, to see if it would be interested in joining this venture. Following several meetings between the two companies, an agreement was reached whereby the tour would be operated every half hour during the Spring Bank Holiday period and again through the peak summer holiday season initially using one of Guide Friday's open-top buses. Quickly proving successful, Eastern Counties replaced the Guide Friday vehicles from 20 July with two of its own open-top Bristol VRTs, both of which had been repainted into the Stratford-based company's green and cream livery for their new duties. Another innovation on the opposite side of Britain which had commenced on 20 May came at the behest of the cycling campaign group 'Wheelwrights 2000' who persuaded South Wales Transport to provide a service for the riders of pedal-powered machines wishing to explore parts of the West Country and South Wales. As a result of their pleas, SWT introduced what was believed to be the first cycle **carrying coach service in Britain by adapting its Duple 425 coaches to** accommodate cycles in their luggage holds. Employed on its Wales - West Country Shuttle service from Tenby to Bath, these coaches soon began to justify their modification and particularly at weekends carried a full compliment of cycles in both directions. Meanwhile, following a controversial suspension by the Ministry of Transport of Swansea-based Brian Isaac Coaches operators licence pending the testing of its entire fleet, such was the feeling over this ruling that South Wales Transport along with several other local operators offered a hand of friendship by taking over Isaacs services for five days until his licence was restored.

Confirming that investment was a cornerstone of FirstBus policy, in

Although its lower panels had been repainted red and its front cream by its new owner Eastern Counties, former Thamesway ECW-bodied Leyland Olympian 103 (XHK273X) still retained the yellow sides and maroon between decks band of its former operator Thamesway ***when seen at Ipswich in April 1996. (M.H.A.Flynn)***

Peeping out of Greyfriars bus station, Northampton is Plaxton Paramount 3200-bodied Leyland Tiger 18 (BUY18Y) which was transferred to Northampton Transport from Leicester Citybus in ***1996. (K.A.Jenkinson)***

CityBus from Timeline in 1996, 406 (G56RND) is seen in August 1997 after being repainted into the livery of its new owner. (K.A.Jenkinson)

With a school bus sign in its windscreen, Bristol Omnibus Co. dual-door ECW-bodied Bristol VRT 5150 (AHW201V) seen resting at Lawrence Hill depot had rejoined the City Line fleet from Durbins in 1996. (K.A.Jenkinson)

addition to placing massive orders for new vehicles, the group also acknowledged the need to progressively upgrade the premises of its operating companies. To this end, Leeds City Link opened a new depot at Cherry Row close to Leeds city centre on 19 April which was to replace that at Torre Road after operations on the following day. Built at a cost of £1.5 million, the new depot which comprised a large open-air parking area, a well-equipped eight-bay workshop and new office block was far more secure than the 59-year old Torre Road premises which had been a constant target for vandalism and the seat of several fires. Less than two months later on 21 June, the Rider Group closed its headquarters at Cleckheaton, to which it had moved less than a year earlier, and relocated its functions to its depots at Kirkstall Road, Leeds and Skircoat Road, Halifax.

After a long period of conflict, a truce was called in Southend by Thamesway and Southend Transport on 18 May when the FirstBus subsidiary withdrew from Shoeburyness in exchange for Southend Transport vacating Canvey and the tickets of each company became inter-available. Earlier on 4 May Thamesway had introduced fifteen new Plaxton Pointer-bodied Darts on London Transport contracted service 191 while service revisions by Eastern Counties brought about the closure of three of its long-standing outstations at Aylsham, Dereham and Long Stratton. At around this same time Eastern National moved its Maldon outstation to new premises at Station Road and on 24 May closed its small depot at Walton-on-the-Naze, its four bus allocation then being transferred to its parent depot at Clacton. Although no longer operational, this depot remained in use for the storage of delicensed vehicles etc. pending a buyer being found. Soon after the integration of Badgerline and City Line's operations had taken place at the start of the year, a number of surveys were undertaken in preparation for the reorganisation of many of the company's services which it was hoped would halt the decline in the number of people using public transport. The first of these changes related to the Yate corridor where routes around that town and Sodbury were simplified, speeded up and increased in frequency. The second phase which took place on 28 July involved the Gloucester/Dursley/Thornbury routes which in addition to being altered were also changed as far as the types of vehicles used was concerned. Amongst these were the X10/X14 from Bristol to Magor/Monmouth via the M32 and M48 motorways to which Dennis Lances were now allocated; the 300 from Bristol - Chepstow which was maintained by Dennis Darts and the 308/309 Bristol - Gloucester/Dursley routes which were now placed under the control of the Optare StarRiders. Badgerline had also gained the contract to operate the new Bath park & ride service from Odd Down whilst additionally it had its contracts for the other park & ride services in the town extended until the end of the year.

South Wales Transport Duple 425 coach 132 (ACY178A) arrives at Cardiff bus station on the "Shuttle" service from Swansea for which it is appropriately liveried and lettered. (K.A.Jenkinson)

Painted in its owner's new mauve & yellow livery, Thamesway Leyland Lynx 1411 (F411MNO) prepares to take its passengers onboard at Southend Central bus station. (D.W.Rhodes)

THE THREAT OF DIVESTMENT

Seeking to further strengthen its position in Scotland, FirstBus made an offer of £110 million to SB Holdings Ltd. in April in a bid to purchase all its assets which included Strathclyde Buses Ltd., Comlaw No.313 Ltd. (GCT) and Kelvin Central Buses Ltd. Included in the bid was Stagecoach's 21.7% stake in the company which it had been instructed to divest by the Office of Fair Trading a few weeks earlier. Born from Strathclyde PTE in 1993, SB Holdings operated two-thirds of the bus services in and to the south-east of Glasgow and operated a combined fleet of around 1,250 buses. Concluding the deal on 3 June, this acquisition moved FirstBus into pole position above Stagecoach as Britain's largest bus operator in terms of both market share and fleet size. Hardly before the ink had dried on this acquisition, however, Strathclyde PTA asked the Office of Fair Trading to refer the takeover to the Monopolies and Mergers Commission on the grounds that if FirstBus acquired a 66% market share in Greater Glasgow, it could make service cuts that would seriously affect the PTA's already tight budget. Additionally, assurances were sought that FirstBus would co-operate with the PTA and that it would consult with it before introducing any fares increases. As will be seen later, this move prompted action from the OFT which led to FirstBus being instructed to divest of Midland Bluebird and part of its operations in Glasgow........ In the meantime, however, Strathclyde buses began to receive the first of its 120 low-emission double and single deck Alexander-bodied Volvos which it had ordered prior to joining the FirstBus group.

The progressive upgrading of the combined FirstBus fleet continued throughout the early summer with the arrival of four more Plaxton Premiere 350 Expressliner-bodied Dennis Javelins for South Wales Transport in June, these being painted in National Express Rapide livery for operation on the company's high-mileage routes from Haverfordwest to London and Birmingham. As part of its plan to modernise its Greater Manchester fleet, 10 Alexander Dash-bodied Volvo B6s made their debut in July soon after the arrival of 10 low-floor Wright-bodied Volvo B6LEs and 5 low-floor Wright Liberator-bodied Volvo B10Ls whilst in addition, 7 one-year old Mercedes Benz 709Ds were acquired from Yorkshire Rider together with a quantity of MCW Metrobuses which were surplus to requirements in Leeds. Apart from the continued flow of new vehicles and the inter-company movements of others, both Eastern Counties and Eastern National embarked upon programmes to extend the lives of a number of their Bristol VRTs by differing degrees of refurbishment. In the case of Eastern Counties, after dispatching a small number to Mainline's workshops at Rotherham where they were given a major rebuild, it was then decided to undertake this work 'in-house' on a reduced scale. Eastern National, however, contracted Marshall S.P.V. at Cambridge to undertake the refurbishment of its VRTs, this work resulting in a total body overhaul to an extremely high standard. To cover for this work, one of Thamesway's driver training Bristol VRTs (3101) was returned to full passenger-carrying status and placed back in service with Eastern National. In the interim period, South

Immaculately presented in Strathclyde Buses pre-FirstBus orange & black livery is Alexander-bodied Volvo Citybus AH14 (F96JYS). (M.Currie)

Acquired by Strathclyde Buses from Busways, Newcastle following the devastating fire at its Larkfield depot in 1993, Alexander-bodied Leyland Atlantean GLA35 (SCN272S) is seen at Croftfoot painted in the attractive green & yellow livery of low-cost unit GCT. (M.Currie)

Passing through Newport bus station on its way to London's Heathrow and Gatwick airports, South Wales Transport Plaxton Expressliner-bodied Dennis Javelin 111 (M111PWN) wore the attractive National Express Airlink livery to which route details were added along its side panels. (K.A.Jenkinson)

Following its acquisition by Strathclyde Buses, Kelvin's fleet was enhanced with several secondhand double deckers one of which, Roe-bodied Leyland Atlantean LA546 (WAG378X) seen leaving Buchanan bus station, Glasgow originated with Kingston-upon-Hull City Transport. (K.A.Jenkinson)

Painted in the orange, black & white livery of GM Buses North and adorned with logos and lettering to signify its low-floor configuration is Wright Crusader-bodied Volvo B6 1071 (N71YNF) which joined the fleet in 1995. (Mark Fitzgerald)

Greater Manchester purchased a number of minibuses and double deckers from the Rider Group during 1996/7 including former Leeds City Link MCW Metrobus 5568 (B568RWY) seen in its new owner's orange livery at Manchester Piccadilly. (K.S.E.Till)

Wales Transport repainted three of its Bristol VRTs into an all-red livery and adorned them with the fleet name 'The Original Big Red Bus' for use on two new low-cost 70p flat fare services numbered 426/7 from Swansea to Blaen-y-Maes and Penlan/Clase started on 28 May in retaliation to competition from local operator Pullman.

Pursuing its experiments into the operation of compressed natural gas-powered buses, FirstBus decided to extend its trials to Northampton and to this end announced that it was to purchase 6 CNG-powered full-size low-floor single deckers for Northampton Transport and install a fast-fill refuelling pump at its depot. With support from the local council and British Gas, it was planned to introduce the new vehicles in the spring of 1997 on a route serving the Kingsthorpe area of the town which operates through several housing developments and although the actual type of vehicle to be purchased had yet to be decided, talks were initiated with Volvo in respect of its B10L model and Mercedes Benz for its 0405. A further development in Northampton initiated by the County Council was the installation in Abingdon Square of selective vehicle detection equipment which allowed buses fitted with special tags to be identified and given priority at traffic lights. Buses owned by both Northampton Transport and Stagecoach United Counties were fitted with the necessary equipment to enable them to trigger the traffic lights and thus speed up their journeys and the County Council promised that if this proved successful, they would install SVD equipment at a further six sites by the end of March 1997.

When released early in July. the results of the first full trading year of FirstBus showed that the city would have to wait a little longer for substantial improvements despite it becoming impatient for immediate gains. Nevertheless, as a consequence of its acquisitions, the Group's turnover had grown by 8.3% from £329.1 million in 1994 to £356.3 million, although pre-tax profits had fallen from £24.8 million to £22 million. During the year, FirstBus had invested a new total of £40.4 million for 524 new buses, £4.1 million on secondhand vehicles and vehicle refurbishment and £5.2 million in depots and other plant and equipment. In addition, commitments were made to invest £21 million in 252 additional new buses and coaches plus £9.8 million for 120 new vehicles for Greater Manchester and £21 million for 210 new buses for SB Holdings. Commenting on the year's results, Moir Lockhead said that the general drift of passengers was downwards despite there having been real passenger growth in some areas and that the greatest decline was on the urban networks where, perhaps, the Group had most to lose. Still confident about its future, however, it was stated that the operating profit margin of 15% by March 1997 in the original bus companies - a target set only twelve months earlier - was now likely to be the margin rate for the whole trading period in those companies. Apart from its bus operations, FirstBus was also looking towards the railways as a means of further expansion and having already gained experience in this field through its 24.5% interest in Great Western Holdings now involved itself in a joint venture with the management team of The South Eastern Train Company to enter a bid for the forthcoming South East Trains franchise. Under the title of Arrow Railways Limited, the new joint company was confident that, if given the opportunity, it could vastly improve the performance and profitability of the suburban services in South London and Kent still operated at that time by British Rail.

On a more personal note Moir Lockhead, FirstBus's deputy chairman and chief executive, was awarded the OBE for services to the bus industry in the recent Queen's Birthday Honours. Having started his career in the industry as an apprentice fitter with United Automobile Services at Darlington and later holding various positions

One of three ECW-bodied Bristol VRTs repainted into an all-red livery and adorned with 'The Original Big Red Bus' fleet names for operation on dedicated services in the Swansea area, South Wales Transport 976 (BEP976V) heads out of Swansea on the 426 service to Blaen y Maes in May 1996. (D.P.B.Davies)

Loaned by its bodybuilder to South Wales Transport to cover for the absence of its own buses of this type which were progressively returned for remedial attention, all-white liveried Plaxton Pointer-bodied Dennis Dart N742GKH was given temporary fleet number 560 during its stay in Swansea where it is seen here working the 224 service to Margam. (Travelscene)

Standing in Reading station is one of Great Western Railways Inter-City 125 high speed trains. (F.W.York)

Grampian's coach-seated Alexander-bodied Renault S56 141 (E110JNH) seen here sporting Beaver Bus fleet names joined the fleet in 1994 from Northampton Transport. (B.Newsome)

in the industry, he had taken over the general managership of Grampian Regional Transport in 1985 and led its employee buyout four years later. Guiding GRT through its flotation in 1994 as GRT Bus Group Plc, he was instrumental in the merger with Badgerline during the following year which resulted in the creation of FirstBus and thus his elevation to the higher echelons in June was richly deserved.

In an attempt to encourage passengers back into the heart of Manchester in the wake of the IRA's devastating attack on the city's Arndale Centre on 15 June, FirstBus subsidiary Greater Manchester at the beginning of July introduced a special £1 return fare on Saturdays for all journeys terminating in the city centre. These fares applied all day so that people could enjoy all the shopping and entertainment facilities on offer and support the city at the same time. Following this move, early in August Greater Manchester teamed up with Manchester Metrolink to offer a reduced price tram ticket which was also available for use on its buses to allow passengers to get nearer the city centre shops. Although Greater Manchester had, as mentioned earlier, revised its livery to all-over orange with a blue band, the latter was replaced by a yellow band on low-floor single deckers to provide easier recognition to passengers of their easier access. Another FirstBus subsidiary to alter its livery and fleet name was Strathclyde Buses who adopted an all-over red scheme and although this was not officially launched until 27 November, one of the company's Alexander-bodied Leyland Olympians was thus repainted in August and given Greater Glasgow fleet names in corporate FirstBus-style lettering. Prior to this, Strathclyde Buses on 17 July received a low-floor Alexander Ultra-bodied Volvo B10L demonstrator which it operated from its Parkhead depot for a month

Illustrating Strathclyde Buses new all-red livery and Greater Glasgow fleet names is Alexander-bodied Volvo Olympian VO101 (P202TGD) at Summerston on its first day in service. (M.Currie)

Resting in Greater Manchester's Oldham depot a few days before entering service, Wright Crusader-bodied Volvo B6LE 1085 (N385CRJ) had a yellow band and Superbus lettering added to its orange livery. (B.Newsome)

Next page, top to bottom left :

Wearing Thames Transit livery to which FirstBus-style Provincial fleet names have been added, former Blue Admiral dual-door Mellor-bodied Iveco 59.12 231 (K715UTT) heads through Southsea enroute to Paulsgrove in June 1996. (T.S.Blackman)

Fresh from the paintshop, Bradford Traveller Roe-bodied Leyland Olympians 5098 (A98KUM) and 5114 (A114KUM) both wore experimental liveries. In the event neither were adopted, the scheme settled upon using the same shades of blue as 5098 but in the style of 5114. (K.A.Jenkinson)

Painted in standard Eastern Counties colours but given Rosemary Coaches fleet names for operation in the Kings Lynn area is Leyland National 1770 (XNG770S). (P.Kay)

Having had its rear panels repainted blue for operation in PMT's Pennine fleet, PMT-bodied Mercedes Benz L608D MMM155 (D155BEH) leaves Ashton-under-Lyne on a journey to Glossop in 1994. (K.A.Jenkinson)

A unique vehicle in the PMT fleet is Talbot Pullman MXP449 (K449XRF) which was purchased new in 1992 and is seen here sporting Red Rider fleet names at Moreton depot. (P.Kay)

Top to bottom right :

One of several Alexander-bodied Leyland Atlanteans acquired by Greater Glasgow from Grampian Transport in 1997, LA1452 (HSD290V) at Clydebank bus station shows off the all-red livery of its new owner. (M.McClintock)

Carrying Leicester Citybus's new livery and corporate FirstBus-style fleet names, Northern Counties-bodied Renault S56 752 (H752ENR) passes St.Margaret's bus station, Leicester in August 1997 on its way to Birstall. (K.A.Jenkinson)

One of a pair of Midland Bluebird low-floor Plaxton Pointer-bodied Dennis Dart SLFs painted in Easyboarder livery, 202 (P202NSC) poses for the photographer on the forecourt of Bannockburn depot in September 1997. (K.A.Jenkinson)

Leaving St.Andrew bus station, Edinburgh at the start of its journey to Ballingry in September 1997 is Lowland's Wright Axcess Ultralow-bodied Scania L113CRL 576 (P576DMS) which carries FifeFirst fleet names. (K.A.Jenkinson)

PAULSGROVE
Provincial
K715 UTT

EXACT FARE
6
Greater Glasgow
HSO 290V

Hirst Wood 640
5098
Bradford Traveller
A98 KUM

Birstall
Leicester Citybus
752
H752 ENR

770
Rosemary Coaches
XNG 770S

E68 University (Macrobert Centre)
EASYBOARDER
202
P202 NSC
PLAXTON

Red Rider

BALLINGRY via DUNFERMLINE 56
EDINBURGH - ROSYTH - DUNFERMLINE - CROSSGATES - HILL OF BEATH - COWDENBEATH - LOCHGELLY - LOCHORE - BALLINGRY
FifeFirst
576
SCANIA
P576 DMS

Grampian's Optare Prisma-bodied Mercedes Benz 0405 542 (P542BSS) with Gold Service lettering on its cove panels, stands outside Marshall College in Broad Street, Aberdeen whilst operating service 19 to Culter. (J.L.Hobbs)

on service 61. Another FirstBus company to place low-floor single deckers in service was Bristol Omnibus Company who put seven new Plaxton Pointer-bodied Dennis Dart SLFs into service at Weston-super-Mare on 1 August. Specifically purchased for operation on route 7 from North Worle to Oldmixon Estate and painted in Badgerline livery, these 10.7m 35-seat buses were equipped with a kneeling facility to provide easier access for less able bodied passengers and those with pushchairs etc.

Earlier in the summer, PMT had launched a new innovative service in partnership with Stoke-on-Trent City Council and local industry under the title of 'China Link'. This incorporated 36 different pottery factories, shops and museums including such famous names as Wedgewood and Royal Doulton and was aimed at boosting the number of visitors to the area. Continuing on the tourist trail, Western National had also introduced a number of summer services which were designed to encourage an increased number of passengers and provide the company with extra revenue. With the support of Devon County Council and the Dartmoor National Park Authority, a special network of Sunday and summer holiday services was launched which served Dartmoor and its surrounding area while similarly in Cornwall the route pattern was modified and enhanced to serve even more places of beauty and historic interest. Extending its Gold Service network yet further, Grampian Transport converted a further four routes on 12 May using recently delivered Optare Prisma-bodied Mercedes Benz 0405s and a number of refurbished Leyland Olympians and from 1 July to 25 August operated the summertime subsidised service 14A from Rose Street to Sea Beach which it had lost to Mairs in 1995. Another supported service gained was the M22 Bridgeton Cross - Castlemilk Monday to Saturday evening operation in Glasgow won by Strathclyde Buses' low-cost GCT unit. Proving that some you win, some you lose, upon retendering Lowland lost the contract for the Borders Rail Link service from Galashiels to Carlisle. This was taken over by MacEwans of Amisfield on 2 June, although Lowland retained some commercially operated Saturday journeys on this route. Leicester CityBus once again offered a full programme of summer day tours to an enlarged range of destinations and to assist with this development it acquired four additional coaches from other members of the FirstBus group - 2 LAG Galaxys from Durbins and 2 Duple Caribbean-bodied Leyland Tigers from SMT. Also joining the Leicester fleet was a Leyland Leopard from Kelvin Central Buses and a number of Dodge S56 minibuses from Rider York.

In a move to further consolidate its position in East Anglia, FirstBus made an offer via its Eastern Counties subsidiary in August for the business and assets of municipally-owned Great Yarmouth Transport who operated a fleet of some 41 vehicles. This was accepted and immediately following the takeover on 29 September an announcement was made that the former municipal company would eventually be fully merged with Eastern Counties Yarmouth operations with the combined fleet being rebranded as 'Blue Bus' with its own individual livery of cream and blue applied in Eastern Counties fashion. The two different fare structures were, however, standardised straight away with price reductions resulting on several urban routes and early in November Eastern Counties vacated its Wellington Street depot in the town, moving its operations to the former Great Yarmouth Transport premises. Despite giving FirstBus a larger share of the bus market in Norfolk and Suffolk, the deal was approved by the Secretary of State for Transport.

In order to enable staff to be given 'on site' instruction on the use of FirstBus's new computerised stores system, two of City Line's Mercedes Benz L608D minibuses were converted into mobile classroom/instruction units and, painted in a Grampian-style livery of ivory and green with FirstBus and Lombard lettering, visited various companies within the group. Around this same time, FirstBus used one of Lowland's new low-floor Wright-bodied Scania L113CRL single deckers to assess passenger reaction to a choice of three different interior designs in order to produce a standard interior decor for all the Group's future vehicles. Together with one of Eastern Counties new low-floor Plaxton Pointer-bodied Dennis SLFs which was used in

It obviously pays to advertise. Displaying posters in almost every available position, Great Yarmouth Transport ECW-bodied Bristol VRT 30 (CVF30T) in its owner's blue & cream livery is seen in the centre of its home town on a journey to North Denes. (T.S.Blackman)

Repainted in Eastern Counties-style livery but using cream and two-tone blue and given Blue Bus fleet names and FirstBus logos is former Great Yarmouth Transport MCW Metrorider 781 (D604AFR) which originated with Blackburn Transport. (S.R.Procter)

One of a pair of former Bristol City Line Mercedes Benz L608D minibuses converted into mobile classrooms, D515FAE seen at the Great Yarmouth depot of Eastern Counties carried FirstBus fleet names on its ivory & green livery as well as lettering for Lombard finance. (M.H.A.Flynn)

a similar role, between them they toured all FirstBus's subsidiaries around Britain for a few weeks before settling down in normal service with their intended operators. Additionally, to assist it with its summer coaching programme Lowland hired a LAG Eos and 9 Van Hool-bodied DAF coaches from Hughes DAF (dealers) at Cleckheaton, operating these in an all-white livery until their return in the early autumn. Joining these at the beginning of the summer on a permanent basis were 3 Van Hool-bodied Scania K113 coaches which, rather than being painted in Lowland's coaching livery were instead given an attractive dark green and silver scheme and were appropriately lettered for use on Prestige Tours duties.

Continuing the steady merging of Badgerline and City Line's functions within the FirstBus empire, August 1 saw existing City Line managers put in charge at each Badgerline depot and following the departure of Les Birchley, Badgerline's fleet engineer, to Provincial, this position was added to the duties of City Line fleet engineer Stuart Bond. Soon after these moves took place, Martin Curtis who had recently moved from Badgerline to Bristol Omnibus Company as its business development manager left the company whilst Martin Sutton, Badgerline's managing director, had resigned his post in July. Stuart Bond was elevated to become engineering director of Bristol Omnibus Company with Chris Jones assuming his vacated role. With the personnel reorganisation in Bristol now completed it was decided that the time had come when some form of co-ordination should be implemented between FirstBus and some of the independent operators with which it competed in the city. Following an approach by A-Bus who operated between Bristol and Keynsham in competition with Badgerline, agreement was reached to co-ordinate their services so that frequencies could be enhanced and long term stability be achieved. Thus, from 28 September A-Bus increased its

Painted in a dark green & white livery with yellow waistband for the Air Shuttle service from Cardiff to the city's airport is Brewers Plaxton Pointer-bodied Dennis Dart 616 (N616MHB). (S.R.Procter)

Next page, top to bottom left :

Still painted in Great Yarmouth Transport's pre-FirstBus livery is Carlyle-bodied Dennis Dart G457KNG seen at prior to leaving for Ipswich on Suffolk Sunday Bus route 645. (M.H.A.Flynn)

Carrying a yellow & blue version of PMT's standard livery for dedicated operation on the Bradwell to Hanley service, ECW-bodied Leyland Olympian DOG734 (A734GFA) is seen leaving Hanley bus station on the route concerned. (K.A.Jenkinson)

Eastern National Plaxton-bodied Mercedes Benz 0814 2702 (P702PWC) passes along Duke Street, Chelmsford on service 41 to Galleywood in July 1997. (J.Podgorski)

Purchased by Strathclyde Buses from Kingston-upon-Hull in 1995 for operation in its Kelvin fleet, Roe-bodied Leyland Atlantean LA546 (WAG378X) leaves Buchanan bus station, Glasgow on a journey to Harestanes. (K.A.Jenkinson)

Top to bottom right :

Badgerline 8610 (A810THW), a convertible open-top Roe-bodied Leyland Olympian in Coast Rider livery makes its way from Weston-super-Mare to Burnham-on-Sea which is incorrectly quoted on its electronic destination screen. (F.W.York)

Illustrating one of the liveries used by Midland Bluebird subsidiary Kings of Dunblane, Plaxton Paramount 3200-bodied Leyland Tiger 160 (D591MVR)seen at Bannockburn depot in September 1997 was acquired from Rover of Horsley in 1993 but was new to Shearings of Wigan. (K.A.Jenkinson)

Seen at Liverpool Street Station is CentreWest Routemaster RML2609 which carries details of route 23 above its lower deck side windows. (J.A.Godwin)

Passing through shadows in The Quadrant bus station, Swansea is South Wales Transport Leyland National 808 (WWN808T). (D.P.B.Davies)

Passing through Shelf on its way to Newlands on route 534 whilst being evaluated by Calderline on 3 August 1996 is Plaxton Pointer-bodied Dennis Dart SLF demonstrator N305DHE. (B.Newsome)

645 IPSWICH VIA
Diss & Woodbridge
G457 KNG

Badgerline
COASTRIDER
A810 THW

417 BRADWELL
every 30 minutes
ERIC ALCOCK
Panasonic

Midland Bluebird
KINGS of Dunblane
KINGS
D591 MVR

GALLEYWOOD
via Gt. Baddow
41
Eastern National
2702
P702 PWC

23
LIVERPOOL STREET
CENTREWEST
Oxford Street Marble Arch Paddington Station Westbourne Grove Ladbroke Grove
RML 2609

NETWORK
Make the first move!
HARESTANES
23

Townhill Circular
SWT
808
WWN 808T

FLY TO FLORIDA FROM LEEDS BRADFORD AIRPORT

Castlemilk
19
GCT
MVK 503R

FAREHAM
5
Provincial
601
N601 EBP

Great Yarmouth
BlueBus
Blue Bus
PLAXTON

Lowland
HAWICK
95
P508 XSH

16
Southend
Bus Station
Thamesway
P703 HPU

Belhaven Best. Smooth beyond belief.
Auchinairn Circle
45
Greater Glasgow

3
Rider York

Kelvin
First Express
Express Service
Kelvin

Western National low-floor Plaxton Pointer-bodied Dennis Dart SLF 433 (P433ORL) had a yellow sash incorporated in its livery to which promotional lettering was later to be added. (J.L.Hobbs)

fares on its services 347 and 349 whilst Badgerline reduced its charges to passengers to reach a common scale and tickets of the two operators became interchangeable. Soon after the changes in Bristol came into being, Brewers launched a new service from Cardiff Station to the city's Airport, running this on an hourly frequency with a Plaxton Pointer-bodied Dennis Dart which for the purpose was down-seated to carry 36 passengers, given extra luggage capacity and repainted into a special green, gold and white livery with appropriate lettering. Meanwhile, over in Essex following the sudden withdrawal of Fargo Coach Lines from local bus work in the Braintree area, Eastern National began the operation of a new temporary service from Braintree to Raine using a pair of Mercedes Benz L608Ds as well as a school service abandoned by Fargo.

Although September was proving to be a month of considerable activity, not all the events were of a pleasant nature as on the 16th of the month an arson attack on the yard of PMT's Rock Ferry depot on the Wirral peninsula destroyed 5 Leyland Olympians together with a withdrawn Bristol VRT and caused minor damage to 3 other vehicles. In order to assist the depot to maintain its services on the following day, Calderline loaned the company one of its ECW-bodied Olympians while PMT's Crosville depots at Ellesmere Port and

New to PMT and ultimately converted to a mobile information unit, ECW-bodied Bristol RESL6L JEH198K is now with Greater Manchester who has repainted it into an attractive red & yellow livery and continue to use it in this role. (S.R.Procter)

Acquired by Greater Manchester and now used as a driver training bus in a white livery with blue bands is ex.Grampian Alexander-bodied Leyland Atlantean 1422 (DSA254T) seen at Atherton depot in February 1997. (B.Newsome)

Previous page, top to bottom left :

Operating the special shuttle to Huddersfield University's halls of residence is Kingfisher Huddersfield 6339 (VWW339X), one of its first Roe-bodied Leyland Atlanteans to be painted in its new two-tone green & cream livery. (K.A.Jenkinson)

Passing St.Enoch Square, Glasgow on its way to Castlemilk is GCT GLA33 (MVK503R), one of a number of Alexander-bodied Leyland Atlanteans acquired from Busways, Newcastle in 1993. (K.A.Jenkinson)

Painted in Provincial's new cream & red livery, UVG Urban Star-bodied Dennis Dart 601 (N601EBP) makes its way to Fareham on route 5. As can be seen, although it carries a conventional roller destination blind it is fitted with an electronic route number. (F.W.York)

Painted in Eastern Counties-style livery but using two-tone blue instead of red & orange is Blue Bus low-floor Plaxton Pointer-bodied Dennis Dart 453 (P453RPW) which was new in 1997. (P.Kay)

Top to bottom right :

Lowland Wright Axcess Ultralow-bodied Scania L113CRL 506 (P506XSH) in its owner's yellow & green livery leaves St.Andrew bus station, Edinburgh on a journey to Hawick in February 1997. (Travelscene)

Making its way through St.Andrew Square, Edinburgh while undertaking a tour is Lowland Van Hool Alizee-bodied DAF MB200 2307 (ESX257, originally WFR612Y) painted in Ian Glass Coaches livery. (P.Kay)

Seen in Chichester Road, Southend-on-Sea in September 1996 is Thamesway low-floor Plaxton Pointer-bodied Dennis Dart SLF 703 (P703HPU). (D.W.Rhodes)

Although still painted in the orange & black livery of Strathclyde Buses, Alexander-bodied Volvo Citybus AH28 (G413OGD) seen passing Buchanan bus station, Glasgow in September 1997 had gained new corporate FirstBus-style Greater Glasgow fleet names. (K.A.Jenkinson)

Looking smart in its owner's new-style livery as it turns at York railway station in September 1997 is Rider York Wright Axcess Ultralow-bodied Scania L113CRL 8437 (R437GSF). (D.Robinson)

Leaving Buchanan bus station, Glasgow on the X3 service to Cumbernauld in September 1997 is Kelvin East Lancs-bodied Scania K93CRB SS4 (TIB8512) sporting First Express fleet names. (K.A.Jenkinson)

Stotts of Oldham's double deck fleet comprised mainly ex.GM Buses and Mainline Fleetlines. One of the former, Northern Counties-bodied YNA287M prepares to leave Ashton-under-Lyne bus station on a journey to Grotton on the 398 service. (K.S.E.Till)

Parked in Swansea after a journey from its home town is Porthcawl Omnibus Co. Duple-bodied Bedford YMT PWN339R which had been purchased from Jenkins of Skewen in 1980. (D.P.B.Davies)

Chester also provided a number of replacement vehicles. Additionally Greater Manchester dispatched one of its recently acquired but as yet unused ex.Strathclyde Buses Atlanteans to Rock Ferry although this was immediately returned from whence it came without having been operated.

Appearing to have lost patience with the slow progress of its light rail plans and its alternative transit schemes, FirstBus closed its Bath-based Transit Development Division in September as part of a restructuring programme under which development work on specific projects would be devolved to subsidiary operating companies under the aegis of business development director Ian Buchan at Leeds. As a result, James Freeman who had headed the Transit Development Division left FirstBus leaving such schemes as the Westway guided busway and Avon Gorge Expressway in the hands of City Line. Meanwhile, overseas franchising opportunities were continuing to be examined despite FirstBus having been unsuccessful in its recent bid to introduce a 50-bus operation in Wroclaw, Poland.

Having retained its contracts for the operation of London Transport local routes 362 and 462 in the Barking, Ilford and Hainault areas of Essex, Thamesway indicated that it would be introducing new low-floor midibuses to these services when the new contracts commenced in March 1997. Western National had in the meantime become the latest FirstBus subsidiary to introduce low-floor buses when in August it placed in service fourteen new Plaxton Pointer-bodied Dennis Dart SLFs on its service 18 between Truro and Penzance. Painted in a dedicated livery with a yellow flash added to the standard colour scheme, these broke new ground by being fitted with a rearward-facing baby seat over the front nearside wheel-arch to give parents the opportunity to put their infant in a safe, secure, purpose-designed seat and as such gave these buses an unusual seating capacity of 35 and a half! A further innovation was the introduction on 23 September by Eastern Counties of its Excel Service between Norwich, Kings Lynn and Peterborough. Operated by new Plaxton Premiere-bodied Volvo B10M coaches painted in a dedicated livery, this offered passengers a new package of service standards with a promise of compensation if these were not met. Eastern National also introduced a new service when on 30 September it commenced operations between Colchester bus station and the University of Essex. Using Bristol VRTs and operating during term times only, this route broke new ground by using roads previously unserved by public transport and on Saturday nights continuing to run beyond midnight, the latest a scheduled bus service had ever operated in the town. On the other side of the coin, however, Greater Manchester made significant changes to 85 of its commercial services on 1 October in a move which was designed to save around two million service miles per year. Included amongst these were 50 services which had frequency cuts or evening and Sunday withdrawals, several which were re-routed in Manchester city centre and ten which were completely discontinued. Blaming these revisions on customer usage and changing travel patterns, it was also stated by the company that it needed to catch up on profit targets which had been severely dented in the aftermath of the Arndale Centre bombing. These moves not surprisingly angered Manchester politicians who accused FirstBus of pursuing 'narrow commercial concerns' and forcing Greater Manchester PTA to having to further support services in order to maintain them. In the meantime, despite its moves to trim its operations in Greater Manchester, the FirstBus subsidiary of that name was continuing talks with Stotts of Oldham, an independent company who had expanded rapidly since its entry into the local bus market on deregulation day in 1986, with a view to purchasing a large part of its business. These eventually reached a conclusion on 23 November when Greater Manchester purchased four of Stotts' five local bus services in the Oldham and Tameside area (the fifth instead being discontinued) together with a number of its buses, leaving the independent to continue its schools contracts and develop its coaching operation. Prior to this move, FirstBus had further strengthened its position in South Wales when on 20 October its subsidiary Brewers purchased the local bus operations of old-established independent Porthcawl Omnibus whose owner John

Adorned with Gold Rider livery, Yorkshire Rider Jonckhere-bodied Volvo B10M 1403 (NIB4905, originally D403LUA) was one of the vehicles which passed to AJC of Leeds in exchange for its Angloblue operation and a number of Leyland Nationals.

Amongst the Leyland Nationals taken over by the Rider Group with the local services of AJC (Angloblue), Leeds was former Merseybus 6001 (SKF1T which had been registered BOK258T) seen here in Leeds city centre. Immediately placed in store by its new owner, it was eventually dispatched in April 1997 to join the Sky Blue fleet of Wessex at Bristol. (K.A.Jenkinson)

54
Leicester Citybus
627
C107 SDX

Bradford
576
Calderline
F167 XYG

HAIN STORE SECONDS
48A
Superbus

Greater Manchester

WESTERN NATIONAL
ODT 232

FLEXI EXPRESS
FLEXI

GOLD service
Grampian

Braunstone 160
Leicester Citybus
R2 LCB

305
"HAMTUN"
Citybus
G305 XCR

74
Slough &
High Wycombe
Slough-Heathrow 74-75
THE BEE LINE
L206 GMO

One of a trio of Northern Counties Paladin-bodied Dennis Darts acquired by the Rider Group from Greater Manchester in 1996, two of which were allocated to the Kingfisher Huddersfield fleet, 3299 (M615SBA) leaves Huddersfield bus station on a journey to Quarmby after being repainted into the two-tone green & cream livery of its new owner. (K.A.Jenkinson)

Painted in a white, red & blue livery and carrying Flexi fleet names and FirstBus logos, PMT Dormobile-bodied Ford Transit MFF178 (D166DNT) joined the fleet from Shropshire County Council in 1994. (P.Kay)

Williams was planning to retire. Included in the deal were ten vehicles (of which none were retained) and seven services, leaving Porthcawl's coaching and contract activities with Williams' family who were to continue their operation. Further pursuing its consolidation programme, FirstBus whose subsidiary Leeds City Link had been facing increasing competition from local independent AJC for more than a year had reached an agreement to exchange Yorkshire Rider's coaching unit which traded as Gold Rider for AJC's local Angloblue bus operations. Under this deal, Quickstep acquired all AJC's commercial bus services together with a number of its Leyland Nationals on 23 September in return for five of the Rider Group's Jonckheere-bodied Volvo B10M coaches, Gold Rider's order book and the right to use its name for an agreed period of time. In actuality, Quickstep had already been operating some of Angloblue's services on its behalf since 15 July due to staff shortages experienced by the independent. Following this deal, the only coaching activities to remain with Yorkshire Rider were its National Express operations and its subsidiary operations at Halifax and Bradford, the latter two of which were maintained with a small number of dual-purpose Leyland Tigers. For a brief period the acquired Leyland Nationals continued to be used by Quickstep (technically on hire to AJC) but were immediately withdrawn and placed in store for eventual disposal on 16 October when the deregistration of the Angloblue services became effective. Soon after these events, Yorkshire Rider's Huddersfield subsidiary Kingfisher regained its prominence in the town on 25 October when Horwich-based independent's Yorkshire Blue Bus ceased operation of all its services. Having crossed the Pennines in 1994 to start up operations in competition with Yorkshire Rider, it had introduced a number of competitive routes in Huddersfield and in addition had gained a handful of West Yorkshire tendered services. Having later also moved into Bradford on a small scale again in competition to Rider, it had even experimented briefly on a Calderline route before retrenching to Huddersfield. Following the ending of this mini bus war, Kingfisher reduced its frequencies on a number of services upon which it had previously suffered from Blue Bus's incursion and was simultaneously able to additionally reduce its fleet. As a result of the above and the conversion of a number of services from minibus to conventional size vehicles, more of its Mercedes Benz 709Ds were sold to Greater Manchester from whom a pair of Northern Counties-bodied Dennis Darts were acquired in part exchange.

October also witnessed the opening by Stoke-on-Trent City Council of its first all-year round park and ride site at Hinde Street, Hanley in partnership with PMT which tailored a package of fares and service levels to encourage use of the 600 space facility. Assisted by a package of bus priority measures in Hanley town centre, PMT diverted a number of its existing services to pick up at the Hinde Street on a four minute frequency between 8.30am and 6.30pm and every 15 minutes in the evenings and on Sundays. An inclusive £1 per day charge covered both parking and return travel for up to four car passengers with additional passengers paying 25p single or 45p return. Coinciding with the opening of this new facility, PMT placed in service 25 new Plaxton-bodied Mercedes Benz 709Ds which replaced some of the companies earlier generation Mercedes Benz L608D minibuses. Additionally, PMT's Crosville unit further strengthened its position in the southern part of the Wirral penninsula following the decision by independent Devaway to abandon all its out-stations and concentrate on services from its main operating centre at Bretton on the outskirts of Chester. As a consequence of this move, Crosville took over Devaway's Ellesmere Port services F4 and F7 together with three of that company's Optare City Pacers which were immediately

Previous page, top to bottom left :

Leicester Citybus 627 (C107SDX), a Northern Counties-bodied Dennis Falcon acquired from Ipswich Buses in 1997 still wears the livery of its previous owner albeit with the addition of new corporate FirstBus-style fleet names. (P.T.Stokes)

New to Badgerline registered D505GHY, Western National Van Hool Alizee-bodied Volvo B10M 2504 (ODT232) rests at Plymouth after completing a schools duty in April 1997. (I.H.Winchester)

8647 (L647PWR), one of Leeds City Link's Alexander Strider-bodied Scania N113CRBs used on the guided busway routes shows off its Superbus livery as it passes along Vicar Lane, Leeds on its way to City Square. (K.A.Jenkinson)

Borrowed by Leeds City Link for operation on its guided busway services, Grampian Transport Wright Cityranger-bodied Mercedes Benz 0405 514 (L514KSA) stands in City Square, Leeds. In addition to displaying FirstBus-style Grampian fleet names, it also has Gold Service lettering on its cove panels and Advance lettering above its front wheel arch. (P.Kay)

Southampton Citybus Carlyle-bodied Dennis Dart 305 picks up its passengers in its home city.

Top to bottom right :

Wearing Calderline's attractive new livery, Northern Counties-bodied Leyland Olympian 5167 (F167XYG) descends through Clayton heights on its way to Bradford on the Flagship 576 service in August 1997. (K.A.Jenkinson)

Still painted in GM Buses North livery but having gained new FirstBus-style Greater Manchester fleet names, one of the company's remaining Northern Counties-bodied Dodge S56s 1845 (D845LND) turns into Bolton bus station in February 1997. (K.A.Jenkinson)

Acquired by PMT from C & M, Aintree in 1992, North West Coach Sales-bodied Mercedes Benz 811D 102 (F452YHF) is part of its owner's Flexi fleet based at Newcastle depot where it is seen here. (P.Kay)

302 (R2LCB), one of Leicester Citybus's new low-floor Optare Excels passes through the centre of Leicester on its way to Braunstone in August 1997. (P.Kay)

Given lettering on its side panels for the 74 & 75 services is Berks Bucks Plaxton Pointer-bodied Dennis Dart 206 (L206GMO).

Pictured at Ipswich displaying a Suffolk County Connections board in jits windscreen is Waylands Marshall-bodied Mercedes Benz 709D M242AEX which became 804 in the Eastern Counties fleet. (J.Podgorski)

Standing at the entrance to Burslem depot in May 1996 are PMT Plaxton Pointer-bodied Dennis Darts IDC960/1 (M960/1XVT), both of which display new corporate FirstBus-style fleet names. (R.Williams)

One of nine Plaxton Beaver-bodied Mercedes Benz 709Ds transferred from Kingfisher Huddersfield to Rider York, 2231 (M231VWU) was still painted in its original owner's colours when photographed travelling along Station Avenue, York with an uninformative destination display. (K.A.Jenkinson)

withdrawn and placed in store by their new owner pending disposal. In the meantime, following a lengthy saga dating back to February 1992 when Bridgend bus station was closed by the receiver following the collapse of National Welsh, its long-awaited replacement finally opened on 14 October after several delays with Brewers having the honour of undertaking the first departure, the 6.20am X1 service to Port Talbot.

After operating from two sites in Aberdeen and Weston-super-Mare since its formation, FirstBus took the decision to set up new corporate headquarters in London so as to be closer to the City business community and be more easily accessible to all its operating companies. Establishing its new base at Weymouth Street close to Harley Street in October, as well as providing office accommodation for the executive chairman, chief executive, finance director and head of investor relations, the property incorporated a board room, general offices, spare office accommodation for the use of other FirstBus personnel visiting London and even a flat where staff involved in late meetings could stay overnight.

Having consolidated its position in Great Yarmouth, Eastern

Counties now turned its attention to Beccles, some ten miles away, and on 27 October purchased the business of Berry of Warlingham who traded under the title of Waylands Minibus. Its ten vehicles - nine minibuses and a Leyland Tiger coach - were all included in the deal and for at least the time being it was decided to maintain Waylands as a separate operating unit. Four weeks later on 27 November, Eastern Counties introduced new low-floor Plaxton Pointer-bodied Dennis Darts to its Hellesdon - City - University and City - Sprowston services in Norwich and gained approval for the introduction of a new service between Clayton and Ipswich which was to be branded 'Superoute 88' and would operate along a special road controlled by retractable bollards. It was, however, to be some time before this new service became operational, of which more later. With an eye on the future as far as its vehicle requirement was concerned, Eastern Counties borrowed two demonstrators - a UVG Urbanstar-bodied Dennis Dart and a Plaxton Pointer-bodied Volvo B6 - for evaluation at Norwich and Ipswich respectively, although neither of these appeared to generate orders for FirstBus's East Anglian subsidiaries.

Adorned in Scottish Citylink colours and resting in St.Andrew bus station following its journey from Aberdeen, Edinburgh is Mairs Irizar-bodied Scania P20GRT. (S.R.Procter)

QUALITY PARTNERSHIPS

Seeing Quality Transport Partnerships as the most effective way forward to easing traffic congestion and improving bus reliability, following the local partnerships established earlier in the year in Hereford, Leicester, Norwich and Worcester, FirstBus subsidiary Strathclyde Buses entered into a similar agreement with Strathclyde PTA and Glasgow City Council in October. Under this new partnership Strathclyde Buses undertook to purchase 200 new buses over the next two years and provide a higher standard of services to its passengers whilst the PTA and Glasgow City Council pledged their support by introducing traffic management on the main routes into the city, bus priority measures which would speed-up services, provide high-tech information systems at bus stops and make passenger waiting areas more pleasant and secure. As stated earlier, on 27 November Strathclyde Buses officially launched its new livery of all-over red which was to be applied to all its buses including those of GCT and Kelvin and replaced its Strathclyde's Buses fleet name with a new Greater Glasgow identity which, along with GCT and Kelvin was to be applied in corporate-style lettering along with the FirstBus logo. Confirming its promises, the first of the new buses - low-floor Alexander-bodied Volvo B10Ls - made their debut on that same day on the 61 service between Maryhill and Tollcross wearing Greater Glasgow's new colours. A week later, Strathclyde PTA switched on its new 'BusTime' passenger information system which was transmitted to 57 bus stops along Maryhill Road and in Glasgow city centre. For this purpose, around half of Strathclyde Buses vehicles were fitted with small tags above their passenger entrance doors which transmitted information to a central control room via 88 roadside beacons.

Looking further ahead, at the start of November FirstBus who had already submitted indicative bids for the Thameslink and Regional Railways North East rail franchises and were in the process of completing final bids for the Great Eastern, Anglia, and West Anglia Great Northern franchises, formed a joint venture with the management team of Birmingham-based Central Trains Limited and lodged a bid for the Central Trains franchise which comprised both urban and inter-urban services. At this same time, FirstBus was also making moves to further enhance its bus operations by placing an offer for the purchase of Dundee-based Tayside Public Transport Company. Also expressing interest were Stagecoach, Yorkshire Traction, Cowie, The Go-Ahead Group and National Express subsidiary Travel West Midlands and thus FirstBus had to play the waiting game until the outcome was announced at the start of the new year. In the event it was unsuccessful in its attempt to increase its share of the Scottish bus market with the Tayside company passing to the ownership of Travel West Midlands. In the meantime, however, FirstBus announced its order for 914 new buses at a cost of £80 million. Of these, 584 were scheduled for delivery during the year ending 31 March 1998 with the balance arriving during the remainder of that year and early in 1999. The order comprised 176 Volvo Olympian double deckers of which 134 were to be bodied by Alexander and 42 by Northern Counties; 10 Optare Excels, 145 Wright-bodied Scania L113s, 102 Wright-bodied Volvo B10BLEs, 257 Plaxton-bodied Dennis Darts, 207 Plaxton-bodied Mercedes Benz 810Ds and 6 Optare MetroRiders with the remaining 11 still to be decided upon. Announcing soaring pre-tax profits up 65% at £23.5 million on an increased turnover of £246.8 million for the six months to 30 September 1996, FirstBus stated that without restructuring and other exceptional costs of £2.2 million, the interim result would have been 81% ahead at £25.7 million. The most profitable region by margin was Scotland with 17.6% whilst the North of England followed with 14.3%, Midlands and South East with 13.7% and Wales and the South West with 13.5%. These strong results reflected the considerable progress made during the period concerned which were in part due to marketing initiatives such as Smartcards, travel shops

Pictured at Summerston on its first day in service (4 December 1996) is Greater Glasgow's low-floor Wright-bodied Volvo B10L SV553 (P188UNS) adorned with its owner's new all-red livery. (M.Currie)

Travelling along the Scott Hall Road guided busway on its way to Alwoodley is Leeds City Link silver & blue Superbus-liveried Alexander Strider-bodied Scania N113CRB 8641 (L641PWR). (K.A.Jenkinson)

Despite having Green Line Park & Ride lettering added to its side panels, Rider York Ikarus-bodied DAF SB220 1202 (J422NCP) which had received its owner's new livery was caught by the camera at Bootham Bar, York operating normal service 12 to Wiggington. (K.A.Jenkinson)

Painted in FirstBus-style Grampian livery, Alexander-bodied Leyland Atlantean 339 (XSS339Y) collects its passengers in Guild Street, Aberdeen in September 1997 before continuing its journey to Cove on the 13 service. (J.L.Hobbs)

One of a pair of open-top Series II ECW-bodied Bristol VRTs operated in the fleet of Eastern National, 3500 (WNO546L) seen at Epsom Downs on Derby Day in 1993 was, together with its sister, sadly destroyed by fire whilst in winter storage at Walton on the Naze depot in 1996. (T.S.Blackman)

and premium services which all attracted more passengers back to bus travel.

Further consolidating its operations on the Leeds to Morley corridor, Leeds City Link took over Miramare of Morley's solitary route between these two points on 4 November, although no vehicles were involved in the deal. Seven days later, Leeds City Link brought phase two of the Scott Hall guided busway into operation between Stainbeck Lane and Potternewton Lane, and following the 30% increase in traffic achieved after the opening of phase one, it was confidently expected that this would continue to grow to an even greater figure. The 450m phase one and 400m phase two sections of the Superbusway were both developed by Leeds City Council with government funding in partnership with the West Yorkshire PTA and Yorkshire Rider and with another three phases yet to be built it would, when eventually completed comprise 1500m of guideway and 800m of bus lane.

Despite 1996 now being in its final phase, activity throughout the FirstBus group continued unabated with new developments taking place, new vehicles being delivered, and the sad loss in Essex of two open-top buses. Benefiting from the sudden collapse of Barry Breeze Travel, City Line gained the Avon County Council contract for the tendered 559 service around Brislington which required one minibus while Badgerline undertook a major revision of its services in both Bath and Weston-super-Mare. This, however, proved to be less successful than had been anticipated and led to further changes being made early in 1997. A few weeks before this event, Grampian Transport cut its 19 service back from Tillydrone to the Bon Accord Centre in Aberdeen on 28 October in preparation for its conversion to Gold Service status when sufficient new Optare Prisma-bodied Mercedes Benz 0405s arrived while in mid-November PMT disbanded its Stoniers unit during a reorganisation of services in Newcastle-under-Lyme and Hanley. In an attempt to increase ridership following a general fares increase, Brewers introduced a new Bridgend Town Rider Ticket on 1 December which allowed unlimited travel around the town for £4.95 per week while in conjunction with the local Chamber of Trade, a lower fares promotion

Preserved by Essex Buses (Thamesway) is 1939 ex.Westcliff-on-Sea ECW-bodied Bristol K5G AJN825 which has been restored in its original owner's red & cream livery. Sadly this bus was damaged by fire at Walton-on-the-Naze depot, although it is intended to be repaired when time allows. (J.Whitmore)

Still wearing the white, red & orange livery of its former owner MC Travel of Melksham. Plaxton Paramount-bodied 2214 (B826KRY) of Western National works a schools duty in Plymouth in April 1997. (I.H.Winchester)

Caught by the camera at St.Andrew bus station, Edinburgh in February 1997 is Mairs Coaches Jonckheere-bodied Volvo B10M 705 (PSU628) which was acquired from Budden of Woodfalls in 1990 registered D95BNV. Sporting FirstBus logos, it wore an all-cream livery with three coloured ticks aft of its rear wheel arch. (K.A.Jenkinson)

was launched which enabled a return journey to be made for the price of a single fare on Sundays up to Christmas. Another FirstBus subsidiary to offer a joint fares promotion was Midland Red West who teamed up with Marks & Spencers in Redditch in a promotion designed to benefit both companies. Under this novel scheme, on production of a used Midland Red West bus ticket at the food hall of Marks & Spencers store in the town, a £1 M&S gift voucher was given in exchange.

Property continued to feature in the news in December when on the 6th of the month Kingfisher Huddersfield officially opened its new depot and offices at Old Fieldhouse Lane. Comprising a large secure outdoor parking area, office and maintenance blocks, this replaced the old Huddersfield Corporation Tramways depot and workshops close to the town centre which, following the closure by West Yorkshire PTE of its Longroyd Bridge depot some years earlier and the advent of longer buses had become more than a little overcrowded. Coinciding with this move, Kingfisher also undertook a widespread reorganisation of its service network which included the replacement of more of its minibuses with conventional-size vehicles. Sadly, little more than a week later Eastern National suffered the loss of two of its open-top Bristol VRTs when its depot at Walton-on-the-Naze was badly damaged by fire on 14 December. Although closed operationally, the depot had still been used to store unlicenced vehicles and in addition to the two open-toppers contained the company's beautifully preserved 1939 Bristol K5G. Although this suffered damage in the fire, fortunately the extent of this did not result in its total destruction and it is planned to eventually rebuild it to its former glory, although to date this work has yet to commence.

New buses were received by a large number of FirstBus group companies as well as a number of secondhand examples passing between them. Amongst these were 31 new Alexander PS-bodied Volvo B10Ms for Kelvin, 4 Scania L113s, 6 Volvo B10Ls and 9 Volvo Olympians for Greater Glasgow, 36 low-floor Dennis Dart SLFs for Greater Manchester of which 11 were bodied by Wrights and 25 by Plaxton, 10 Mercedes Benz 709Ds for each of Thamesway and PMT, the latter of whom also received 7 Optare MetroRiders and 3 Plaxton-

Great Eastern's single coach Sudbury 'bubble car' diesel L131 stands at Marks Tey station on 1 November 1997. Fitted with a FirstBus-style fleet name and logo, it also carries a Chappel Viaduct pictogram. (Jim Hardwick)

Repainted in GNER train livery for operation on the rail link service between Bradford and Wakefield is Bradford Traveller Jonckheere-bodied Volvo B10M 1422 (YR3939) which began life in 1993 registered L22YRL. Appropriately lettered, it is seen resting at Bradford's Forster Square railway station in August 1997. (D.Robinson)

Fitted with a large pod on its roof to hide its gas cylinders and displaying Ecobus lettering, Southampton Citybus gas-powered Plaxton Pointer-bodied Dennis Dart 331 (N160GOT) makes its way to the city centre on the 16A service. (F.W.York)

Converted to open-top configuration in 1984 and seen here painted in Guide Friday's green & cream livery, Southampton Citybus East Lancs-bodied Leyland Atlantean 900 (WOW529J) is used almost exclusively on the hourly Southampton Tour. (G.T.W.Carter)

bodied Dennis Darts for Brewers. In addition, Brewers received 4 Leyland Leopards from PMT and a Plaxton Paramount-bodied Tiger from Yorkshire Rider while Mair's of Aberdeen gained 3 Atlanteans cascaded by Grampian. Due to a reduced need for minibuses, Yorkshire Rider transferred 7 of its one year old Mercedes Benz 709Ds to Greater Manchester and I to Western National while Greater Glasgow took into stock a trio of Alexander Ultra-bodied Volvo B10Ls which had previously served as demonstrators. Perhaps the most unexpected move, however, was that of an NCME-bodied Fleetline which Yorkshire Rider had purchased from Manchester-based GM Buses in 1988. Having resold this to GM Buses North in 1994 it was surprisingly repurchased by Calderline on 6 December and after being repainted into its new owner's white, blue and yellow livery, was given its old fleet number and returned to service in Halifax. In the meantime, Grampian's coaches and those of Mair's and Kirkpatrick were to be given with an ivory colour scheme adorned with three ticks in the colours of their operating company, the only exception being the executive coaches which would use silver as their base colour.

Further success was achieved in December when it was announced that FirstBus had been successful in its bid for the Great Eastern Railway franchise, thus strengthening its earlier foothold in Britain's rail network. Commencing on 5 January 1997 for a period of seven years three months, Great Eastern operated 576 mainly electric multiple units on services between London's Liverpool Street station and Gidea Park, Southend, Clacton, Colchester and Ipswich comprising 164 miles of route and the operation of 56 stations. In view of Anglia Trains also providing some services between Liverpool Street, Colchester and Ipswich, however, FirstBus's success in gaining Great Eastern precluded it from pursuing its bid for the former for which the franchise was concurrently awarded to GB Railways. Receiving a £29 million subsidy from OPRAF for the first two years of its franchise, FirstBus guaranteed to maintain the current level of service on Great Eastern for the first three years under its control and additionally pledged to introduce a number of service improvements including new hourly fast services between London and Harwich and London and Walton, more peak hour journeys between London and Ipswich and better off-peak, Saturday and Sunday services particularly between London and Southend. Although having no financial interest in Great North Eastern Railways, FirstBus through its Yorkshire Rider subsidiary Leeds City Link had entered into an agreement with the railway company to operate a road feeder service between Bradford's Interchange and Forster Square railway stations and Wakefield Westgate station to provide connections with the mainline service to London. For this purpose Leeds City Link dedicated one of its Volvo coaches to this duty after repainting it into GNER's dark blue livery and adding that operators lettering to its panels.

1997

As the new year opened, it was made known that FirstBus had made an indicative offer to buy Southampton CityBus from its management and employees who had acquired the company from Southampton City Council in a closed sale in 1993. Operating within Southampton and on some interurban services to Portsmouth, FirstBus saw this as a valuable addition to its growing south coast

Painted in Quickstep's ivory & cherry livery but adorned with Leeds City Link fleet names, Kinsley depot's Ikarus-bodied DAF SB220 17 (L517EHD) stands outside Wakefield bus station prior to its departure to Doncaster on the former United Services route 498. (K.A.Jenkinson)

Painted in an all-white livery and appropriately lettered to allow it to work on park and ride duties as well as its customary Flagship operations, Rider York Wright Axcess Ultralow-bodied Scania L113CRL 8417 (N417ENW) arrives at Askham Bar parking area with an almost full load of passengers. (K.A.Jenkinson)

Converted into a mobile workshop for Thamesway's engineering department is Reeve Burgess-bodied Mercedes Benz L608D 9305 (B42AAF) which began life with Western National and is seen here at its new owner's Basildon depot. (K.A.Jenkinson)

South Wales Transport is currently replacing its array of local fleet names with standard SWT lettering and a large FirstBus logo as illustrated on Reeve Burgess-bodied Mercedes Benz 709D 309 (F309AWN) at Swansea. (D.P.B.Davies)

network which already included the former Peoples Provincial and Portsmouth Transit operations. Additionally, CityBus already operated a number of CNG-powered buses and had its own gas station which would thus allow FirstBus to continue its experiments into more environmentally friendly forms of transport. Before talks between the two companies were started, however, Southampton CityBus sold its Red Ensign coaching operations to the expanding Coachline of Rotherham, leaving it with 150 buses running from its Portswood depot and a further 10 at its Hants & Sussex unit at Havant. Seeking to establish its position if its acquisition went ahead, FirstBus made contact with the Office of Fair Trading in order to gain its approval and after this was given early in April, negotiations were able to proceed to an ultimate conclusion at the end of July. Unfortunately, however, the good news had been overshadowed on 24 January by the long-awaited result of the investigation by the Monopolies and Mergers Commission into FirstBus's acquisition of SB Holdings. Despite FirstBus having entered into a Quality Partnership Agreement in Glasgow and committed itself to a £21 million investment in new buses for Greater Glasgow, GCT and Kelvin, the Monopolies and Mergers Commission believed that the acquisition of SB Holdings was against the public interest and thus instructed FirstBus to divest itself of one of its Glasgow depots and the whole of its Midland Bluebird operation. Given nine months to comply with this directive, if the sale of the specified parts of the FirstBus empire was not completed within that time span, then it would be required to dispose of the whole of SB Holdings. Putting on a brave face, FirstBus chairman Trevor Smallwood expressed disappointment that the MMC had not been satisfied with the divestment of Midland Bluebird, which had been offered as a palliative by the group. Prior to this, Midland Bluebird on 6 January had withdrawn its unusual Pentland Rambler service from Livingston to Balerno which had operated only on the fourth Sunday of every month.

After several weeks of speculation, Midland Red West closed its Midland Red Coaches unit on 25 January and dispersed most of its fleet of Leyland Tigers to other members of the FirstBus Group with Eastern Counties taking 5, Brewers 6 and Western National 4. Following quickly on the heels of this move, Midland Red West gave notice to cancel all its commercial services and most of its supported routes in Shropshire following plans by the County Council to axe services in Shrewsbury and Telford in a bid to keep its spending within agreed budgetary limits. If this move went ahead, Midland Red West's presence in the county after May would only comprise its Hereford to Birmingham trunk route and its low-floor vehicle supported services around Bridgnorth leaving the county's main towns of Shrewsbury and Telford in the hands of independent operators and Midland Red North. Only days before the closure of Midland Red Coaches took place, one of the company's Plaxton Paramount-bodied Leyland Tigers (B103JAB) was stolen from Redditch depot and sadly, it has never been recovered!

Taking a further step in its restructuring process, early in the new year the FirstBus announced that it was to reduce its Rider York subsidiary to the status of an operating unit of the Yorkshire Rider Group, this being marked by the departure of its managing director Lorraine Goulding and operations director Peter Drew. Placed under the control of Leeds City Link, Rider York which had remained a separate legal entity since its acquisition by Rider Holdings in 1990 was to be wound up, although its name and livery would continue to be used for the York-based fleet. Soon after this announcement was made, Leeds City Link took the decision to close its Kinsley depot which was located away from the company's main area of operation and under an exchange deal, pass its Wakefield to Doncaster services and a local route around Hemsworth to the Cowie-owned Yorkshire Bus Group. This resulted in Kinsley's former operations being taken over by the Wakefield depot of West Riding Automobile Services on 24 February and in exchange, Leeds City Link acquiring the Leeds to Halifax services of Yorkshire Woollen District Transport. Kinsley's Oulton to Morley service was, however, not included in the deal and was instead transferred to Leeds City Link's Cherry Row depot for continued operation. A week prior to the above events, Yorkshire Rider subsidiary Bradford Traveller experimentally introduced stored value Smartcard tickets on its Bradford Moor to Clayton group of services in a bid to improve the attractiveness and convenience of bus travel. For this purpose, twelve Olympians were fitted with 'Smart Traveller' Wayfarer 3 cancellors in addition to retaining their passenger unfriendly 'no-change' fare boxes, although only eight were required for operation of the four routes concerned. It was not only in West Yorkshire, however, that changes were taking place as in South Wales, SWT began to phase out the use of local identity names, replacing these with standard SWT fleet names and logos, the only exceptions being the company's 'Shuttle' and 'Timecutter' names which were both to be retained.

Meanwhile, amid much publicity, FirstBus had launched its revolutionary new HybridBus in Portsmouth on 3 February, this being a 20-seat Mercedes Benz 709D which could be operated either diesel or electric power. Developed under a £110,000 Hampshire County

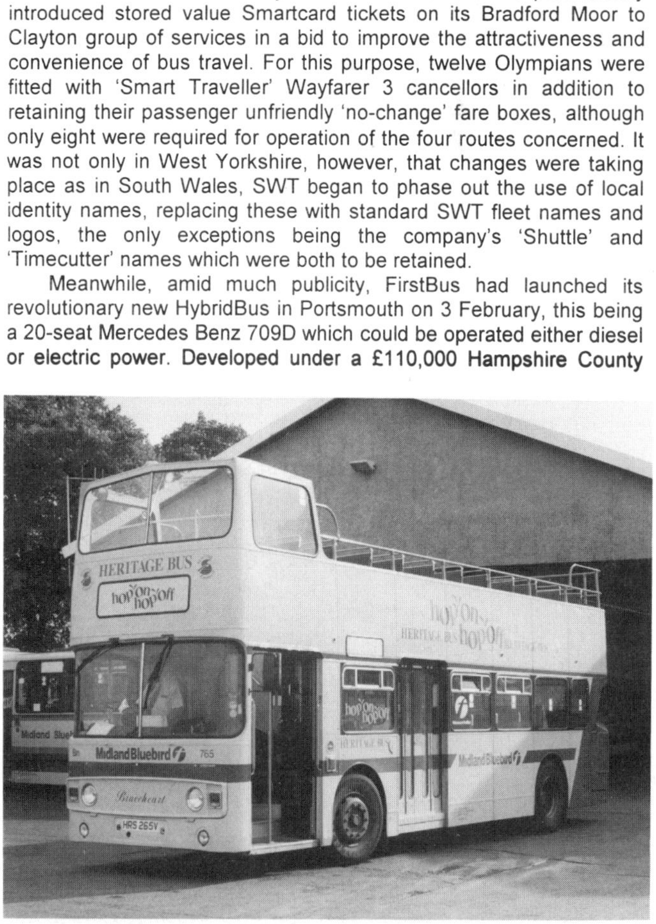

Converted to open-top configuration for use on the Stirling Heritage Tour, Midland Bluebird's ex.Grampian Transport dual-door Alexander-bodied Atlantean 765 (HRS265V) leaves Bannockburn depot to take up its day's duties on a September Sunday in 1997. (K.A.Jenkinson)

Provincial's Plaxton Beaver-bodied diesel-electric Mercedes Benz 709D 100 (VCL461) painted in a silver & green livery and carrying Hybridbus fleet names together with FirstBus logos is demonstrated to the press at its launch in Portsmouth.

Council programme jointly funded by the European Union, Hampshire County Council, FirstBus and Hybrid Vehicles Ltd., this bus which was to be put to use on the 14 service to Baffins Pond was capable of running silently on electricity in the city centre for 25% of its working day and on diesel fuel for the rest of the time outside the city when its auxiliary batteries would be recharged. Under the development deal, the bus was committed to run for three years with FirstBus subsidiary Provincial in order that it could be extensively evaluated. On the subject of alternative fuels, following the first year of operation of its CNG-powered Dennis Dart in Bristol, FirstBus stated that this had proved to be 33% more expensive to run than a comparable diesel bus in terms of pence per kilometre. The bus itself, however had run almost faultlessly since its original electrical problems were resolved and it was confirmed that the bus would continue its trials with City Line throughout 1997 before a final decision was made as to the future of such vehicles within the FirstBus fleet.

A FOOTHOLD GAINED IN THE METROPOLIS

Having been conspicuous in not bidding for any of the former London Transport subsidiaries when they were privatised in 1994 and still having no major interests in the capital, FirstBus on 19 February took steps to address this situation by making a £54 million offer for the purchase CentreWest from its management and employees. In addition to maintaining five depots at Acton Tram Depot, Alperton, Greenford, Uxbridge and Westbourne Park from which it operated almost 500 buses, CentreWest also maintained a network of tendered services at Orpington which it had gained in December 1995 and owned the Berks Bucks Bus Company Limited with depots at Bracknell, Maidenhead and Slough and London Buslines at Isleworth and Southall which had been acquired from Len Wright's Q-Drive in March 1996. In addition, CentreWest held a 20% share in Tramtrack Croydon Limited, a consortium of companies which had been awarded the contract to design, build, operate and maintain the Croydon Tramlink. CentreWest's wholly-owned subsidiary Tram Operations Limited had been awarded the contract to operate and maintain the system for 30 years from its anticipated opening in November 1999 from a new depot and workshops at Therapia Lane, Croydon using trams built by Bombardier Eurorail. Following an Extraordinary General Meeting of CentreWest's shareholders, the deal was confirmed on 26 March and FirstBus was at last able to claim a sizable stake of London's bus market where its adversaries Cowie, Stagecoach and MTL already had a major presence.

In the final round of the Government's rail privatisation process in February 1997 when the remaining seven franchises were announced, FirstBus learned that Great Western Holdings in which it

Passing through Edgware on the London Transport-contracted 79 service is London Buslines Northern Counties-bodied Leyland Olympian 40 (H140FLX). (G.T.W.Carter)

RML2378, one of CentreWest's 30ft.long Routemasters threads its way through central London on its way to East Acton Station and carries route details above its lower deck side windows.

Berks Bucks Northern Counties-bodied Scania L113CLL 810 (M810PGM) shows off its attractive new livery in 1997. (T.W.W.Knowles)

had a 24.5% share had been successful in gaining North West Regional Railways which operated over a vast area including North West England, North Wales, Manchester and Liverpool. Under this deal which was to commence on 2 March, Great Western Holdings who renamed its new acquisition North West Railways, gave a commitment to improve services between Liverpool and Manchester and Manchester, Wigan, Bolton and Preston and introduce new services to London from Rochdale and North Wales. Additionally it announced that it was to purchase 70 new 100mph diesel multiple units before March 2000 and spend £6.5 million on the refurbishment of stations and existing rolling stock. With Britain's rail privatisation having now been completed, despite its disappointment in 1996 when it attempted to gain its first foothold in overseas bus operations, it was decided to continue in its quest to expand outside Britain and to this end appointed Graeme Varley as Director for Overseas Development with Robbie Duncan taking the position of Director U.K. Bus. Under this restructuring, five Divisional Directors were appointed - London & South East : Peter Hendy; North West : Mike Mitchell; Scotland : John McCormick; South Wales : Bob Holland and Yorkshire : Ray O'Toole to whom the Managing Directors of the individual operating subsidiaries would report. In the meantime, FirstBus had continued to enhance its bus services in various parts of the country, extending its Eastern Counties service 24 (Norwich city centre to Vulcan Road) to Norwich Airport and upgrading Grampian Transport's 19 service between the Bonn Accord Centre in Aberdeen and Culter to Gold Service standard using new Optare Prisma-bodied Mercedes Benz 0405s.

Property continued to feature on FirstBus's agenda and after opening its new Kingfisher Huddersfield depot in December 1996, consideration was given to a standard format for all future new depots. Amongst the first to be given this attention was a planned new depot at Hengrove for Bristol Omnibus Company which would allow the closure of City Line's Winterstoke Road and Badgerline's Marlborough Street, Bristol depots. Indeed, despite still being in the planning stage, 'For Sale' notices had already appeared at Marlborough Street, although it was made known that when the site was redeveloped it had to contain a new bus station to replace the existing facility. Similarly, plans were announced in February for a new 16-bay bus station at Norwich on the site of the old Surrey Street garage which would additionally include a travel office, shops and multi-screen cinema. Still on the subject of property, Grampian Transport regained the full extent of its depot at King Street, Aberdeen on 23 February when Stagecoach subsidiary Bluebird Buses vacated the area it had rented and moved to a new site on the fringe of the city. On the reverse side of the coin, however, planning permission was refused for Brewers' proposed new depot at Bryncethin near Bridgend in South Wales leaving the company to return to the drawing board.

BATTLELINES DRAWN IN SCOTLAND

Continuing its policy of forming quality partnerships, FirstBus joined with Scottish local authority West Lothian Council to provide a better standard of local public transport in two separate ventures, both of which involved Midland Bluebird. In one of these, six local services running along the Edinburgh to Livingston corridor were upgraded to 'Diamond Service' standards on 14 February using new vehicles backed by a new customer charter whilst the other saw the X14 express service from East Calder and Livingston to Glasgow being operated from this same date by refurbished coaches and given new fare bargains. The latter were given a special livery of green, white and coral and carried West Express fleet names together with SMT and West Lothian Council logos. Another new partnership formed in March saw FirstBus team up with Strathclyde Police in an attempt to stamp out bus vandalism. Under this new scheme, the partnership approach would be able to identify the 'hot spots' for vandalism and enable the police to maintain a uniformed presence on the problem routes as well as community officers visiting schools to explain the dangers of vandalism etc. Meanwhile, Strathclyde Buses had in February taken delivery of 26 new single deckers as part of its ongoing fleet replacement programme. Of these, 10 were low-floor Alexander-bodied Dennis Dart SLF's for the GCT fleet (8 of which were East Lancs Spryte-bodied examples from a cancelled Cowie Group order, the remaining 2 being fitted with Plaxton Pointer bodywork) while the remaining 16 were Alexander PS-bodied Volvo B10Ms for Kelvin. All were painted in Strathclyde's new all-red livery including the GCT examples which were dedicated to the Duntocher to Clydebank and Parkhall to Clydebank services and the Kelvin vehicles which were put to work on the 67 service from Glasgow city centre to Newmains and Wishaw. Despite these moves to increase patronage on its services and reduce mindless damage to its vehicles, all was not well, however, in Glasgow as early in March it was learned that Stagecoach intended to set up a new operating company in the city with 150 buses which would compete directly with services operated by Strathclyde Buses. To be introduced

Painted in a special green & white livery and carrying West Express lettering for operation on the X14 service to Livingston, Midland Bluebird's ex.SMT Plaxton Paramount-bodied Leyland Tiger 335 (A13SMT) is seen leaving Buchanan bus station, Glasgow in heavy rain. (B.Newsome)

Painted in Greater Glasgow's all-red livery but fitted with GCT fleet names, East Lancs Spryte-bodied Dennis Dart MD1 (P852VUS) prepares to leave Govan bus station on a journey to Pollock Centre in July 1997. (A.Blagburn)

Painted in a dedicated red & buff livery for the X1 Gold Line service from Hillhouse to Glasgow, Kelvin's coach-seated Alexander-bodied Volvo Olympian 1848 (M848DUS) approaches its Glasgow terminal at Buchanan bus station in September 1997. (K.A.Jenkinson)

progressively, the first four routes were to begin on 24 April from Buchanan bus station to Nitshill, Darnley, Kennishead and Cumbernauld using the motorway network around Glasgow and were to operate seven days a week. Although undoubtedly the re-emergence of Stagecoach in the city would abstract passengers from areas where Strathclyde Buses had in more recent times reigned supreme, it also gave FirstBus hope in its ongoing battle with the Monopolies and Mergers Commission by the fact that as it no longer had a monopoly in the area it had no need to divest its Midland Bluebird operations or one of its Glasgow depots. In retaliation to Stagecoach's move, FirstBus decided to launch an attack on that group's services in Fife and Ayrshire and to this end registered a service from Ardrossan to Kilmarnock which was to begin on 25 May and one between Ballingry and Dunfermline which was to commence on 9 June. That in Ayrshire was to be placed under Kelvin's control and operate on a 10 minute frequency along A1 Service's old-established route while the new operation in Fife, which competed with Fife Scottish, was to run at 10 minute intervals with every third journey continuing through to Edinburgh and was to be maintained by Lowland. Using FifeFirst as its fleet name and an all-red livery the latter utilised seventeen buses (3 Plaxton Pointer-bodied Dennis Dart SLFs and 14 Wright Access Ultralow-bodied Scania L113CRLs) from Midland Bluebird's Westfield depot and a new outstation at Halbeath whilst the Ayrshire operation was maintained by 15 UVG-bodied and 3 Plaxton Pointer-bodied Dennis Dart SLFs based at Eagle Coaches depot at Stevenston. In addition to the above new ventures, Strathclyde Buses also set about to strengthen its position in Glasgow ahead of Stagecoach's arrival in the city by allowing holders of Transcard, Supergran and network travel cards to use them on any Greater Glasgow, GCT or Kelvin services instead of restricting them to the operating company marked on their ticket. Pre-empting possible Stagecoach expansion in Glasgow (which indeed became a reality), Greater Glasgow began two new express services (marketed under the title First Express) in the city during May, the X77 running between Buchanan bus station and Newton Mearns via the M8 and M77 motorways and the X93 between the city centre and Drumchapel via the Clydeside Expressway and in June introduced a new service numbered 75 from St.Enoch Square to Castlemilk, another numbered X19 between the city centre and Easterhouse via the M8 motorway and one numbered 19 from Castlemilk to Garthamlock. Following Stagecoach Glasgow's incursions into East Kilbride, Kelvin on 7 July began two new local services linking Calderwood with Greenhills on a basic 10-minute headway and two limited stop services branded Gold Line (X1/X2) between Glasgow and Hairmyres and High Whitehills whilst further retaliatory measures on 21 July saw Kelvin further expand in Ayrshire with five new local services radiating from the Safeway store at Stevenston, each operating on a 30-minute frequency. The Cumbernauld - Glasgow corridor also saw Kelvin enhance its services using new vehicles adorned with First Express fleet names to compete with Stagecoach's newly introduced express routes while Greater Glasgow also used the fleet name SuperBus on some of its new low-floor single deckers.

As if Strathclyde's announcement of ventures into pastures new had not been enough for one month, South Wales Transport introduced a new innovative service on 1 March under the brand name 'FlightPath'. Running every 90 minutes between Swansea and

Leaving Buchanan bus station, Glasgow on the X3 service to Cumbernauld is Kelvin Plaxton Premiere-bodied Volvo B10M P766XHS painted in an all-red livery with the addition of First Express lettering. (K.A.Jenkinson)

Standing in Irvine whilst operating the service from Ardrossan to Kilmarnock which was introduced in competition to the Stagecoach A1 Service between these same two points is Kelvin UVG-bodied Dennis Dart SLF MD38 (P757XUS) which carries the legend 'Super Low Fleet Easy Access Bus' along its cove panels. (K.A.Jenkinson)

Dressed in Welsh costume, a group of children stand alongside South Wales Transport Ford Galaxy People Mover P36HEW for a publicity photograph when the FlightPath service was launched. In the background, the luggage trailer hauled by these vehicles can be seen. (South Wales Transport)

South Wales Transport used several Brian Isaac Coaches for a short time during a period of vehicle shortages. One of these was Duple-bodied Bedford YMT MDV143W which is seen here resting between duties in Swansea. (Travelscene)

Cardiff Airport using Ford Galaxy people movers with luggage trailers, a fare of £14 return was charged, this including free travel on SWT buses to and from the Quadrant Bus Station, Swansea at the start and finish of their airport journeys. Towards the end of that month, GM Buses North and Greater Manchester PTA launched their first quality partnership on the 600/601 services between Wigan and Leigh, the last phase of an overall 'easy access' initiative introduced by the PTA in 1995. For operation on the new partnership routes, Greater Manchester purchased five low-floor Wright-bodied Volvo B10Ls which were adorned with Superbus and other promotional lettering lettering on their cove panels and the legend 'Easy Access' on the upper part of their windscreens and, in common with the company's other Superbuses, were given a narrow yellow band along their side panels. A further initiative launched by FirstBus jointly with Stagecoach was a £4.99 Multisaver ticket which allowed unlimited travel after 9.30am on weekdays and all day on Saturdays, Sundays and Bank Holidays on all services in Northampton operated by Northampton Transport and United Counties.

Still in expansive mood, FirstBus further consolidated its position in South Wales in March when on the second day of the month South Wales Transport took over operation of Davies of Pencader's six local bus services in the Llanelli/Trimsaran area, of which five were tendered routes which operated only during the evenings. Although no vehicles were involved in this deal, seven of Davies' drivers transferred to the FirstBus subsidiary. United Welsh also gained some additional work when it took over some of the services operated by Waterhall Coaches and in addition was awarded a five-year contract from Great Western Trains and South Wales and the West Railway to provide rail replacement services between Cardiff and Fishguard. To meet this new requirement, despite United Welsh Coaches having acquired a number of secondhand Leyland Tigers from Midland Red Coaches and the Yorkshire Rider Group, it found it necessary to supplement these with coaches hired from Brian Isaacs of Swansea until further vehicles of its own could be obtained. Later, on 21 March Bristol Omnibus Company acquired the operations and 22 vehicles of Keynsham-based independent Streamline Buses (Bath) Ltd. who operated a service from Bath city centre to the University in competition to Badgerline and several tendered routes and two local services in Keynsham. Although the Streamline's garage and office at Keynsham were included in the deal, both were immediately closed leaving only its premises at Station Road, Lower Weston still in use by its new owners. The acquired fleet, all of which was initially taken into stock and allocated fleet numbers, included a Setra and a Volvo B10M coach, several minibuses including 5 coach-seated Plaxton-bodied Mercedes Benz 709Ds and 4 Marshall-bodied Mercedes Benz 811Ds purchased new in 1993/4 and a trio of 49-seat Ikarus-bodied DAF SB220 buses which were less than a year old. Surprisingly, rather than absorb the newly acquired operations into those of Badgerline it was instead decided to retain Streamline as a separate operating unit under its own name, although all vehicle maintenance was to be carried out by Badgerline at its Bath depot.

Resting between its duties on a local service is Streamline Buses of Bath Dormobile-bodied Iveco 49.10 F965FKP. (F.W.York)

Displaying Ealing Buses fleet names, CentreWest low-floor Marshall-bodied Dennis Dart P136NLW is seen operating the E7 service to Ealing Broadway. (P.Kay)

Throughout the FirstBus empire services continued to undergo revision in order to meet public demand and achieve greater efficiency and on 23 March a large number of those operated by South Wales Transport at Llanelli were recast following the arrival of twelve new Dennis Darts. Prior to this on 3 March South Wales Transport had made alterations to several of its Swansea area routes and an announcement was made to the effect that the city's park and ride operation would be reintroduced for the summer period. On 1 April a massive reorganisation of services was undertaken in Bristol by both Badgerline and City Line, largely as a result of gains through local authority retendering although a substantial amount of routes were cut by Badgerline in Bath and North East Somerset. The network at Weston-super-Mare, however, remained virtually unchanged. Following the transfer of City Line's 8 and 9 services (Temple Meads to Clifton) from Muller Road to Lawrence Hill depot, a number of its Dennis Darts had Rail-Link branding applied while on 1 April the Long Ashton park and ride site finally opened after lying idle for almost two years. Although the new park and ride services were initially operated by six of Badgerline's Dennis Lances, these were replaced at the end of June by a similar number of new Northern Counties Palatine 2-bodied Volvo Olympians which were given a special silver and burgundy livery for this purpose. Prior to this, on 10 March Badgerline's 'veteran' open-top Bristol VRT 8617 (JHW109P) after being repainted into the new Cheddar Gorge livery of blue & mauve set off from Weston-super-Mare on a week's promotion tour for this attraction which took it, amongst other places, to Gloucester, Worcester, Kidderminster, Coventry., Leicester, Derby, Stoke-on-Trent, Birmingham and Cardiff. Despite its age and the fact that it covered 633 miles on its circuitous journey, it performed faultlessly throughout and at the beginning of the summer season took up its duties on the Gorge Tour and Park & Ride at Cheddar.

Before the month ended, Western National also expanded its operations when on the 30th it took over a number of local services in the Bude area from Jennings of Bude together with that company's Bude to Exeter and Bude to Plymouth express services. In this instance, however, no vehicles changed ownership with Jennings retaining these for the continuation of its coaching activities. PMT had also strengthened its position on when on 8 February it took over the Chester operations of comparative newcomer South Lancashire Transport who withdrew to from whence it had come (St.Helens). No vehicles were included in the deal, however, and the acquired routes were mostly withdrawn due to the fact that they replicated those already operated by Chester City Transport. Despite all these advances, Midland Red West was still experiencing difficulties with a number of its services following financial cuts made by some of the local authorities within its area and on 26 April it closed its outstations at Birmingham's Bull Ring and Bridgnorth, an action which sparked off a large scale reallocation of its fleet.

Resting at Uxbridge are CentreWest Wright-bodied Dennis Dart ODZ8911 and Northern Counties-bodied Volvo Olympian V44 (P844UCW), both of which carry Uxbridge Buses fleet names. (P.Kay)

Amongst the buses given dedicated lettering for the joint Kingfisher Huddersfield/Calderline Swiftlink service X36 between Halifax and Huddersfield is Calderline Alexander Strider-bodied Volvo B10B 1023 (L123PWR) seen here at Halifax bus station. (K.A.Jenkinson)

*Painted in an all-white livery with FirstBus Quality Service lettering on its side panels is Rider York low-floor Plaxton Pointer-bodied Dennis Dart 3303 (P303AUM) seen outside the city's railway station. **(C.F.Wood)***

Eastern National Northern Counties-bodied Dennis Lance 1509 (P509MNO) hurries towards Highwoods Tesco on route 65A. (J.Podgorski)

What must be one of the most unusual buses to be found in a FirstBus fleet in June 1997 was the sole surviving ex.Great Yarmouth Transport ECW-bodied AEC Swift 83 (WEX683M) which had surprisingly been recertified in April for further service. Seen here at the Second Avenue, Caister terminus of service 8 it has, however, since been withdrawn. (A.Bagshaw)

Four Alexander-bodied Leyland Atlanteans acquired by Brewers from Greater Glasgow in 1997 are seen standing at the Port Talbot depot of their new owner still in the liveries in which they were received. The two buses on the left wear Strathclyde Buses orange & black while the other two are painted in Kelvin and GCT colours respectively. (D.P.B.Davies)

During April, Lowland Omnibuses successfully secured the unusual contract subsidised by the Borders Health Board and Scottish Borders Council for the operation of the Border Courier service which had previously been worked by Buskers of Galashiels and Munros of Jedburgh. This ferried medical supplies across the Borders region as well as transporting passengers to and from hospitals and required buses with enormous luggage capacity at the rear. For its operation Lowland placed an order for 5 specially modified 22-seat Optare MetroRiders for delivery in July immediately prior to the commencement of this five-year contract. Meanwhile, FirstBus's new London subsidiary CentreWest retained the LT contract for the 83 service between Golders Green and Ealing on a net cost tender while in May 41 new low-floor Marshall-bodied Dennis Dart SLFs were placed in service on the Ealing Buses network (which had also been retained upon retendering) along with 16 new Marshall Minibuses, all which had been ordered prior to CentreWest's acquisition by FirstBus. Back in northern England, on 14 April Yorkshire Rider subsidiaries Calderline and Kingfisher Huddersfield launched a new joint express limited stop service between Halifax and Huddersfield numbered X36 and branded 'SwiftLink'. Designed to reduce congestion in both towns by encouraging commuters to leave their cars at home and use the bus, a £2 return fare was offered and the through journey time reduced by 10 minutes. To publicise the new service upon which alternate Saturday journeys continued to Meadowhall, Sheffield, Kingfisher added SwiftLink branding to six of its Plaxton Verde-bodied Dennis Lances whilst Calderline likewise adorned some of its Alexander Strider-bodied Volvo B10Bs and a couple of its Plaxton Paramount 3200-bodied Leyland Tigers. Nearby in Leeds, the third phase of the Scott Hall Road guided busway was officially opened on Monday 28 April, this comprising a 350 metre section for use by city-bound buses bringing the total length of the guideway to 1,200 metres. Used by up to twenty buses per hour, the opening of the new section cut around three minutes of peak journey times and further strengthened the venture which had since the opening of the initial section two years earlier increased patronage of

Although borrowed by Leeds City Link for a three-month evaluation in the spring of 1997, Grampian Alexander-bodied Mercedes Benz 0405G bendibus K1GRT saw little use during its period in West Yorkshire. Fitted with guide wheels, Leeds Super Busway logos and temporary fleet number 101 it is seen at City Link's Cherry Row depot where it spent most of its time resting. (K.A.Jenkinson)

Painted in Western National's simplified livery which omitted the red & blue flags, ECW-bodied Bristol VRT 1230 (VTH942T) which had been acquired from South Wales Transport in 1990 rests in Plymouth bus station in April 1997. (I.H.Winchester)

Seen at Northern Counties factory at Wigan in February 1997 prior to delivery to PMT is one of its new Dennis Lances. (B.Newsome)

the Leeds City Link services using the busway by 40%.

During the first four months of 1997 the flow of new vehicles to FirstBus had continued without respite with numerous low-floor examples being placed in service to further enhance passenger comfort etc. In addition to those already mentioned with Greater Manchester and the Strathclyde Buses subsidiaries, Greater Manchester had received the first 25 of its 80 low-floor Plaxton Pointer-bodied Dennis Dart SLFs, Rider York had taken delivery of 4 similar vehicles together with 6 Wright-bodied Scania L113CRLs for its park and ride operations, Midland Bluebird had accepted 13 Plaxton-bodied Dennis Dart SLFs for its SMT unit, Eastern Counties gained 10 Wright Axcess Ultralow-bodied Scania L113CRLs and PMT had taken into stock 6 long-wheelbase Optare MetroRiders which conformed to the latest DiPTAC step regulations together with a trio of Northern Counties-bodied Dennis Lances. Eastern National received 11 new Northern Counties-bodied Dennis Lances which allowed the withdrawal of more Leyland Nationals while Badgerline rid itself of all but 3 of its Iveco 49.10s. In addition to replacing several time-expired vehicles which were offered for sale, these new arrivals allowed a number of buses to be cascaded to other FirstBus subsidiaries amongst which were Brewers who received another Plaxton Paramount-bodied Leyland Tiger from Bradford Traveller and, more surprisingly 4 Atlanteans from GCT/Greater Glasgow, Kingfisher Huddersfield and Bradford Traveller who between them gained 16 Leyland Atlanteans from Greater Manchester (one of which was acquired by Kingfisher solely for cannibalisation) and Leicester CityBus whose fleet was expanded by 4 Leyland Atlanteans borrowed from Grampian Transport. Perhaps more surprising, however, was the passage of 6 of Rider York's youthful Wright-bodied Scania L113CRLs which despite being less than two years old were during April dispersed two each to Lowland in preparation for its new operations in Fife. Earlier in the year, a loan-based exchange was undertaken by Leeds City Link and Grampian Transport which resulted in the latter's Mercedes Benz bendibus K1GRT arriving at Leeds City Link's Cherry Row depot with Wright Pathfinder-bodied Dennis Lance SLF M221EAF going to Aberdeen. The exchange which was to last three months was supposedly to enable Leeds City Link to evaluate the bendibus on the Scott Hall Road guided busway, although in the event it spent almost all of its time parked at Cherry Row depot, making only two trips during the evening peak each day from Leeds city centre to Chapeltown, a route which ironically does not use the guideway! Both buses returned to their rightful owners on 24 May.

In April, FirstBus train operating company Great Eastern launched a new corporate identity and grey blue and green livery at the same time that it announced a £9.25 million investment programme and

Wearing a silver livery with red & yellow bands for dedicated operation on the 320 service between Hanley and Crewe, PMT's Plaxton Verde-bodied Dennis Lance SDC866 (N866CEH) rests between duties at Hanley bus station. (R.Williams)

Joining the Sky Blue fleet of Wessex from the Rider Group who in turn had acquired it with the local bus operations of AJC Angloblue of Leeds, Volvo-engined Leyland National 801 (RKA869T) which began life with Merseybus received a new livery of blue with red & white bands before entering service in its new Bristol home early in 1997. (S.R.Procter)

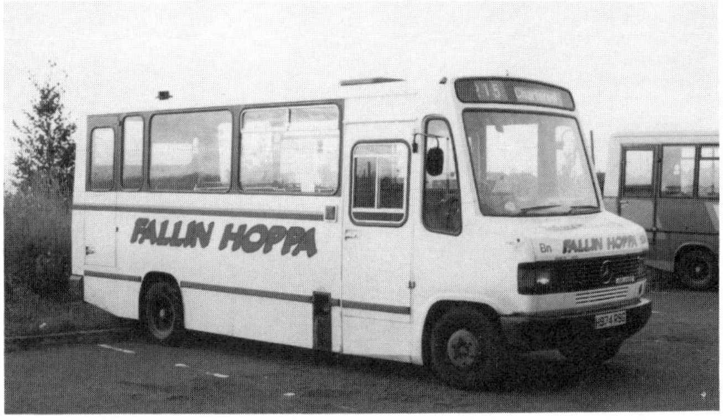

Painted in a predominantly white livery and carrying Fallin Hoppa fleet names. Midland Bluebird Alexander-bodied Mercedes Benz 709D 634 (H974RSG) takes its Sunday rest at Bannockburn depot in September 1997. (K.A.Jenkinson)

Having been repainted in Grampian's latest livery of ivory with dark green & gold stripes, Alexander-bodied Mercedes Benz 709D 436 (H36USO) seen in Guild Street, Aberdeen in September 1997 also carries corporate FirstBus-style fleet names and logos. (J.L.Hobbs)

plans to promote closer bus and rail integration with through ticketing on many journeys. In the pilot scheme which was to start with the summer timetable, through season tickets were to be made available from Chelmsford and Maldon which was not served by a rail service. By the autumn through tickets were expected to be available from new computerised ticket machines on Eastern National and Thamesway buses and FirstBus was also looking at the possibility of incorporating a London Underground add on to the tickets. A dedicated commuter bus link would also run at peak times between Maldon, Heybridge and Hatfield Peveril with through ticketing and it was additionally proposed to link with Thamesway services at Rayleigh to places such as Hadleigh and Thundersley. At the end of May, Sunday rail services were doubled in frequency and the Maningtree to Harwich service reintroduced and to promote its return, Great Eastern ran a free shuttle service on Sunday 25 May between Harwich International, Dovercourt and Harwich Town to take crowds of spectators to a lifeboat naming ceremony. Further security measures were to be taken across the network to enhance passenger safety whilst all stations were to be repainted by the year

Beautifully restored and repainted into its original Tilling green & cream livery, Western National's preserved ECW-bodied Series I Bristol VRT 1056 (OTA290G) is regularly used on its owner's heritage services in Devon. ***(J.L.Hobbs)***

2002 and many were to be refurbished as well. Meanwhile, in South Wales a joint venture was set up by Brewers and the Cardiff Railway Company under which Brewers was to sell and accept Valley Day Ranger tickets (which allowed unlimited travel on the entire Valley Lines rail network) between Maesteg, Afan Valley and Treorchy. At around this same time Brewers also revised its services operating to the Sandfields Estate area of Port Talbot and introduced fares based on a zonal system which gave a maximum day return fare within the zones of 60p, 70p and £1 after 9.00am each day.

A further quality partnership was announced during April between PMT, Mersey Travel and Wirral Metropolitan Borough Council covering two corridors into Birkenhead. These would be served by 14 new low-floor Scania single deckers and would benefit from new bus priorities and quality stops provided by the Council and PTE. These would be served by 14 new low-floor Scania single deckers and would benefit from new bus priorities and quality stops provided by the three councils. Having already replaced a large number of its Mercedes Benz L608D minibuses with 33 new Mercedes 810s and Optare MetroRiders during the first four months of 1997, PMT promised to purchase at least 100 new buses before the millennium in order to continue the upgrading of its fleet. Meanwhile, in north-east Scotland Grampian Transport pledged to continue commercial operation of Aberdeen's City Quick park and ride services for at least

Being repainted at Bury St.Edmunds depot from its Rider Group colours into the livery of its new owner Eastern Counties is ECW-bodied Bristol VRT 232 (JWT762V) whilst in the background stands withdrawn Robin Hood-bodied Ford Transit 851 (E851PEX). ***(M.H.A.Flynn)***

Eastern Counties new Wright Axcess Ultralow-bodied Scania L113CRL 543 (P543RNG) lettered for Superoute 88 is seen in Ipswich on its first day in service. (J.Podgorski)

Preserved by the Rider Group is HUM401, a 1940 Roe-bodied AEC Regent which has been superbly restored in the pre-war livery of its original owner Leeds City Transport. Now maintained by Leeds City Link, it is seen here at the opening of the new Kingfisher Huddersfield depot. (K.A.Jenkinson)

another twelve months despite them remaining loss making. Launched in October 1994 the services were currently attracting 7,500 passengers per week compared with 3,000 in 1995 and thus had hopes that their viability could perhaps at last be achieved during 1997/8. To further improve its services, Grampian fitted a satellite operated Automatic Vehicle Location System (funded by the Scottish Office) to its 10 new Optare Prisma single deckers dedicated to Springhall - Cove route 16 upon which Real Time information displays were installed and it was planned that ultimately all sixty buses operating Gold Services would be so equipped.

Liveries once again became the subject of change amongst some FirstBus subsidiaries when in the spring Western National simplified its colour scheme by omitting the flags which had adorned its vehicles for several years. PMT continued its policy of using different liveries for the vehicles employed on certain of its routes and on inter-urban operations while Wessex adopted a new light blue, red and white scheme for its Sky Blue fleet and Badgerline repainted its Bath-based open-top double deckers in standard Guide Friday colours. Bradford Traveller, however, who had settled on a two-tone blue and red livery following various experiments with differing shades of blue altered its standard application by omitting the red band below the upper deck windows of its double deckers and instead, adding this to its lower panels. After only a handful of buses had been repainted thus, however, a further amendment was made in May by the addition of a white band along the lower deck panels and at the same time the colour of the corporate FirstBus style fleet name was changed from red to blue! Whether this proves to be the new standard livery or whether it will be altered yet again remains to be seen.

Returning to operations, it was pleasing to see that Western National continued its heritage operations during 1997 when on 25 May it introduced a new service (numbered 118) between Gunnislake Station and Okehampton Station via Tavistock and Dartmoor connecting with trains to Exeter and Plymouth. For operation on this route which travelled through breathtaking scenery and encountered some steep gradients, the company extensively restored its preserved Bristol FLF-type Lodekka and used its vintage Bristol VRT as its back-up vehicle, both types which were familiar in the area for a great many years. Unfortunately, however, South Wales Transport took the decision not to operate its popular open-top service to Limeslade during 1997 and thus although it had no plans to withdraw its venerable Bristol KSW, it appeared that it would see little use during 1997. More fortunate was the company's Gower Tour which was reinstated on Sundays until 28 September and was to be maintained by a Dennis Dart equipped with a recorded commentary. Sadly, however, as a consequence of the fire at Eastern National's Walton-on-the-Naze depot in December 1996 which destroyed the company's two open-top Bristol VRTs, the Clacton services 1 and 2 upon which they had previously worked during successive years had to be maintained by conventional Leyland Nationals 1833/51 for the summer period in 1997.

Northampton Transport's gas-powered Alexander (Belfast)-bodied Volvo B10L 506 (P506MVV) wearing a silver livery and promotional lettering leaves Greyfriars bus station on a journey to Ecton Brook in July 1997. (G.T.W.Carter)

Carrying lettering for the Stansted Airport - Bishops Stortford service on its cove panels and Venturer fleet names is Eastern National 1002 (EWR652Y), a coach-seated Duple Dominant-bodied Leyland Tiger acquired from Yorkshire Rider in 1995. (G.T.W.Carter)

One of a number of Leyland Tigers acquired by Brewers from the Rider Group, Plaxton Paramount 3200-bodied 132 (F615XWY) which previously served with Bradford Traveller is seen in its new owner's colours at Port Talbot. (D.P.B.Davies)

After acquiring some further Leyland Nationals (from Rider York) for its Sky Blue operation, Wessex repainted some of its coaches into the new National Express FlightLink livery and also took back into stock some of its original coaches which were hired from the dealer to which they had earlier been sold. These were required for use on some additional National Express contracts during the summer months although under this reorganisation Wessex lost its Eurolines contract. As far as local bus services were concerned, FirstBus continued to look for ways in which car users could be persuaded to switch to public transport and believed that this could, at least, be partly achieved if buses were more comfortable, accessible and journey times were reduced. To this end Eastern Counties with the support of Suffolk County Council at the start of June replaced its elderly Bristol VRT double deckers with 10 new Wright Axcess Ultralow-bodied Scania L113CRL low-floor single deckers on one of its interurban route corridors between Ipswich and Stowmarket. Branded 'Superoute 88', journey times between the two towns was reduced by a third by routing the service along the A14 trunk road and making use of a number of bus priority measures in Ipswich. Meanwhile, following the success of its guided busway in the Scott Hall Road area of Leeds which was used by several Leeds City Link services, in July Leeds City Council announced plans to build a second busway (along York Road) and agreed to spend £80,000 on preparatory legal work for the scheme. Continuing the theme of guided busways, Northampton County and Borough Councils approved a plan submitted by the consortium Rapid Transit International for the construction of privately financed busways based on a park and ride scheme and using low-floor gas-powered single deckers while a similar scheme was put to Nottingham City Council for its consideration.

Announcing an operating profit of £73.7 million (before paying employee profit shares, restructuring and other exceptional costs) on a turnover of £551.5 million, FirstBus had been able to increase its operating profit to 15.2% and conclude that it has enjoyed a satisfactory year. Whilst moving ahead with confidence, it did, however, acknowledge that there was 'still much to be done' and was pursuing its expansion strategy not only through acquisitions in both the UK and overseas but also through solid sustained organic growth. Now having 22% of the UK bus market and with for £80 million-worth of new buses on order (914 vehicles) for delivery in 1997, its improvement to service and aims to transfer travellers from their private cars to public transport remained at the top of its agenda.

In an unusual move, Sheffield-based Mainline in which FirstBus hold a 20% stake linked up with supermarket giant Tesco to provide a peak hour and all-day Saturday park and ride service to its new store on Abbeydale Road, Sheffield and at other times free shoppers services from various housing estates. Under this arrangement, Tesco purchased two low-floor Wright-bodied Volvo B6LEs which it painted in its own colours and entered into a nominal rental agreement with Mainline who was to operate them on behalf of the supermarket chain for two years. Additionally. Mainline agree to purchase the buses after the two year contract ended and expressed a wish to then commercially register the park and ride services if they had proved successful. In the meantime, north of the border Grampian Transport had increased its open-top double deck fleet to five buses with the conversion of four more Atlanteans to this configuration for operation on the increasingly popular city tour as

Parked in Chelmsford bus station after completing a private hire duty is Eastern National's coach-seated ECW-bodied long wheelbase Leyland Olympian 4510 (D510PPU) which still displayed its pre-FirstBus style fleetnames and logo. (M.H.A.Flynn)

Acquired by Provincial from Western National in 1993, freshly repainted open-top ECW-bodied Bristol VRT 594 (MOD571P) shows off its new FirstBus corporate style fleet names as it stands outside Fareham depot.

Once numerous in the SMT fleet, the Ailsa Volvo is now disappearing with some speed, the remaining examples all now being part of the Lowland fleet. Here, Alexander-bodied HSF89X in the old SMT green & cream livery makes its way along Princes Street, Edinburgh on its way to St.Andrew Square. (D.P.B.Davies)

well as on a special service between 12 and 15 July when the Cutty Sark Tall Ships event was to come to Aberdeen.

June 26 heralded the long-awaited appearance of Northampton Transport's low-floor Alexander (Belfast) Ultra-bodied compressed natural gas-powered Volvo B10Ls which, in a silver livery, entered service on the 21, 29 and 79 routes which served the Acre Lane and Kingsthorpe areas of the town. Introduced as part of a new quality partnership initiative with Northampton County and Borough Councils, the buses were wheelchair accessible and were fuelled from a new British Gas NGV filling station installed at Northampton Transport's depot. Further new vehicles received towards the end of June were 6 new Northern Counties Palatine 2-bodied Volvo Olympians painted in a special silver and burgundy livery for operation by Badgerline on the Long Ashton park and ride service in Bristol. Continuing in its belief that quality partnerships were the best way forward in improving public transport and attracting more passengers, FirstBus joined with Edinburgh City Council and Lothian Regional Transport in a new partnership in Edinburgh which promised mutual agreement of bus services in the city with joint projects to improve bus priority and provide better service information to passengers. Meanwhile, looking towards further expansion, FirstBus began talks with Ireland's state-owned bus and coach operator CIE in the hope that it may at some time in the future either acquire this or become involved in some form of partnership. It must, however, be stated that at this moment of time the Irish Government had no immediate plans to privatise its transport network and thus the talks between the two concerns were only of an exploratory nature.

Continuing its assault on FirstBus in retaliation to its moves in Ayrshire and Dunfermline, Stagecoach moved its battle south of the border to Greater Manchester at the end of June and introduced a new £5 all-week MegaRider ticket which was available from Stagecoach Manchester and Ribble but was not available on its inter-urban express routes. At around this same time, Great Eastern Railways introduced a multi-modal ticket for Essex commuters which enabled them to connect their railway journeys to Thamesway bus services. For a small supplement, season ticket holders were able to reach Rayleigh station from outlying areas using 12 different Thamesway services, thus enabling them to leave their cars at home rather than use them for the initial part of their journeys. While this move was welcomed by all concerned, less popular was the proposal by Great Eastern Railways to invite commuters to become part-time train guards on the peak-time services upon which they travelled. The offer which included free travel to and from work, £5.25 per hour and a uniform in return for duties such as making platform announcements, checking slam-doors were properly closed and signalling the driver to depart was as a result of Great Eastern experiencing difficulty in recruiting full-time guards. While accepted by the trade union, the proposed scheme was met with some concern by the Health and Safety Executive who was not wholly happy with it despite it being copied from a similar one in Hong Kong which had proved successful. Following difficulties in the operation of its services into the Ravenscliffe Estate as a result of attacks on its drivers and vehicles, Bradford Traveller after suspending evening operations on the routes concerned took the decision to reintroduce conductors to that area of the city. As one of three customer-orientated initiatives launched on 7 July, the 'Bus Buddies' as they were known took up their duties on the Greengates Circular services 608. 609 and 688 to not only collect fares but also to assist passengers boarding and alighting and provide information about the services concerned. In a separate exercise started on the same date, the unpopular fareboxes were removed from the West Bowling to Baildon group of routes upon which the drivers then gave change as well as issuing tickets while on the Bradford Moor to Clayton services upon which Smartcard stored valued tickets could be used, an extra 20% worth of travel was added each time the cards were recharged. Although the Smartcard offer was for a limited period of three weeks, the farebox discontinuation and Bus Buddies experiments were to be continued for three months after which a decision would be taken on their future based on results. While innovations such as those above were designed to attract more passengers, not all FirstBus's actions were successful and in a new round of tendering Badgerline lost its Bristol/Bath to Burnham on Sea services 490/1 to Bakers of Weston-super-Mare while due to financial cuts by Bridgend Borough Council, Brewers lost several of its schools contracts.

PROGRESSING TOWARDS THE MILLENNIUM

Continuing its quest to further improve the standard of its vehicles, FirstBus unveiled its new standard single deck bus interior towards the end of July following a period of consultation with passengers dating back to August 1996. This incorporated green-tinted bonded double glazing, individual Scanflex seats, improved leg-room, high quality Altro flooring and a Sutrak integrated heating and ventilation system. Employing lilac trim for seats and interior panels, the new standard specification included aqua green handrails to meet DiPTAC requirements while the cove panels incorporated a new clear polycarbonate lighting system. The first vehicles delivered featuring this new interior were Plaxton Pointer 2-bodied Dennis Dart SLFs and Plaxton Beaver 2-bodied Mercedes Benz Varios and it was stated that the new standard would also be fitted to Palatine double deckers in due course. Following this innovative move, FirstBus quickly turned

Leaving Crewe bus station in August 1997 on a local journey to Coppenhall is PMT ECW-bodied Bristol VRT DVL709 (GRF709V) painted in Pennine's blue & yellow livery but sporting corporate FirstBus-style fleet names and logos. (K.S.E.Till)

This lower deck view of one of Leeds City Link's new Alexander Royale-bodied Volvo Olympians shows the new standard FirstBus interior which has lilac moquette seats, lilac gangway and light green handrails. (Leeds City Link)

One of a number of Carlyle-bodied Mercedes Benz 811Ds new to Portsmouth Transit which during 1997 were acquired by Brewers from Provincial, 443 (H178GTA) still wore its former owner's cream & red livery when photographed at Port Talbot but had received its fleet names on its bonnet and side panels, although the latter were in white and thus were barely visible. (D.P.B.Davies)

at the end of June the Yorkshire Rider Group took delivery of the first of 18 new Plaxton Pointer-bodied Dennis Darts which were painted in an unrelieved red livery and were all placed in service during July and August without fleet names. One of these was immediately loaned to Grampian Transport while 3 had initially been delivered to Western National, by whom 2 had been registered in June and used in service for three to four weeks. The initial 6 took up their duties on 14 July with Leeds City Link who gained a further 5 (including the example which had seen service in Aberdeen) in August while 2 were allocated to the Quickstep fleet and 5 to Rider York. Additionally, Kingfisher Huddersfield and Bradford Traveller both received more Leyland Atlanteans from Greater Manchester, some of which were repainted by Mainline at Rotherham prior to their arrival with their new owners. Meanwhile, after spending a period in store Yorkshire Rider's last Leyland National (except for those in the Rider York fleet) was returned to service with Calderline on 6 July after having been repainted into that subsidiary's livery. Interestingly, this bus (1367) which was new to Eastern National has since served with Rider York, Quickstep Travel and Leeds City Link before finally joining Calderline!

Still painted in the red livery of its original owner CentreWest but having received a cream bonnet and cream side vinyl along with the fleet names of its new operator Leicester Citybus, Wright-bodied Renault S75 791 (HDZ5465) is seen in the centre of its new home city whilst undertaking a journey to Evington on the 36 service. (S.R.Procter)

its attention to measuring customer satisfaction on all aspects of its service provided by its 28 subsidiaries by appointing a top UK market research company to conduct a survey amongst passengers. This, it was believed, would enable it to understand precisely what customers expected in all aspects of service and enable it to address these needs in its future plans. Despite the continuing arrival of new buses in a number of FirstBus fleets, not all of those which they replaced were sold and instead a number were cascaded to other members of the Group to increase their fleets or allow the withdrawal of older vehicles. Following the arrival of CentreWest's new Dennis Dart SLFs, several of its Wright-bodied Renault S75s were dispatched to join the fleets of Beeline and Leicester CityBus while a number of Alexander-bodied Mercedes Benz 811Ds were transferred to Eastern Counties. Thamesway received 4 Leyland Lynxes from London Buslines while Provincial has disposed of a large number of minibuses with 19 Carlyle-bodied Mercedes Benz 709Ds passing to Brewers and 6 Carlyle/Marshall-bodied Ivecos being cascaded to Badgerline. North of the border Grampian Transport loaned some of its Atlanteans to Kelvin and permanently transferred others to Midland Bluebird while in order to provide extra coaches for the summer season, Greater Glasgow hired a couple of Plaxton Paramount-bodied Volvo B10Ms from Parks of Hamilton and Kelvin took a similar vehicle from the same source. Somewhat surprisingly,

Seen passing through Windsor on its way to London's Heathrow Airport on the 191 service is Berks Bucks (Beeline) Leyland Lynx 802 (K802CAN). (J.A.Godwin)

Painted in corporate National Express livery and carrying Rapide Airlink lettering above its windscreens, Wessex Plaxton Expressliner-bodied Volvo B10M 158 (J204HWS) stands at its owner's depot ready for its next duty. (K.A.Jenkinson)

Painted in a grey & green livery and lettered for the Heathrow Airport service is CentreWest subsidiary Berks Bucks Northern Counties-bodied Leyland Olympian 605 (F176LBL). (T.W.W.Knowles)

Greater Glasgow Alexander-bodied Dennis Dart SLF P817YUM carries SuperBus fleet names and Super Low Floor Easy Access Bus lettering on its cove panels. Painted in an all-red livery with black window surrounds, it is seen approaching Buchanan bus station, Glasgow in September 1997. (K.A.Jenkinson)

After Lowland and Midland Bluebird successfully retained the majority of the contracts in the Borders and Central Regions of Scotland and Badgerline its contracts in North Somerset in recent rounds of retendering, FirstBus further expanded its operations in August when its Leicester CityBus subsidiary took over some Rutland County Council tendered services following the sudden decision by Blands of Cottesmore to cease trading. These coincided with the arrival of Leicester's 10 new low floor Optare Excel single deckers which were placed in service on the first day of the month, although they were used on city services rather than on those taken over from Blands. Despite the purchase of these Leeds-built vehicles, FirstBus continued to favour Wrights of Ballymena in Northern Ireland for its future low-floor single deck deliveries and increased its existing 247 vehicle order by 16% to 287. Of these, 112 were to be Renown-bodied Volvo B10BLEs whilst the remaining 175 were to be Axcess Ultralow-bodied Scania L113CRLs. All were to incorporate FirstBus's new standard interior and in a major meet-the-people exercise a Greater Manchester Renown and a Greater Glasgow Axcess Ultralow set out together with a Greater Glasgow Alexander Royale-bodied Volvo Olympian to visit towns and cities throughout the FirstBus operating territory. The Greater Manchester example which was one of 21 scheduled to join that company was painted in a new ivory livery with passion blue flash similar to that used by the group's Scottish subsidiaries, this being designed to replace Greater Manchester's existing deep orange livery but on dedicated services which will be operated as Gold Services.

Delivered with the registration P571PBA and painted in Greater Manchester's new Gold Service livery of cream with a deep blue side flash and gold band on its cove panels, low-floor Wright Renown-bodied Volvo B10BLE 571 was re-registered R571YNC prior to its entry into service at Wigan. (A.Blagburn)

Painted in an unrelieved red livery and devoid of fleet names, Leeds City Link Plaxton Pointer-bodied Dennis Dart SLF 3006 (P813YUM) was being operated by Quickstep Travel when photographed in Larkfield Road, Rawdon on the 731 service from Otley to Leeds in August 1997. (K.A.Jenkinson)

Adorned with easiaccess lettering, Mainline Wright-bodied Volvo B6 443 (N443BKY) rests at Olive Grove depot, Sheffield in the spring of 1997. (B.Newsome)

Having gained corporate FirstBus-style fleet names and logos, Southampton CityBus East Lancs-bodied Leyland Atlantean 260 (YRV260V) passes through the centre of its home city in August 1997. (F.W.York)

On loan to Calderline from Volvo Bus & Coach to provide cover for its Volvo B10Bs whilst they received remedial attention, all-white liveried Volvo-engined Leyland National CWX666T was given Calderline fleet names during its stay with the company. New to West Riding, it is seen here at Calderline's Skircoat Road depot in May 1997. (D.Robinson)

Resting outside Leeds City Link's Kirkstall Road depot on 10 August 1997 whilst visiting the city to demonstrate the new FirstBus standard bus interior is Greater Glasgow Alexander-bodied Volvo Olympian VO141 (R141EHS). (D.Robinson)

During July, Great Western Holdings in which FirstBus had a 24.5% share announced a profit of £5 million on a turnover of £327.8 million in its first full year of trading which ended on 31 March. During this time it had made significant progress in refurbishing its high-speed 125 fleet and had achieved a 9% reduction in staff levels through voluntary severance. Another company in which FirstBus had a minority stake - Mainline of Sheffield - was also involved in a refurbishment programme under which 12 of its seven-year old Alexander-bodied Volvo B10Ms had been down-seated from 51 to 37 in order to improve their internal ambiance. Upon completion of this work they were, in October, placed on the 51 service from Lodge Moor to Charnock which was upgraded to the company's Silver Standard in an attempt to woo passengers back to the buses.

Having now completed its purchase of Southampton CityBus on 31 July, its new owners immediately set about adding FirstBus logos to all the acquired vehicles and began to look at the future of the company, although detailed plans have yet to be formulated. Indicating that its interests stretched further than road and rail transport, in August FirstBus made a bid for the 51% stake in Bristol International Airport which was at that time being offered by its owner, Bristol City Council. Current figures showed that the airport had produced £5 million profit on a turnover of £25.5 million and although

Displaying corporate FirstBus-style fleet names and logos and with a route diagram for service 10 on its cove panels and additional lettering below its windows, Southampton CityBus Leyland Lynx 105 (G105WRV) passes through its home city on its way to Thornhill in September 1997. (F.W.York)

Illustrated earlier with Red Rider names, PMT Dormobile-bodied Mercedes Benz 709D MMM489 (K489CVT) is seen at Stockport bus station in August 1997 after receiving new corporate FirstBus-style Pennine fleet names. (K.S.E.Till)

a condition of the sale was the building of a new £24 million terminal, this did not deter FirstBus or National Express who was also launching a bid. In the end, however, it was FirstBus who in November was named as the preferred bidder and it was expected that the acquisition would be completed before the end of the year.

Having now had time to assess some of its more recent innovations, whilst several had proved highly successful FirstBus conceded that its experimental FlightPath service from Swansea to Cardiff Airport which had been operated by South Wales Transport using Ford Galaxy people movers had failed to attract sufficient passengers. As a consequence no bookings for the service were taken after 30 May, although it was not until September that the final journey was undertaken. Similarly, having concluded its trials using 'Bus Buddies' on selected services, Bradford Traveller converted these back to one-person-operation with fareboxes from Sunday 28 September despite their apparent success. Earlier in the month, Streamline of Bath joint with Badgerline introduced some new services which linked Newton St.Loe (Bath Spa University College) to the University of Bath and operated until 2.40 am. Marketed under the title 'Bright Orange Bus Service' they were operated by 4 Ikarus-bodied DAF SB220s and 3 Plaxton Verde-bodied Dennis Lances which were all repainted into an all-over orange livery with yellow above the windows. At this same time, Streamline altered its livery to white with a red wedge at the rear in similar fashion to Durbins who used a blue wedge. Also involved in a service change was Wessex whose National Express 400 from Bristol to London was converted to shuttle operation from 14 September for which all Wessex's Dennis Javelins and 2 of its Volvo B10Ms were repainted into shuttle livery. From that date the coaches employed on this route were fitted with Wayfarer ticket machines and although advance reservations could still be made and seats were held until five minutes before departure, after this time payment could be made onboard to the driver.

PMT moved to a new depot on 1 August when it relocated its Pennine base at Dukinfield from Platt Street to the former Stuart Bus & Coach premises at Broadway. In the meantime, following the closure of a large part of Bradford's Transport Interchange for redevelopment which additionally affected part of Bradford Traveller's Hall Ings depot (situated beneath the Interchange), it had been necessary to park a large number of the company's buses on the nearby redundant coach station or in the bus station itself overnight and at weekends. This was, however, only a temporary measure as construction of Bradford Traveller's new £4 million depot around half a mile away was nearing completion and was brought into use on 21 September allowing Hall Ings depot to be vacated completely. It was not until 27 October, however, that the 'official' opening of the new depot took place when the Minister for Transport, Dr.Gavin Strang MP performed the ceremony accompanied by Trevor Smallwood and invited guests. As one depot opened, so the announcement was made of the closure in November of Kelvin's premises at Airdrie after which its vehicles and staff would be transferred to other Greater Glasgow/Kelvin depots. Meanwhile, following negotiations with Cardiff University, towards the end of September Brewers began a new service supported by the University of Wales Institute between the campuses and the halls of residence using three ex.Greater Manchester Atlanteans painted in an all-blue livery and adorned with dedicated lettering. North of the border, while news was still awaited relating to the divestment order made against Greater Glasgow and Midland Bluebird at the start of the year, in a competitive response to Stagecoach's service 5 to Milton, Greater Glasgow introduced a new route (numbered 52) from Glasgow city centre to Milton using low-floor single deckers branded with SuperBus fleet names. On the other side of the coin, however, on 13 October Kelvin ceased operation on

Despite displaying posters for its usual duty, pale blue & cream liveried Bournemouth Christchurch Buses open-top Alexander-bodied Daimler Fleetline 133 (NFX133P) is seen at Portsmouth in August 1997 while on loan to Provincial whose fleet name has been temporarily applied on its sides and front. (Paul Savage)

Branded for route 285, London Buslines Plaxton Pointer-bodied Dennis Dart 625 (N625XJM) awaits its passengers at London's Heathrow airport before setting out for Kingston. (P.Kay)

Bristol Omnibus Co. Plaxton Pointer 2-bodied Dennis Dart SLF 1713 (R713BAE) is seen here painted in City Line livery when new. (P.Kay)

In March 1997 two former Bradford Traveller Plaxton Paramount 3200-bodied Leyland Tigers were dispatched to Midland Bluebird to assist it with a vehicle shortage before travelling south to join their new permanent owner Brewers. Displaying temporary Midland fleet number 190 but still in the livery of its former owner and carryng its fleet names, F622XWY stands in the yard of Larbert depot alongside Midland Bluebird Wright Endurance-bodied Scania N113CRB 565 (L565JLS). (K.A.Jenkinson)

Yorkshire Rider painted a small number of its buses in the old liveries of their consituent companies under the banner 'Building on a Great Tradition'. Wearing the old light blue & cream colours of Bradford City Transport, Roe-bodied Leyland Olympian 5134 (B134RWY) which has since been repainted into standard Bradford Traveller livery is seen at Lidget Green heading to Clayton on the 637 service. (K.A.Jenkinson)

its five local services radiating from the Safeway store at Stevenston which it had started in competition to Stagecoach in July. In yet another innovative move, Great Western Trains joined with car hire company Avis in November to provide a rail-drive package for travellers in the west of England. Under this scheme first class rail passengers are to be offered preferential car rental rates for business and leisure package trips initially from Bristol, Swindon, Reading, Plymouth and Exeter stations.

Returning to FirstBus's combined fleet, in addition to receiving a large number of new vehicles, many older examples continued to be cascaded between fleets to meet increased operating needs or enable the withdrawal of time expired buses and coaches. Amongst these moves, PMT surprisingly gained 4 MCW Metrobuses from Greater Manchester and as these were of full height and thus unable to be universally used in the Potteries due to numerous low bridges, they were dispatched to Chester for operation by PMT's Crosville unit. Berks Bucks was able to withdraw a large number of its Leyland Nationals, Bristol VRTs and Mercedes Benz minis following its receipt of a quantity of Wright-bodied Renault S75s from CentreWest while Bradford Traveller withdrew the last of its Plaxton Paramount-bodied Leyland Tigers. Although destined to join several of their sisters at

Painted in an all-white livery is Greater Manchester low-floor Plaxton Pointer 2-bodied Dennis Dart SLF 6028 (R228SBA) seen here at Wigan in October 1997.

Brewers, these 2 coaches were instead dispatched to Midland Bluebird in mid-August to assist it during a temporary vehicle shortage. On the new bus front Leeds City Link received a number of new Alexander Royale-bodied Volvo Olympians in mid-September while Provincial gained 16 Plaxton Pointer 2-bodied Dennis Dart SLFs. After gradually reducing its fleet of Great Tradition-liveried buses during the spring and early summer, the sale of Calderline's Halifax Joint Omnibus Committee-liveried Plaxton-bodied Leyland Tiger to Brewers at the end of August and the repainting into standard Calderline fleet colours of its Halifax and Todmorden-liveried Olympians, left only Kingfisher Huddersfield Atlantean 6299 and semi-preserved Leyland Leopard 8534 still in the livery of Yorkshire Rider's predecessors (Huddersfield Corporation and Todmorden Joint Omnibus Committee respectively) and it was wondered just how much longer these would survive. As far as FirstBus's railway interests were concerned, North Western Trains introduced new blue and gold-liveried Class 323 electric trains on its Glossop/Hadfield line from Manchester Piccadilly on 3 November to further reflect its commitment to a better quality of services to its passengers.

Since the merging of Badgerline Holdings and GRT Bus Group in June 1995, FirstBus plc has grown to become Britain's largest bus operator with a 22% market share, a fleet of almost 9,000 vehicles

Painted in its owner's attractive new livery, Great Eastern class 321 unit 321-340 accelerates away from Romford on 1 November 1997. (Jim Hardwick)

The newest additions to the Leeds City Link fleet are Alexander Royale-bodied Volvo Olympians, one of which - 5606 (R606JUB) - is seen in the Headrow, Leeds before its entry into service in October 1997. (Leeds City Link)

Displayed at the Coach & Bus Show at Birmingham's National Exhibition Centre in October 1997 is Thamesway 415 (P415VPU), a Marshall-bodied Mercedes Benz 0814. (K.A.Jenkinson)

and employing some 23,500 people. In addition it has added a number of railway franchises to its portfolio and has diversified into airports and to reflect its expanding role, in November 1997 it changed its name to FirstGroup. Although it does not yet have a presence overseas, opportunities in this area are currently being sought which, if achieved, will give FirstGroup international status. Environmental and community issues continue to be strongly supported and during 1996 FirstBus announced five-year funding for a Chair in Transport Management at the Robert Gordon University in Aberdeen as well as becoming a Patron Company sponsor of the Outward Bound organisation for young people. Looking to the future, FirstGroup is confident that through its ongoing programme of investment, its involvement in quality partnerships and its firm commitment to a cleaner environment, it will enter the millennium with even greater strength and thus maintain its position as Britain's largest public transport operator.